Fresh Ways
with Terrines & Pâtés

Time-Life Books Inc.
is a wholly owned subsidiary of
TIME INCORPORATED

FOUNDER: Henry R. Luce 1898-1967

Editor-in-Chief: Jason McManus
Chairman and Chief Executive Officer: J. Richard Munro
President and Chief Operating Officer: N. J. Nicholas, Jr.
Editorial Director: Richard B. Stolley
Executive Vice President, Books: Kelso F. Sutton
Vice President, Books: Paul V. McLaughlin

COVER

Encased in a golden crust (technique, page 36), this squab pâté is an elegant dish that offers the hearty texture and flavor of traditional pâtés, while keeping fat content low. This recipe (pages 36-37) serves 12 as a main course and is prepared one day in advance, adding to its appeal as a dinner-party choice.

TIME-LIFE BOOKS INC.

EDITOR: George Constable
Executive Editor: Ellen Phillips
Director of Design: Louis Klein
Director of Editorial Resources: Phyllis K. Wise
Editorial Board: Russell B. Adams, Jr., Dale M. Brown, Roberta Conlan, Thomas H. Flaherty, Lee Hassig, Donia Ann Steele, Rosalind Stubenberg
Director of Photography and Research: John Conrad Weiser
Assistant Director of Editorial Resources: Elise Ritter Gibson

European Executive Editor: Gillian Moore
Design Director: Ed Skyner
Assistant Design Director: Mary Staples
Chief of Research: Vanessa Kramer
Chief Sub-Editor: Ilse Gray

PRESIDENT: Christopher T. Linen
Chief Operating Officer: John M. Fahey, Jr.
Senior Vice Presidents: Robert M. DeSena, James L. Mercer, Paul R. Stewart
Vice Presidents: Stephen L. Bair, Ralph J. Cuomo, Neal Goff, Stephen L. Goldstein, Juanita T. James, Carol Kaplan, Susan J. Maruyama, Robert H. Smith, Joseph J. Ward
Director of Production Services: Robert J. Passantino
Supervisor of Quality Control: James King

Library of Congress Cataloging in Publication Data
Fresh ways with terrines & pâtés / by the editors of Time-Life Books.
　　　p.　　cm. — (Healthy home cooking)
　　　Includes index.
　　　ISBN 0-8094-6079-3. — ISBN 0-8094-6080-7 (lib. bdg.)
　　　1. Terrines. 2. Pâtés (Cookery)
I. Time-Life Books.　　II. Title: Fresh ways with terrines and pâtés.　　III. Series.
TX749.F757 1989　　　　　　　　　　　　89-4723
641.8'12—dc19　　　　　　　　　　　　　　CIP

For information on and a full description of any Time-Life Books series, please call 1-800-621-7026 or write:
Reader Information
Time-Life Customer Service
P.O. Box C-32068
Richmond, Virginia 23261-2068

HEALTHY HOME COOKING

SERIES DIRECTOR: Jackie Matthews
Studio Stylist: Liz Hodgson

Editorial Staff for *Fresh Ways with Terrines & Pâtés:*
Editor: Frances Dixon
Researcher: Ellen Dupont
Designer: Mike Snell
Sub-Editors: Wendy Gibbons, Eugénie Romer
Indexer: Myra Clark

PICTURE DEPARTMENT:
Administrator: Patricia Murray
Picture Coordinator: Amanda Hindley

EDITORIAL PRODUCTION:
Chief: Maureen Kelly
Assistant: Samantha Hill
Editorial Department: Theresa John, Debra Lelliott

U.S. Edition:
Assistant Editor: Barbara Fairchild Quarmby
Copy Coordinators: Marfé Ferguson Delano, Ann Bruen, Anne Farr
Picture Coordinator: Betty H. Weatherley

Editorial Operations
Copy Chief: Diane Ullius
Production: Celia Beattie
Library: Louise D. Forstall

Correspondents: Elisabeth Kraemer-Singh (Bonn); Maria Vincenza Aloisi (Paris); Ann Natanson (Rome).

THE CONTRIBUTORS

JOANNA BLYTHMAN is an amateur cook and recipe writer who owns a specialty food shop in Edinburgh, Scotland. She contributes articles on cooking to a number of newspapers and periodicals.

LISA CHERKASKY has worked as a chef at numerous restaurants in Washington, D.C., and in Madison, Wisconsin, including nationally known Le Pavillon and Le Lion d'Or. A graduate of The Culinary Institute of America at Hyde Park, New York, she has also taught classes in French cooking technique.

SILVIJA DAVIDSON studied at Leith's School of Food and Wine in London and specializes in the development of recipes from Latvia, as well as other international cuisines.

JOANNA FARROW, a home economist and recipe writer who contributes regularly to food magazines, is especially interested in the decorative presentation of food. Her books include *Creative Cake Decorating* and *Novelty Cakes for Children.*

ANTONY KWOK, originally a fashion designer from Hong Kong, has won several awards for his Asian-inspired style of cooking and was the *London Standard* Gastronomic Seafish Cook of 1986.

STEVEN WHEELER is a chef and the author of three books on desserts. He has also written a book about seasonal English cooking.

The following people also have contributed recipes to this volume: Pat Alburey, Maddalena Bonino, Carole Clements, Jill Eggleton, Scott Ewing, Anne Gains, Sally Major, Colin Spencer, and Susie Theodorou.

THE COOKS

The recipes in this book were prepared for photographing by Pat Alburey, Allyson Birch, Jane Bird, Jill Eggleton, Anne Gains, Antony Kwok, Lesley Sendall, Jane Suthering, Rosemary Wadey, and Steven Wheeler. *Studio Assistant:* Rita Walters.

THE CONSULTANT

PAT ALBUREY is a home economist with a wide experience in preparing foods for photography, teaching cooking, and creating recipes. She has written a number of cookbooks, and she was the studio consultant for the Time-Life Books series The Good Cook. She has created a number of the recipes in this volume.

THE NUTRITION CONSULTANT

PATRICIA JUDD trained as a dietitian and worked in hospital nutrition before returning to college to earn her M.Sc. and Ph.D. degrees. She has since lectured in Nutrition and Dietetics at London University.

Nutritional analyses for *Fresh Ways with Terrines & Pâtés* were derived from McCance and Widdowson's *The Composition of Food* by A. A. Paul and D. A. T. Southgate, and other current data.

Other Publications:

This volume is one of a series of illustrated cookbooks that emphasize the preparation of healthful dishes for today's weight-conscious, nutrition-minded eaters.

Fresh Ways with Terrines & Pâtés

BY

THE EDITORS OF TIME-LIFE BOOKS

TIME-LIFE BOOKS / ALEXANDRIA, VIRGINIA

Contents

Terrine of Rabbit with Mixed Lentils and Peas

Potted Pheasant with Chestnuts

Terrine of Pheasant, Squab, and Quail with Wild Mushrooms

Fresh and Smoked Mackerel Pâté

3 Vegetables in Novel Guises 84

4 Terrines for Dessert 110

Two-Lentil Terrine

Terrine of Prunes and Almonds

5 Microwaved Terrines and Pâtés 128

The New Terrines and Pâtés

The intriguing pâtés, terrines, and galantines displayed in the windows of good delicatessens are often regretfully forsworn by health-conscious food lovers. When made in the conventional manner, these delicacies almost always fall into the category of forbidden fruit: They are rich in pork fat, laden with salt, and packed with exquisite morsels of meat or seafood whose savor is exceeded only by their cholesterol count. The good news, however, is that help is at hand. A new style of cooking renders these delights accessible even to those who wish to keep to a lighter, leaner diet.

Justifiably or not, a certain mystique surrounds the making of these dishes. Cooks debate, often heatedly, about their very names. To the purist, a pâté—French for a pie or turnover—is entitled to that label only if it is a savory assemblage of ingredients presented in some form of pastry crust. A terrine, taking its name from the French *terre* for earth, after the earthenware vessel in which it was traditionally baked, is a loaf based on meat, fish, or vegetables that have been cut into small pieces, or finely minced, to form the mixture known as a forcemeat. Nevertheless, contemporary common usage has blurred the distinction between the two, and the terms ''pâté'' and ''terrine'' are now often used interchangeably for any spreadable, savory paste. Indeed, even the old division between sweet and savory is breaking down, as a rising generation of adventurous cooks uses fruits, yogurt, low-fat cheeses, liqueurs, and chocolate to explore a hitherto little-known avenue—the dessert terrine.

Still more linguistic and culinary debate surrounds the galantine. Some culinary historians contend that the name is derived from an old French word for hen, and that the only true galantine is a boned, stuffed bird, poached in gelatinous stock, glazed with its own jelly, ornately decorated, and served cold. A more liberal interpretation applies the term to other boned, stuffed meats and fishes. Some of these creations, in the hands of chefs with a penchant for showmanship, can take on an extravagant, even barbarous, splendor: a whole suckling pig, for instance, or the head of a boar, cleverly boned and stuffed to keep its shape,

sauced, and painted with a gilded glaze. Yet the galantine possesses a set of humbler cousins, devised in thrifty farmhouse kitchens: robust headcheese and other jellied meats, such as parslied duck *(page 139)* or morsels of chicken in a lemon-tarragon aspic *(page 49)*.

Whatever names their admirers give them, all these dishes share one common characteristic: They are food for those who genuinely like to cook. They invite imaginative marriages of flavors and textures, encourage a free hand with spices and herbs, and offer generous rewards for those of experimental disposition. Of the 105 original recipes in this volume, some, such as the broccoli and blue cheese pâté *(page 88)* or the mackerel pâté *(page 68),* take little time to prepare; others, more complex, require a modicum of patience. But even the most elaborate are easily achieved by following a sequence of simple procedures that can be accomplished in advance, and in easy stages. The results amply repay the effort expended: These dishes look as wonderful as they taste, whether intended as the glamorous centerpiece of a formal buffet or as the inviting mainstay of a rustic lunch, needing no accompaniment other than crusty bread, with a little cheese and fruit to follow.

A new approach to an old tradition

Any attempt to create pâtés and terrines that respect the contemporary preference for lighter, more healthful eating has to begin by addressing the problem of fat. Traditional terrines and pâtés have always relied heavily on animal fats. Egg yolks, butter, cream, and, most particularly, pork fat—minced, cubed, or cut into sheets—play many roles: They bind and moisten, enhance flavor, produce a pleasant suavity of texture, and in some cases, act as a preservative. Indeed, to some cooks, the very notion of a low-fat pâté would be incomprehensible.

The recipes in this volume have been designed to reduce fat content substantially, without making an unrealistic attempt to eliminate it altogether. Less emphasis is placed on pork and other fatty meats; more use is made of poultry, naturally lean game, fish, and vegetables. When the use of some form of enrichment or lubrication is necessary, alternative sources of more modest fat content are found. Bacon, for instance, provides a leaner alternative to pork fat for lining baking dishes and covering terrines; so, too, does caul, the pliable, lacy membrane that surrounds the stomach of the pig. Wrapped around a mixture of highly spiced meat and vegetables to form a single large terrine *(page 25)*, caul will gradually melt in the oven's heat, basting the filling as it cooks, and crisping and browning into an attractive lattice pattern on the surface of the finished dish. Caul is available, either fresh, dry-salted, or frozen, from butchers who manufacture their own sausages and pâtés.

Classic fish and vegetable terrines are often based on a mousseline, an amalgam of cream and egg whites—sometimes further enriched with egg yolks and butter—blended with pounded fish or chicken. Yet the mousseline's delicate flavor and silken texture need not be renounced by the health-conscious: A lighter but highly satisfactory version can be made with low-fat ricotta cheese or yogurt, using only the whites of egg. Not only does this variant contain appreciably less fat, but it is also easier to handle: It is less prone to break or curdle, and it does not need to be kept as cold as ordinary mousselines, which will often fall apart unless prepared over a bowl of ice.

Even less fat is required for potted meats, poultry, and seafood. These quickly made preparations are moistened instead with stock, fruit juice, or yogurt. The marinated pheasant on page 40, for instance, is packed in a reduction of its own aromatic cooking juices; the deviled crab on page 81 relies on yogurt.

Another approach to reducing fat content is to modify the doughs and pastries used for covering pâtés. The simple short crust that forms part of the beef and veal en croûte on page 16, for instance, uses polyunsaturated margarine instead of butter or lard to reduce the amount of saturated fat. A brioche dough, as used in the salmon coulibiac on page 60, is a delicious low-fat alternative to classic puff paste with its heavy content of butter. The Healthy Home Cooking version of this dough calls for only two egg yolks instead of the usual seven per one pound of flour.

Raised savory pies, a hallmark of old English cooking, are characterized by their sturdy hot-water crusts. Indeed, so robust is this casing that it was used in the 18th century as the packaging for a celebrated regional specialty known as Yorkshire goose pie. This delicacy consisted of a whole tongue embedded in forcemeat and enclosed within a boned chicken, which, in turn, was placed inside a hollowed-out goose. The entire assemblage was then sealed into its hot-water crust and mailed to distant friends as a gift for Christmas. The modern hot-water crust on page 36 may be less suitable for shipping across the Yorkshire moors in a horse-drawn coach, but it is considerably lower in cholesterol than its prototype and is again made with polyunsaturated margarine instead of lard.

Such substantial structures as these would seem to have little in common with fragile aspic glazes and the shimmering surfaces of galantines. Yet jelly, in its various forms, plays a part equal to that of pastry in covering, sealing, and decorating terrines and pâtés. In headcheese and other jellied preparations, such as the molded rabbit and spring vegetables on page 30, jelly serves as the binding element that holds the other ingredients together. A topping of jellied glaze keeps terrines moist, while pastry-wrapped pâtés are often made with a layer of jellied stock interposed between filling and crust. For the sweet terrines that are the subject of Chapter 4, jelly is indispensable, both as binder and as decoration. Indeed, it is only the imaginative use of gelatin that has made it possible to develop the new style of light dessert terrine, as typified by the loaf of exotic fruits in champagne jelly *(page 125)* or the gingered melon mousse *(page 119)*.

The starting point for any savory jelly is a good, full-bodied, and virtually fat-free stock *(pages 10 and 11)*. Meat and fish stocks derive their substance from the natural gelatin in bones and meat; vegetable stocks require the addition of powdered gelatin if they are to set. So, too, do sweet jellies, which are based on a fruit juice or purée.

An aspic is a brilliantly clear meat, fish, or vegetable jelly that is produced by adding gelatin to stock and clarifying it. Even scrupulously skimmed and degreased stocks may be muddy; to clarify, or clear, them, egg whites and crushed egg shells are added, and the mixture is then simmered and strained *(page 12)*. For cooks in a hurry, commercially prepared aspic is available, but it is far higher in salt content and will not produce the same purity of flavor or lightness of texture as an aspic that has been prepared from homemade stock.

For the best results, jellies and aspics need to be given sufficient time to set, in cold conditions. The setting times indicated in this volume are those required if the jelly is to be set in the refrigerator. However, it is also possible to set jellies in the freezer, or in a fairly cool room over a bowl of ice. In all cases, these mixtures will chill more rapidly if they are placed in metal containers. When assembling layered jellies in contrasting hues, such as the cassis, peach, and raspberry layered pudding on page 124, it is essential to allow each layer to set thoroughly before adding the next, to avoid the risk of one color seeping into another.

Tools and techniques

There was a time when every kitchen, whether of the grand hotel or of the farmhouse, had plenty of helping hands. Those days are over; the modern cook relies on food processors and microwave ovens instead of kitchenmaids. The new style of cooking takes full advantage of this technology; mousselines, for instance, or layered terrines based on several different purées, take minutes to prepare instead of the hours they once required.

The Key to Better Eating

Healthy Home Cooking addresses the concerns of today's weight-conscious, health-minded cooks with recipes developed within strict nutritional guidelines.

The chart at right shows the National Research Council's Recommended Dietary Allowances of calories and protein for healthy men, women, and children, along with the council's recommendations for the "safe and adequate" intake of sodium. Although the council has not established recommendations for either cholesterol or fat, the chart includes what the National Institutes of Health and the American Heart Association consider the daily maximum amounts for healthy members of the population. The Heart Association, among other groups, has pointed out that Americans derive about 40 percent of their calories from fat; this, it believes, should be cut to less than 30 percent.

The volumes in the Healthy Home Cooking series do not purport to be diet books, nor do they focus on health foods. Rather, the books express a common-sense approach to cooking by offering recipes that use salt, sugar, cream, butter, and oil in moderation while including other ingredients that also contribute flavor and satisfaction.

The recipes make few unusual demands. Naturally they call for fresh ingredients, offering substitutes should these be unavail-

Recommended Dietary Guidelines

		Average Daily Intake		Maximum Daily Intake			
		CALORIES	PROTEIN grams	CHOLESTEROL milligrams	TOTAL FAT grams	SATURATED FAT grams	SODIUM milligrams
Children	7-10	2400	22	240	80	27	1800
Females	11-14	2200	37	220	73	24	2700
	15-18	2100	44	210	70	23	2700
	19-22	2100	44	300	70	23	3300
	23-50	2000	44	300	67	22	3300
	51-75	1800	44	300	60	20	3300
Males	11-14	2700	36	270	90	30	2700
	15-18	2800	56	280	93	31	2700
	19-22	2900	56	300	97	32	3300
	23-50	2700	56	300	90	30	3300
	51-75	2400	56	300	80	27	3300

able. (Only the original ingredient is calculated in the nutrient analysis, however.) The majority of the ingredients can be found in any well-stocked supermarket; the occasional exceptions can be bought in specialty or ethnic food stores.

About cooking times

To help the cook plan ahead effectively, Healthy Home Cooking takes time into account in all its recipes. While recognizing that everyone cooks at a different speed, and that stoves and ovens may differ somewhat in their temperatures, the series provides approximate "working" and "total" times for every dish. Working time stands for the minutes actively spent on preparation; total time includes unattended cooking time, as well as time devoted to marinating, steeping, or soaking various ingredients. Because the recipes emphasize fresh foods, the dishes may take a bit longer to prepare than those that call for canned or packaged products, but the difference in flavor, and often in added nutritional value, should compensate for the little extra time involved.

One great advantage for the hard-pressed cook is that terrines and pâtés can often be assembled, cooked, and served in the same container. Rectangular loaf pans or terrine dishes are classic and easy to unmold but are not compulsory: Oval or round containers, or a set of individual ramekins, are equally suitable. Frequently, the nature of the recipe will dictate the most appropriate serving dish. Earthenware is particularly well suited to robust, country-style mixtures, while porcelain heart-shaped molds or ramekins would be a happier choice for a delicate aspic or mousseline. In all of the recipes that follow, loaf pans and terrines are specified according to their dimensions, molds according to their capacity.

For pâtés with a crust, a hinged metal container—such as an oval mold or a cake pan with a removable base—makes a convenient receptacle. When employing metal pans and dishes, however, be sure to use only those made of nonreactive materials, such as stainless steel, that will not react chemically with vegetables, fruit, and other acidic ingredients to affect the color or flavor of the finished dish. Copper and cast iron, in particular, are best avoided.

The gentle, even cooking required for most of these dishes is achieved most effectively in an easily improvised water bath, sometimes called a bain-marie. To assemble a water bath, set the filled terrine mold in a large, deep roasting pan or baking dish, place the pan in a preheated oven, and pour in enough boiling water to come about two-thirds of the way up the sides of the mold. As the terrine bakes, heat will circulate gently around it, allowing all parts of the mixture to cook at the same rate. Once cooked, many terrines—especially those without a pastry crust—must be cooled to room temperature and chilled under weights to produce the desired firm, compact texture.

Pâtés that have been baked in a pastry-lined mold are not weighted. After baking, they are allowed to cool, then filled with gelatinous stock through a hole made in the top of the pastry, and chilled until the jelly sets. It is vital to check that the baked crust is perfectly intact before adding the stock, to prevent leaks that may ruin the whole composition. If the pastry does crack during baking or unmolding, it is easily rescued: Enclose the pâté in plastic wrap, gently pushing the sides of the crack together to seal the breach, and place the pie in the freezer for about 30 minutes, until it is well chilled but not frozen.

Chilling times for pâtés and terrines vary according to their contents. Meat terrines are often allowed to mature for a day or two to develop their flavors, although the relatively low fat content of the meat terrines in this volume precludes the longer keeping time allowed for traditional, high-fat preparations. Fish and vegetable terrines, however, are generally given only sufficient time to chill and set.

To be enjoyed at their best, terrines should not be served immediately upon removal from the refrigerator. Instead, they should be allowed to reach a cool, rather than frigid, temperature. A large meat terrine may need about an hour at cool room temperature, while small, single-serving pâtés require only 15 to 20 minutes to take the chill off.

Galantines and other jellied preparations are best served cold, since prolonged exposure to warm room temperatures will melt their surfaces, ruining the decorative sheen that renders them so attractive. Unmolding jellies without mishap requires care. The simplest procedure is to dip the bottom and sides of the mold in hot water for a few seconds, place a serving plate on top, invert the mold and plate together, and lift off the mold. Swift though it is, this treatment has one drawback: The outer surface of the jelly will melt slightly upon contact with the heat. If an impeccably neat surface is required, an alternative procedure is to invert the terrine onto its serving plate and wrap the mold in hot towels, changing them as they cool, until the container lifts neatly away, leaving the jelly intact. At times it may be necessary to run a knife or skewer along the sides of the jelly to pry it gently from its mold.

Those pâtés and terrines that look most dramatic in their uncut form should be brought to the table intact and divided just before serving. Some very delicate mixtures, such as the pink trout mousse on page 60, are best served with a spoon. If a terrine is to be served sliced, use a very sharp knife for best results. Owners of electric carving knives may find these tools convenient for producing thin slices, but they run the risk of marking the pâté's surface with the blade.

Delights for all occasions

Pâtés and terrines are not restricted to a single place on the menu. Because of their delicacy, fish and shellfish terrines are most often served as first courses, while those made with vegetables would be equally at home as first courses, as side dishes to accompany a roast, or as main courses for a light lunch. Meat terrines and pâtés, because of their comparative richness and greater complexity of flavor, are, perhaps, less versatile. If they are to serve as a first course, the rest of the menu should be kept fairly light; many, indeed, are substantial enough to provide the centerpiece of a lunch or light supper in their own right, supported by a selection of salads.

On the following pages are dishes to serve all purposes and seasons: lavishly decorated galantines for buffets, sophisticated terrines for intimate dinner parties, robust country-style pâtés and coarse pâtés for informal snacks and picnics. For the most elegant, those which are virtually paintings on a plate, a few lettuce leaves or a spoonful of a carefully chosen sauce are the most appropriate accompaniments. But for the great majority of these preparations, some form of bread is the traditional, and most welcome, partner. Crusty French loaves, dark ryes, and whole-wheat bread all have their partisans. Mixtures of a softer, more delicate texture, liable to be overshadowed by too substantial a crust or crumb, are better spread on lighter, crisper bases, such as Melba toast, warmed pita, small muffins, rolls, or protein-rich sesame sticks. A basket filled with a generous selection of breads and crackers adds to the sense of occasion created by the appearance of a homemade terrine or pâté—heady with herbs and spices, too good to resist, as pleasing to the taste buds as it is delightful to the eye.

Chilies—A Cautionary Note

Both dried and fresh hot chilies should be handled with care; their flesh and seeds contain volatile oils that can make skin tingle and cause eyes to burn. Rubber gloves offer protection—but the cook should still be careful not to touch the face, lips, or eyes when working with chilies.

Soaking fresh chilies in cold, salted water for an hour will remove some of their fire. If canned chilies are substituted for fresh ones, they should be rinsed in cold water in order to eliminate as much of the brine used to preserve them as possible.

Stocks for Full Flavor

A good, well-flavored stock adds moistness and flavor to terrines and pâtés, provides a poaching liquid for galantines, and when mixed with gelatin and clarified, makes aspic *(page 12)*. Producing good stock is a simple procedure. Recipes for five basic stocks appear on the right.

Stock comes from humble beginnings indeed—inexpensive cuts of meat, fish bones, or chicken wings and backs. Attention to details will reward you with a rich and limpid stock: Any large fat deposits should be trimmed away beforehand; large bones, if they are to cede the treasured gelatin that gives body to a stock, should first be cracked. During cooking, take care to skim off the scum that collects on top of the liquid lest it cloud the stock. After its initial rapid cooking, a stock must not be allowed to return to a full boil during preparation; the turbulence would cloud the liquid. For a final cleansing, the stock should be strained through a fine sieve or a colander lined with cheesecloth.

To prepare stock for storage, divide it among containers surrounded with ice water. Wait until the stock has cooled before covering the vessels, otherwise it may sour. Refrigerated in covered containers, any of these stocks will keep for up to three days. Because the fat on top of the stock will form a temporary seal, helping to keep it fresh, you need not degrease the stock *(box, opposite)* until shortly before you are ready to use it. To prolong the life of a refrigerated stock, first remove and discard the congealed fat, then boil the stock for five minutes; either freeze the stock or boil it again every two or three days to keep it fresh. As always, cool it quickly—uncovered—before storing it once more.

Fish stock and vegetable stock may be frozen for two months; the other three may be frozen for as long as four months. Stock destined for the freezer must first be degreased; frozen fat can turn rancid.

The recipes that follow yield differing amounts of stock. Brown stock, for example, is made from large bones, which require more water for cooking. But, like any stock, it freezes well, meaning an abundance is never too much.

Vegetable Stock

Makes about 9 cups
Working time: about 25 minutes
Total time: about 1 hour and 30 minutes

4 celery stalks with leaves, cut into 1-inch pieces
4 carrots, scrubbed and cut into 1-inch pieces
4 large onions, coarsely chopped
3 large broccoli stems, coarsely chopped (optional)
1 medium turnip, peeled and cut into ½-inch cubes
6 garlic cloves, crushed
1 cup loosely packed parsley leaves and stems, coarsely chopped
10 black peppercorns
4 sprigs fresh thyme, or 1 tsp. dried thyme leaves
2 bay leaves

Put the celery, carrots, onions, broccoli, if you are using it, turnip, garlic, parsley, and peppercorns into a heavy stockpot. Pour in enough cold water to cover the contents by about 2 inches. Bring the liquid to a boil over medium heat, skimming off any scum that rises to the surface. When the liquid reaches a boil, stir in the thyme and the bay leaves. Lower the heat and let the stock simmer, undisturbed, for one hour.

Strain the stock into a large bowl, pressing down lightly on the vegetables to extract all their liquid. Discard the vegetables.

Chicken Stock

Makes about 9 cups
Working time: about 20 minutes
Total time: about 3 hours

4 to 5 lb. uncooked chicken trimmings and bones (preferably wings, necks, and backs), the bones cracked with a heavy knife
2 carrots, cut into ½-inch-thick rounds
2 celery stalks, cut into 1-inch pieces
2 large onions, cut in half, one half stuck with 2 cloves
2 sprigs fresh thyme, or ½ tsp. dried thyme leaves
1 or 2 bay leaves
10 to 15 parsley stems
5 black peppercorns

Put the chicken trimmings and bones into a heavy stockpot; pour in enough water to cover them by about 2 inches. Bring the liquid to a boil over medium heat, skimming off the scum that rises to the surface. Lower the heat and simmer the liquid for 10 minutes, skimming and adding a little cold water to help precipitate the scum.

Add the vegetables, herbs, and peppercorns, and submerge them in the liquid. If necessary, pour in enough additional water to cover the contents of the pot. Simmer the stock for two to three hours, skimming as necessary to remove the scum.

Strain the stock, discard the solids, and degrease the stock *(box, opposite)*.

EDITOR'S NOTE: *The chicken gizzard and heart may be added to the stock; the liver, however, should never be used. Wings and necks—rich in natural gelatin—produce a particularly gelatinous stock, ideal for sauces and jellied dishes. [Turkey, duck, or goose stock may be prepared with the same basic recipe.]*

Veal Stock

For a light veal stock, follow the chicken stock recipe, but substitute 5 pounds of veal bones for the chicken trimmings and bones.

Fish Stock

Makes about 9 cups
Working time: about 15 minutes
Total time: about 40 minutes

2 lb. lean-fish bones, fins and tails discarded, the bones rinsed thoroughly and cut into large pieces
2 onions, thinly sliced
2 celery stalks, chopped
1 carrot, thinly sliced
2 cups dry white wine
2 tbsp. fresh lemon juice
1 leek, trimmed, split, washed thoroughly to remove all grit, and sliced (optional)
3 garlic cloves, crushed (optional)
10 parsley stems
4 sprigs fresh thyme, or 1 tsp. dried thyme leaves
1 bay leaf
5 black peppercorns

Put the fish bones, onions, celery, carrot, wine, lemon juice, 9 cups of cold water, and the leek and garlic, if you are using them, into a large, nonreactive stockpot. Bring the liquid to a boil over medium heat, then lower the heat to maintain a strong simmer. Skim off all the scum that rises to the surface.

Add the parsley, thyme, bay leaf, and peppercorns, and gently simmer the stock for 20 minutes more.

Strain the stock; allow the solids to drain thoroughly before discarding them. If necessary, degrease the stock (box, right).

EDITOR'S NOTE: *Because the bones from oily fish produce a strong flavor, be sure to use only the bones from lean fish. Sole, flounder, turbot, and other flatfish are best. Do not include the fish skin; it could discolor the stock.*

Brown Stock

Makes about 3 quarts
Working time: about 40 minutes
Total time: about 5 hours and 30 minutes

3 lb. veal breast (or veal-shank or beef-shank meat), cut into 3-inch pieces
3 lb. uncooked veal or beef bones, cracked
2 onions, quartered
2 celery stalks, chopped
2 carrots, sliced
3 unpeeled garlic cloves, crushed
8 black peppercorns
3 cloves
2 tsp. fresh thyme, or ½ tsp. dried thyme leaves
1 bay leaf

Preheat the oven to 425° F. Place the meat, bones, onions, celery, and carrots in a large roasting pan, and roast them in the oven until they are well browned—about one hour.

Transfer the contents of the roasting pan to a large stockpot. Pour 2 cups of water into the roasting pan; with a spatula, scrape up the browned bits from the bottom of the pan. Pour the liquid into the pot.

Add the garlic, peppercorns, and cloves. Pour in enough water to cover the contents of the pot by about 3 inches. Bring the liquid to a boil, then lower the heat to maintain a simmer and skim any impurities from the surface. Add the thyme and bay leaf, then simmer the stock very gently for four hours, skimming occasionally during the process.

Strain the stock; allow the solids to drain thoroughly into the stock before discarding them. Degrease the stock (box, right).

EDITOR'S NOTE: *Thoroughly browning the meat, bones, and vegetables should produce a stock with a rich mahogany color. If your stock does not seem dark enough, cook 1 tablespoon of tomato paste in a small pan over medium heat, stirring constantly, until it darkens—about three minutes. Add this to the stock about one hour before the end of the cooking time.*

Any combination of meat and bones may be used to make the stock; ideally, the meat and bones together should weigh about 6 pounds. Ask your butcher to crack the bones.

Degreasing Stocks

An essential step in making stocks as healthful as they can be is degreasing—the removal of fat from the surface of the liquid. Stock must always be degreased before it is used in a recipe, frozen, or transformed into aspic.

The easiest and most effective degreasing method is to refrigerate the finished stock, then lift the congealed layer of fat from its surface. To inhibit bacterial growth, a hot stock should be cooled quickly in small containers surrounded by ice water, then covered and refrigerated. The fat may then be spooned off. So that the stock will not sour, it should be covered and refrigerated only after it has cooled.

For a completely fat-free stock, lightly draw an ice cube across the cold stock's surface; the fat will cling to the cube. Alternatively, blot up any remaining fat with paper towels, using the following method: Lay a corner or strip of towel directly on the fat, then immediately lift away the towel. Continue this process, always using a dry section of towel, to rid the surface of every drop of fat.

Crystal-Clear Aspic

Aspic is the clear jelly that is used to glaze many terrines and galantines, to bind the elements in headcheese and other jellied preparations, and to fill the gap between pastry and filling in traditional pâtés. It is derived from stock, set with gelatin and clarified—cleared of its impurities—with egg whites and shells.

Aspic may be made from any type of stock, but in this volume, vegetable stock—usually the most convenient to prepare—is always used. A recipe for vegetable aspic is given on the right, and the techniques for making it are demonstrated below.

The gelatin may be omitted if you wish simply to clarify a stock. But note that if you later add gelatin to clarified stock, the liquid will become cloudy again.

Making Aspic

1 *SCALDING THE EQUIPMENT. Fill a saucepan with water, and place a wire whisk, metal sieve, and length of cheesecloth in the pan. Bring the water to a boil. Remove the whisk, sieve, and cheesecloth, and set them aside. Pour the water into a large bowl, to scald that, too; then empty the bowl. Wring out the cheesecloth. Line the sieve with a double layer of the cheesecloth and set it over the bowl.*

2 *ADDING THE INGREDIENTS. Pour the cold stock into the saucepan. Add the gelatin to the stock, then add the clarification ingredients—the egg whites and shells and the vinegar. Set the pan over medium heat.*

3 *FORMING THE RAFT. Using the scalded whisk, whisk the gelatin, clarification ingredients, and stock together thoroughly. In a few minutes, the egg whites will float to the surface of the stock, forming a thick, foamy layer known as the raft. Remove the whisk from the pan and bring the mixture to a boil.*

4 *COMPLETING THE CLARIFICATION. When the raft rises to the rim of the pan, remove the pan from the heat and let the foam settle. Boil the stock twice more, then let the foam stand for five minutes. Working carefully to avoid breaking up the raft, pour the aspic through the cheesecloth-lined sieve into the bowl. When cool, the aspic will set to a clear jelly.*

Vegetable Aspic

Makes about 1 quart
Working time: about 45 minutes
Total time: about 2 hours and 45 minutes

½ lb. carrots (about 3 medium), sliced
½ lb. leeks (about 2 medium), sliced
2 onions, finely chopped
4 celery stalks, sliced
10 sprigs fresh parsley
1 sprig fresh rosemary
1 sprig fresh thyme
4 garlic cloves, unpeeled
½ tsp. salt
8 black peppercorns
4½ tbsp. powdered gelatin
2 eggs, whites and washed shells only
1 tbsp. red wine vinegar

Put the carrots, leeks, onions, celery, parsley, rosemary, thyme, garlic, salt, and peppercorns into a large saucepan with 2 quarts of cold water. Bring the water to a boil, then lower the heat and partially cover the saucepan with a lid. Simmer gently for about two hours, or until the liquid is reduced by half.

Strain the stock through a fine sieve into a large bowl; discard the vegetables. Pour the stock into a 1-quart container and add water, if necessary, to make 1 quart. Allow the stock to cool, and clean the bowl thoroughly.

Scald a wire whisk, a large metal sieve, and a length of cheesecloth in a saucepan of boiling water, then use the water to scald the bowl (technique, opposite, Step 1). Line the sieve with cheesecloth and place it over the bowl.

Pour the cold stock back into the saucepan, and add the gelatin, egg whites and shells, and vinegar. With the scalded whisk, whisk the stock over medium heat until the egg whites form a thick foam on the surface. Stop whisking, then bring the mixture to a boil so that the foam rises to the top of the saucepan—do not allow it to boil over. Remove the saucepan from the heat and allow the foam to settle back down. Repeat this process twice more, then allow the mixture to stand for five minutes.

Very gently and carefully pour the aspic through the lined sieve, without allowing the foam floating on top of the liquid to break up. Let the aspic cool. Once it has thoroughly cooled, the aspic will assume a firm, jelly-like consistency.

EDITOR'S NOTE: *Vegetable aspic may be kept in the refrigerator for a few days, ready to be used when needed. Once set, it can be quickly melted again by placing the bowl over a saucepan of hot water.*

Dissolving Gelatin

Gelatin is a vital element in many of the terrines made in this book. Although it is available in both leaf and powdered form, the powdered variety is more generally available and has been used throughout this volume. Leaf gelatin may, however, be substituted, in a ratio of 6 leaves to 1 tablespoon powdered gelatin.

To ensure a smooth and lump-free final result, gelatin should be softened in a little cold liquid: Powdered gelatin requires two minutes to soften, leaf gelatin, some 30 minutes. The gelatin is then melted over gentle heat (below). Make sure it does not boil, or its setting power will be reduced.

Softening and Melting Gelatin

1 SOFTENING THE GELATIN. Place the cold liquid, as specified in the recipe, in a flameproof bowl. Sprinkle the gelatin evenly over the surface of the liquid (above, left). Leave it for 2 minutes, to allow the gelatin granules to soften and swell (above, right).

2 MELTING THE GRANULES. Set the bowl over a saucepan of simmering water. Using a metal spoon, stir the mixture constantly for about three minutes, or until the gelatin granules have completely dissolved (above, left). Test for this by lifting the spoon out of the bowl and allowing the liquid to trickle back: It should be completely clear, and no grainy deposits should remain on the spoon (above, right).

1 *Shimmering aspic encases a flavorsome combination of lean marinated pork and wild mushrooms (recipe, page 25).*

Reinterpreting the Classics

In the best tradition of peasant cooking, almost any type of meat or poultry found its way into pâtés and terrines. Miscellaneous portions of farm-raised pigs and rabbits, fowl long past the laying stage, and game brought home by the hunter were transformed into headcheese, herb-flecked terrines and sausages, savory pies, puddings, and potted meats.

The once lovingly fattened pig may now be bred for greater leanness, the quail and venison as likely to be farmed as caught in the wild, but meat terrines and pâtés are still as varied and as versatile as ever. Some of the recipes in this chapter remain close to their rustic origins: The herbed pork and veal terrine on page 22 is not unlike one that once might have been produced in any farmhouse kitchen. Others, such as the layered terrine of mixed game birds and wild mushrooms embedded in a Madeira-flavored jelly *(page 38)*, reflect a more sophisticated, contemporary style.

But all of these dishes demonstrate a departure from tradition in their reliance on a relatively small proportion of fat. Pork, beef, and lamb are not rejected outright, but only lean cuts are used, and then only when scrupulously freed of fat. Greater emphasis is placed on meats that are naturally lean: Game birds, rabbit, venison, and veal are especially suitable. Poultry is usually skinned, with all visible fat cut away.

The recipes employ diverse means of providing the succulence that fat would have lent: Many include a layer of vegetables; some are served with a sauce. In a number of the recipes, the ingredients are marinated in an aromatic infusion of wine, liqueurs, fruit juices, and spices. Meats should be marinated in the refrigerator, loosely covered to allow air to circulate. Game, such as venison, lends itself especially well to this treatment and will benefit from standing for as long as 48 hours in marinade; other meats, and poultry, are best steeped for no more than half that time.

Undeniably, many of the recipes in this chapter call for a long list of ingredients and a considerable number of necessary steps. Yet meat terrines and pâtés are ideally suited for advance preparation; their production can be divided into easy stages and accomplished well ahead of time. An interval of a day or so between cooking and serving will only enhance the complex flavors of the dish.

Moreover, the product of your labors can very often be frozen for later use. The traditional, densely textured meat terrine freezes well, either whole or cut into slices; but do not freeze any that are bound with jelly. If an aspic topping is called for, it can be added at a later stage, after the terrine has been thawed. Pâtés encased in a piecrust are best not frozen because the pastry tends to become soggy when thawed.

Beef and Veal en Croûte

Serves 16 as a main course
Working time: about 1 hour and 15 minutes
Total time: about 2 hours and 50 minutes

Calories **220**
Protein **20g.**
Cholesterol **65mg.**
Total fat **11g.**
Saturated fat **3g.**
Sodium **280mg.**

½ tbsp. virgin olive oil
1 large onion, finely chopped
1 lb. lean veal, trimmed of fat and connective tissue, cut into cubes
6 tbsp. fresh white breadcrumbs
3 tbsp. chopped parsley
1 stick (¼ lb.) plus 2 tbsp. polyunsaturated margarine
3 tbsp. pistachio nuts
1 egg white, beaten
1¼ tsp. salt
freshly ground black pepper
1 lb. beef round, trimmed of fat and connective tissue, very finely chopped
1½ oz. dried ceps, soaked in tepid water for 20 minutes, drained and chopped
2 cups unbleached all-purpose flour
2 eggs

Heat the oil in a skillet over medium heat, add the onion, and cook it until it is soft but not brown—six to eight minutes. Let the onion cool for five minutes.

Meanwhile, process the veal in a food processor until it is finely chopped. Transfer it to a bowl. Add the onions to the veal, together with the breadcrumbs, parsley, 2 tablespoons of the margarine, the pistachio nuts, the beaten egg white, ¼ teaspoon of the salt, and some freshly ground black pepper. Mix these ingredients well and set them aside.

Put the beef in a bowl, and mix in the chopped ceps, ¼ teaspoon of the salt, and some black pepper.

Lay a 15-by-12-inch sheet of plastic wrap flat on the work surface. Spread the beef mixture into a 12-by-8-inch rectangle on top of the plastic wrap. Form the veal mixture into a 12-inch-long sausage shape, and place it along the center of the beef. With the aid of the plastic wrap, wrap the beef around the veal to enclose it completely and form a neat roll. Cover the roll with the plastic wrap, put it onto a flat tray, and refrigerate it while you make the pastry.

Preheat the oven to 425° F.

Lightly grease a baking sheet. Sift the flour and the remaining salt into a mixing bowl. Using your fingertips or the back of a wooden spoon, rub in the remaining margarine until the mixture resembles fine breadcrumbs. Make a well in the center of the flour. Beat one of the eggs with 1 tablespoon of cold water, pour it into the well, and mix it in, using a wooden spoon, to form a dough. Knead the dough lightly on a floured surface until it is smooth.

Roll out the pastry to a 20-by-12-inch rectangle. Carefully remove the plastic wrap from the meat roll and place the roll in the center of the pastry. Cut a 3-inch square from each corner of the pastry.

In a small bowl, beat the remaining egg. Lift the two short ends of the pastry up and over the meat, then brush them with a little of the beaten egg. Lift one of the long sides up and over the meat, and brush it with the egg. Bring the remaining long side up and over the meat to enclose it completely. Press the pastry edges firmly together to seal them.

Place the roll on the baking sheet, with the seam underneath. Reknead and reroll the pastry trimmings to a long rectangle, and cut out two strips of pastry ½ by 18 inches. Brush the roll with beaten egg. Decorate it with the pastry strips and brush these with egg as well. Make three evenly spaced holes in the top of the pastry.

Bake the roll until the pastry is golden brown—30 to 35 minutes. Allow it to stand for one hour before serving. Serve the roll warm or cold, cut into slices.

SUGGESTED ACCOMPANIMENT: *broccoli and cauliflower florets.*

Tomato Sirloin Loaf

Serves 8 as a main course
Working time: about 20 minutes
Total time: about 8 hours (includes chilling)

Calories **285**
Protein **27g.**
Cholesterol **50mg.**
Total fat **12g.**
Saturated fat **4g.**
Sodium **300mg.**

2 tbsp. virgin olive oil
2 onions, finely chopped
14 oz. canned plum tomatoes (about 2 cups), chopped
1 tbsp. fresh oregano, or 1 tsp. dried oregano
1 tsp. fennel seeds
¼ tsp. salt
freshly ground black pepper
1½ lb. beef sirloin, trimmed of fat, and ground or finely chopped
3 garlic cloves, finely chopped
¼ cup chopped parsley, plus parsley sprigs for garnish
1 tsp. hot red-pepper sauce
2 tsp. Worcestershire sauce
1⅓ cups dried breadcrumbs
3 egg whites

Heat 1 tablespoon of the oil in a heavy saucepan over medium-low heat. Add half of the onion, stir, then cover the pan and cook the onion until it is soft—about five minutes. Add the tomatoes, oregano, fennel seeds, salt, and some black pepper. Simmer the tomato sauce, uncovered, stirring occasionally, until it has reduced to about 1 cup—about 40 minutes. Press the sauce through a sieve.

Preheat the oven to 350° F. Brush a loaf pan 9 by 5 by 3 inches with some of the remaining olive oil.

Place the sirloin in a bowl with the tomato sauce. Mix in the garlic, the remaining onion, the parsley, hot red-pepper sauce, Worcestershire sauce, and plenty of black pepper. Add the breadcrumbs and mix well. Last, add the egg whites and blend them thoroughly into the mixture by hand.

Form the mixture into a smooth, fat sausage shape and lay it in the pan, pressing it down firmly on all sides. Brush the top of the loaf with the remaining olive oil, cover it with foil, and bake it until it is cooked throughout and a skewer inserted into the middle is hot to the touch when withdrawn—about one hour.

Let the terrine cool to room temperature—about two hours—then chill it for at least four hours before serving. Garnish with parsley sprigs.

SUGGESTED ACCOMPANIMENTS: *new potatoes; asparagus.*

Smooth Potted Beef

Serves 12 as a first course
Working time: about 40 minutes
Total time: about 8 hours (includes chilling)

Calories **160**
Protein **30g.**
Cholesterol **60mg.**
Total fat **4g.**
Saturated fat **2g.**
Sodium **115mg.**

3 lb. beef round
¾ tsp. salt
½ tsp. grated nutmeg
1½ tsp. ground allspice
1¼ cups unsalted brown stock (recipe, page 11)
1 tsp. powdered gelatin
fresh thyme or parsley sprigs for garnish

Preheat the oven to 400° F. Put the beef into a roasting pan and sprinkle it evenly with ¼ teaspoon of the salt. Roast the beef for 15 minutes, then lower the oven temperature to 350° F., and continue roasting the meat for about one and three quarters hours, basting it frequently, until it is well done. Transfer the beef to a plate, loosely cover it with foil, and allow it to cool. Meanwhile, pour the pan juices into a bowl, allow them to cool for 30 minutes, then put them into the refrigerator until the fat rises to the surface and solidifies—about two hours. Remove the juices from the refrigerator and discard the layer of fat.

Cut away all fat from the roast beef, then cut the meat into small chunks. Put the chunks into a food processor and process them until the meat is finely minced. Add the nutmeg and allspice, the remaining salt, the roasting juices, and ¾ cup of the brown stock. Process the mixture to a smooth paste.

Spoon the beef paste into a serving dish; press it

down firmly, leveling and smoothing the top. Refrigerate the potted beef for one hour.

Meanwhile, dissolve the gelatin in 2 tablespoons of water (technique, page 13). Quickly stir the dissolved gelatin into the remaining brown stock. Chill the stock until it begins to thicken but is not yet set—approximately 30 minutes.

Pour the thickened stock evenly over the potted beef, then garnish it with the thyme or parsley sprigs. Refrigerate the potted beef for two to three hours more, until it is well chilled.

SUGGESTED ACCOMPANIMENT: triangles of hot toast.

Three-Tongue Terrine Perfumed with Five Spices

Serves 20 as a first course
Working time: about 1 hour and 30 minutes
Total time: about 1 day (includes soaking and chilling)

Calories **185**
Protein **14g.**
Cholesterol **80 mg.**
Total fat **13g.**
Saturated fat **3g.**
Sodium **440mg.**

1 calf's tongue (about 2½ lb.)
2 pig's tongues (about 4½ oz. each)
4 lamb's tongues (about 2½ oz. each)
1 calf's foot, quartered
2½ cups dry white wine
3 large garlic cloves, unpeeled
1½ cinnamon sticks
½ tsp. Sichuan pepper
8 cloves
2 star anise pods
2-inch piece fresh ginger, unpeeled and cut into four or five slices
2 carrots, each cut into four or five rounds
1 onion, quartered
3 tsp. salt
1 tsp. light brown sugar

1 bunch watercress for garnish
Caper sauce
1½ cups plain low-fat yogurt
2 tsp. Dijon mustard
4 scallions, finely chopped
6 small pickled gherkins, finely chopped
1 small sweet yellow pepper, peeled (technique, page 90), seeded, deribbed, and finely diced
1 small sweet red pepper, peeled (technique, page 90), seeded, deribbed, and finely diced
2 tsp. capers, rinsed and finely chopped
½ tsp. salt
freshly ground black pepper

Trim any visible fat and cartilage from the tongues, and scrub them well. Soak the tongues in several changes of water for about four hours, to draw out the blood. Put the tongues and the calf's foot into a large pan of cold, fresh water to cover, and bring it to a boil. Rinse the tongues and calf's foot under cold running water, and wash out the pan.

Return the tongues and foot to the pan, and pour

the wine over them. Add the garlic, cinnamon, Sichuan pepper, cloves, star anise, ginger, carrots, onion, salt, sugar, and enough cold water to cover all the ingredients. Bring the liquid to a boil, skim the liquid, and reduce the heat to very low. Cover the pan, and let the tongues simmer very slowly for one hour.

Using a slotted spoon, remove the pig's and lamb's tongues from the pan; continue to simmer the calf's tongue and foot. Peel off and discard the skins of the pig's and lamb's tongues. Return the peeled tongues to the pan to simmer for 30 minutes more, or until they are soft. Test them with a skewer; they should be of an almost melting consistency. Put the pig's and lamb's tongues in a dish, pour several spoons of the stock over them to keep them moist, and cover the dish. Set the dish aside.

Simmer the calf's tongue and foot for 30 minutes more. Remove the tongue, peel it, and return it to the pan. Continue to simmer the calf's tongue and foot for another 45 to 60 minutes, until the tongue is very soft when tested with a skewer.

Remove the calf's tongue and calf's foot from the pan and set them aside; cover the tongue to prevent it from darkening and hardening through exposure to the air. Strain 2½ cups of the stock into another saucepan. Degrease this *(box, page 11),* reduce it by two-thirds, then set it aside.

When the calf's tongue is cool enough to handle, cut it into slices ½ inch thick; reserve enough of the neatest slices to form two layers in a terrine or loaf pan 9 by 5 by 3 inches. Dice the rest of the calf's tongue. Cut the lamb's tongues into slightly smaller dice than the calf's tongue. Neaten the pig's tongues to fit the terrine when laid end to end, and dice any trimmings. Remove the white, gelatinous tendons from the calf's foot and dice them finely; discard the rest of the foot. Mix all the diced meats together.

Line the bottom of the terrine or loaf pan with half of the reserved calf's tongue slices. Spread a layer of the mixed diced meat over the calf's tongue, place the whole pig's tongues along the center of the terrine, then arrange the rest of the diced meat along the sides and on the top. Lay the remaining slices of calf's tongue over this. Pour the warm reduced stock into the terrine to cover the meat, then cover the terrine loosely with plastic wrap, and set it aside to cool for one hour.

Weight the terrine with a 2-pound weight *(box, below),* and chill it in the refrigerator for at least 12 hours before serving. To make the caper sauce, blend all the sauce ingredients together in a large bowl. Serve the terrine cut into very thin slices, garnished with the watercress and accompanied by the sauce.

Weighting a Terrine

Some cooked terrines benefit from being pressed under weights to form a cohesive mass that will make slicing easier and neater. Too heavy a weight, however, would force out the terrine's juices and make it dry. The amount of weight required for terrines in this book is given in each recipe. Place the weights—either scale weights or unopened cans—on a wooden board cut to fit inside the rim of the terrine and sanded smooth. Alternatively, stiff cardboard can be used; but it must be covered with plastic wrap or aluminum foil to keep it dry, and it will not last as long as wood.

Veal and Ham Pâté

MAKE THIS PÂTÉ A DAY IN ADVANCE AND CHILL IT OVER-
NIGHT TO ALLOW THE STOCK TO SET THOROUGHLY AND
THE FLAVORS TO DEVELOP.

Serves 12 as a main course
Working time: about 1 hour
Total time: about 1 day (includes cooling
and overnight chilling)

Calories **300**
Protein **26g.**
Cholesterol **100mg.**
Total fat **11g.**
Saturated fat **3g.**
Sodium **445mg.**

2 lb. lean leg of veal, trimmed of fat and connective tissue, cut into ½-inch cubes
½ lb. lean smoked ham, trimmed of fat and connective tissue, cut into ½-inch cubes
8 scallions (about ¼ lb.), chopped
¼ cup chopped parsley
2 hard-boiled eggs, chopped
¾ cup unsalted brown stock (recipe, page 11)
½ tsp. salt
freshly ground black pepper
1½ tsp. powdered gelatin
Hot-water crust pastry
3 cups unbleached all-purpose flour
¼ tsp. salt
1 egg yolk
6 tbsp. polyunsaturated margarine
1 egg, beaten, for glazing

Put the veal and ham in a bowl together with the scallions, parsley, chopped eggs, and 3 tablespoons of the brown stock. Season with the salt and some black pepper. Mix the ingredients together well, then set them aside while making the pastry.

Sift the flour and salt into a mixing bowl, and make a well in the center. Add the egg yolk. Put the margarine in a saucepan with ½ cup of cold water. Heat slowly until the margarine melts, then bring the mixture to a boil. Immediately pour the hot liquid into the well in the flour, stirring with a wooden spoon at the same time to form a soft dough. Knead the dough on a lightly floured surface until it is smooth.

Preheat the oven to 425° F. Thoroughly grease an 8-inch round springform pan at least 3 inches deep.

Cut off one-third of the pastry, cover it with plastic wrap, and set it aside. Roll out the remaining pastry to a large round, about 13 inches in diameter. Line the greased pan with the pastry, pressing it firmly over the bottom and up the sides, allowing a little excess pastry to overhang the edge.

Fill the pastry-lined pan with the veal and ham mixture. Roll out the reserved pastry to a round large enough to cover the pâté. Brush the overhanging pastry edges with a little cold water, then set the pastry lid in position. Press the edges firmly together to seal them. Using kitchen scissors, trim the pastry to neaten the edges. Reserve the trimmings.

With the tip of a small knife, lightly score the edge all around the pâté. Then press the back of the blade into the edge at intervals to create a scalloped effect. Make three evenly spaced holes in the top of the pâté.

Reroll the pastry trimmings and cut out leaves, or other shapes, to decorate the pâté. Using a pastry brush, brush the top of the pâté with some of the beaten egg, then decorate the pâté with the pastry shapes. Brush the decorations with a little more beaten egg. Reserve the remaining egg.

Place the pâté on a baking sheet and bake it for 20 minutes, then lower the oven temperature to 375° F. Continue cooking for one and a half hours.

Remove the pâté from the oven, and carefully release and remove the outside of the pan. Brush the sides of the pâté with the reserved beaten egg, then return it to the oven for 10 to 15 minutes, or until it is golden brown all over.

Allow the pâté to cool for one hour, then refrigerate it for two to three hours, until cold.

Dissolve the gelatin in 3 tablespoons of water (technique, page 13). Quickly stir the gelatin into the remaining brown stock. Using a funnel, carefully pour the stock into the pâté through the holes in the top. Refrigerate the pâté overnight. Remove the pâté from the bottom of the pan before serving.

SUGGESTED ACCOMPANIMENTS: *boiled potatoes with parsley; grated carrot salad.*

Duck and Pork Terrine with Cranberries

Serves 12 as a main course
Working time: about 1 hour
Total time: about 36 hours (includes marinating
and chilling)

Calories **220**
Protein **25g.**
Cholesterol **105mg.**
Total fat **10g.**
Saturated fat **4g.**
Sodium **415mg.**

1 lb. boneless duck breasts, skinned, trimmed of all fat and connective tissue
¼ cup cognac
½ tsp. green peppercorns, rinsed and crushed
1 cinnamon stick, broken into three pieces
1 lb. pork loin, ground or finely chopped
7 tbsp. fresh whole-wheat breadcrumbs
1 small egg, beaten
1 tsp. ground cinnamon
½ tsp. salt
freshly ground black pepper
5 oz. lean bacon slices
⅔ cup whole fresh or thawed frozen cranberries, rinsed and dried

Cut the duck breasts into ¼-inch-thick slices, then cut the slices into thin, 1-inch-long strips. Place the strips in a bowl. Pour the cognac into a small saucepan, and add the peppercorns and cinnamon stick. Warm the mixture very slowly until hot but not boiling. Allow this marinade to cool until tepid, then pour it over the duck. Cover the bowl, and let the duck marinate in the refrigerator for about six hours. At the end of this time, discard the cinnamon stick from the marinade.

Drain the strips of duck on paper towels and pat them dry. Place the pork in a bowl and pour the marinade over it. Lightly mix the breadcrumbs with the egg, ground cinnamon, salt, and some black pepper. Add them to the pork, and stir the ingredients well to combine them.

Preheat the oven to 350° F.

Lay the bacon slices on the work surface, and using the back of a heavy kitchen knife, stretch them as thin as possible. Line a loaf pan or terrine 7½ by 3¾ by 2 inches with the bacon; lay the slices across the pan with the ends overhanging the rim. Press one-third of the pork mixture into the bottom of the pan. Place half of the duck strips over the pork, then scatter the cranberries over the strips. Press half of the remaining pork mixture over the duck and cranberries, and repeat the layers, finishing with a layer of pork. Fold the ends of the bacon slices over the top of the terrine, and cover it tightly.

Set the terrine in a large roasting pan or dish. Pour boiling water into the roasting pan to come two-thirds of the way up the outside of the terrine. Bake the terrine until a skewer plunged into the center feels hot to the touch—one hour and 15 minutes to one hour and 30 minutes. Weight the terrine with a 1-pound weight *(box, page 19),* and let it cool to room temperature—about one hour. Chill the terrine for 24 hours before serving.

Just before serving the terrine, pour off excess juices, turn it out onto a board, and cut it into slices.

SUGGESTED ACCOMPANIMENT: *orange, fennel, and watercress salad.*

Herbed Pork and Veal Terrine

Serves 10 as a main course
Working time: about 1 hour
Total time: about 14 hours
(includes marinating and chilling)

Calories **200**
Protein **29g.**
Cholesterol **60mg.**
Total fat **7g.**
Saturated fat **3g.**
Sodium **290mg.**

1½ lb. pork loin, trimmed of fat and connective tissue, two-thirds cut into 1-inch cubes, one-third cut into ½-inch cubes
5 oz. lean veal, trimmed of fat and connective tissue, cut into 1-inch cubes
¼ cup cognac
¼ cup dry white wine
1 tbsp. chopped fresh thyme
freshly ground black pepper
¼ lb. fresh spinach, washed and stemmed
¾ cup cooked long-grain rice (¼ cup raw)
1½ tsp. cut chives
1½ tsp. chopped fresh marjoram
¼ tsp. chopped fresh rosemary
1½ tbsp. chopped parsley
2 large garlic cloves, finely chopped
¾ cup finely chopped onion
2 egg whites
½ tsp. dried oregano
½ tsp. dried thyme leaves
½ tsp. grated fresh nutmeg or ground nutmeg
¼ tsp. ground allspice
¼ lb. lean ham, cut into ¼-inch cubes
2 slices lean bacon
1 bay leaf, plus 1 bay leaf for garnish (optional)
watercress for garnish (optional)
tomato wedges for garnish (optional)

Place all the pork and veal cubes in a shallow dish, keeping the small cubes separate from the large ones. In a small bowl, mix the cognac, wine, half of the fresh thyme, and a little black pepper. Pour the liquid evenly over the meat cubes. Cover the dish and let the meat marinate in a cool place for about four hours.

Blanch the spinach in a large saucepan of boiling water for 20 seconds. Drain the spinach, refresh it under cold running water, drain it again, then squeeze all the moisture from the leaves. Chop the spinach in a food processor, add the rice, and process until the rice is reduced to tiny particles. Add the remaining fresh thyme, the chives, marjoram, rosemary, and chopped parsley, and continue processing until the mixture is well combined. Transfer it to a mixing bowl.

Cook the garlic and onion in a small, nonstick frying pan over low heat until they are soft—about five minutes—then add them to the rice mixture.

Drain the marinade from the meat, and add it to the rice mixture together with the small cubes of pork. Place half of the large pork cubes and half of the veal cubes in the food processor with an ice cube. Pulse the processor until the meat is coarsely chopped, then add one of the egg whites and purée the mixture until it is smooth. Remove the purée and add it to the rice mixture. Process the remaining large meat cubes and egg white into a purée in the same way, adding the dried herbs, nutmeg, allspice, and more pepper with another ice cube. Add the ham and process briefly to break it into smaller pieces and to mix it in, but do not purée the ham. Add all the purée to the rice mixture and mix well by hand or with a wooden spoon, removing any filaments of connective tissue.

Preheat the oven to 350° F. Lay the bacon slices flat on a board, and stretch them as thin as possible with the flat blade of a knife. Line the bottom of a 1-quart terrine or loaf pan with the bacon. Pack the meat and rice mixture firmly into the terrine or pan, spooning it in a little at a time and pressing down firmly with the back of the spoon. Place one of the bay leaves on top, and cover with a lid or foil. Set the terrine or loaf pan in a deep roasting pan, and pour in hot water to come halfway up its sides. Bake the terrine until a skewer inserted into the middle of the terrine feels hot to the touch when removed—about one and a half hours. Allow the terrine to cool to room temperature—about three hours—then chill it for at least four hours before serving. Remove the bay leaf and turn the terrine out onto a serving dish. Garnish it with watercress, tomato wedges, and a fresh bay leaf if desired.

EDITOR'S NOTE: *The terrine may be kept in the refrigerator for up to two days. If you have a large-capacity food processor, all the meat can be processed at once.*

Rosemary and Pork Headcheese

MAKE THIS DISH TWO DAYS IN ADVANCE AND CHILL IT TO ALLOW THE FLAVORS TO DEVELOP FULLY.

Serves 10 as a main course
Working time: about 45 minutes
Total time: about 2 days (includes chilling)

Calories **200**
Protein **32g.**
Cholesterol **70mg.**
Total fat **7g.**
Saturated fat **3g.**
Sodium **135mg.**

3 lb. lean pork shoulder, trimmed of fat and connective tissue
2 pig's feet, washed and split
⅔ cup dry white wine
1 small onion, quartered
1 garlic clove, finely chopped
1 small carrot, cut into four pieces
1 celery stalk, cut into four pieces
7 fresh rosemary sprigs
4 lemons, juice only
½ cup white wine vinegar
1 tbsp. powdered gelatin
¼ tsp. salt
ground white pepper
1 fresh hot chili pepper, seeded and cut into thin strips (cautionary note, page 9)

Place the pork, pig's feet, wine, onion, garlic, carrot, celery, and one of the rosemary sprigs in a large, heavy-bottomed saucepan. Pour in 2½ cups of water and bring the liquid gently to a boil, skimming the surface frequently to remove scum. Lower the heat, cover the pan, and simmer the mixture for about two hours, until the pork is tender.

Remove the pork shoulder from the saucepan, and set it aside. Strain the stock through a cheesecloth-lined sieve, discarding the vegetables and feet. Return the stock to the pan, add the lemon juice and wine vinegar, and bring it back to a boil. Boil the stock until it has reduced by half. Cool the reduced stock. Chill it for three to four hours, then discard the fat that has risen to the surface.

Put 3 tablespoons of the degreased stock in a small bowl and sprinkle the gelatin over it. Dissolve the gelatin, following the technique on page 13. Warm the rest of the stock. Add the salt and some pepper, then stir in the dissolved gelatin. Let the stock cool.

Cut the pork into bite-size cubes and place them in a 1½-quart round dish, scattering the strips of chili pepper between the cubes. Pour the cooled stock over the meat and immerse the remaining rosemary sprigs in the stock. Cover the dish and set it aside until it has cooled completely—about one hour. Chill it for about two days before serving.

SUGGESTED ACCOMPANIMENTS: *crusty bread; crisp, tossed green salad.*

EDITOR'S NOTE: *The pig's feet are split not only to yield the maximum flavor but also to ensure a firm set for the finished headcheese. If you do not have a heavy meat cleaver with which to split the pig's feet, ask the butcher to split them for you. If pig's feet are unavailable, double the amount of gelatin in the recipe.*

Gamey Pork Terrine

THE PORK IN THIS RECIPE IS TREATED WITH A LONG MARINADE
TO GIVE IT AN INTENSE GAMEY FLAVOR.

Serves 12 as a main course
Working time: about 1 hour
Total time: about 2 days (includes marinating)

Calories **175**
Protein **26g.**
Cholesterol **60mg.**
Total fat **6g.**
Saturated fat **3g.**
Sodium **160mg.**

2½ lb. lean pork loin, trimmed of fat (1 oz. of soft fat reserved), rubbed all over with 1 tbsp. of coarse salt and left in the refrigerator for 6 to 12 hours
1 oz. dried ceps or other wild mushrooms, soaked for 20 minutes in tepid water
1 lb. Swiss chard leaves, plus ¼ lb. stems
1 garlic clove
½ tsp. salt
6 juniper berries, toasted for 45 seconds under a broiler and crushed
⅛ tsp. allspice
freshly ground black pepper
2½ oz. caul fat, soaked for 15 minutes in warm water and 1 tsp. of white vinegar
⅔ cup vegetable aspic (recipe, page 13), melted (optional)

Red wine marinade

1½ cups red wine
1 tbsp. red wine vinegar
1 tbsp. virgin olive oil
1 onion, sliced
1 large garlic clove
6 juniper berries
6 black peppercorns
4 allspice berries
2 cloves
1 cinnamon stick

First prepare the marinade. Pour the red wine, vinegar, and oil into a nonreactive saucepan. Add the onion, garlic, juniper berries, peppercorns, allspice berries, cloves, and cinnamon stick. Slowly bring the liquid to a boil, then remove the pan from the heat and allow the liquid to cool. Rinse the meat under cold running water to remove the salt and exuded juices, and pat it dry with paper towels. Place the meat in a large bowl and pour the marinade over the meat. Cover the dish and leave it in the refrigerator for 36 hours, turning the meat from time to time.

Rinse the soaked mushrooms to remove any grit, drain them well, then chop them coarsely. Cook the Swiss chard stems in boiling water for three minutes. Add the leaves and cook for two minutes more. Drain the chard, refresh it under cold running water, and drain it again. Keeping them separate, squeeze both leaves and stems in cheesecloth to extract all the water, then finely chop both.

Preheat the oven to 350° F. Drain and dry the marinated meat on paper towels; reserve 1 tablespoon of the marinade. Cut the meat and the reserved fat into ¼-inch cubes. Mix the cubes with the mushrooms, chopped chard leaves and stems, and the tablespoon of marinade. Crush the garlic clove with the salt and add it to the meat mixture, together with the juniper berries, allspice, and some pepper. Mix the ingredients thoroughly, and form the mixture into a shape that will fit into a 1-quart oval terrine or 1-quart loaf pan.

Drain the caul fat thoroughly and stretch it out as thin as possible on a sheet of plastic wrap. Lay a second sheet of plastic wrap over the stretched caul fat and flatten the caul fat with a rolling pin. Remove the top piece of plastic wrap. Place the molded meat mixture on top of the caul fat and wrap it up, cutting away any excess caul fat. Put the parcel into the terrine with the caul seam underneath.

Cover the terrine and place it in a large, ovenproof dish or roasting pan. Pour in boiling water to come two-thirds of the way up the side of the terrine. Bake the terrine until it is cooked through and a skewer inserted in the middle of the terrine feels hot to the touch—about one hour. Remove the terrine from the oven, let it cool—about two hours—then chill it for at least four hours.

If desired, pour the melted aspic over the terrine and chill it again for at least two hours before serving.

SUGGESTED ACCOMPANIMENTS: *whole-wheat bread; fresh mushroom salad.*

Liver and Fruit Pâté

THIS SMOOTH, LIGHT PÂTÉ, IDEAL FOR SPREADING ON BREAD OR
TOAST, IS MADE TWO DAYS IN ADVANCE TO ALLOW THE
FLAVORS TO FULLY DEVELOP. THE LIVER IN THE PÂTÉ IS A RICH
SOURCE OF VITAMINS BUT HAS A RELATIVELY HIGH
CHOLESTEROL CONTENT.

Serves 16 as a first course
Working time: about 40 minutes
Total time: about 3 days (includes chilling)

Calories **150**
Protein **10g.**
Cholesterol **110mg.**
Total fat **6g.**
Saturated fat **2g.**
Sodium **435mg.**

½ cup dried apricots, chopped
½ cup pitted prunes, chopped
4 oranges, juice only
2 tbsp. virgin olive oil
2 large onions, finely chopped
1 lb. pork liver, sliced
3 oz. lean bacon, chopped
2 large cooking apples, peeled, cored, and coarsely chopped
2 tbsp. chopped fresh thyme
2 tbsp. chopped parsley, plus parsley sprigs for garnish
1 scant cup fresh whole-wheat breadcrumbs
1 lemon, juice only
2 eggs, beaten
1 tbsp. green peppercorns, rinsed and coarsely crushed

Place the apricots and prunes in a bowl. Pour in the
orange juice, and let the fruit soak for at least two
hours, or overnight.
    Heat the oil in a large saucepan over medium heat.

Add the onions and cook them until they are transparent—about five minutes. Add the liver and
chopped bacon, and cook them, stirring occasionally,
until the liver is evenly browned—about 10 minutes.
Mix in the apple, thyme, and parsley, and cook for two
to three minutes more. Remove the pan from the heat,
allow the mixture to cool slightly, then transfer it to a
food processor or blender. Add the breadcrumbs, lemon juice, and eggs, and process the ingredients to a
smooth pâté. Turn the pâté into a bowl, then stir in the
prunes and apricots with any orange juice remaining
in the bowl. Add the green peppercorns and mix them
into the pâté lightly.
    Preheat the oven to 350° F.
    Line a terrine or loaf pan 9 by 4 by 2½ inches with
parchment paper. Spoon the pâté into the prepared
pan, pressing it down with the back of the spoon.
Tightly cover the terrine with a lid or foil. Place the
terrine in a large roasting pan or ovenproof dish, and
pour in boiling water to come two-thirds of the way
up the sides of the terrine. Bake the terrine until it is
firm to the touch—about one and a half hours. Let the
pâté cool—about one hour—then weight the terrine
with a 1-pound weight *(box, page 19)*, and chill it for
at least eight hours, or overnight. Remove the weight,
cover the pâté, and leave it in the refrigerator for two
more days before serving. Turn out the terrine and
serve it sliced, garnished with parsley.

SUGGESTED ACCOMPANIMENT: *soft rolls.*

EDITOR'S NOTE: *Because the pâté is soft, a very sharp knife is
essential for cutting thin slices.*

Mediterranean Lamb Wrapped in Grape Leaves

Serves 6 as a main course
Working time: about 45 minutes
Total time: about 9 hours (includes cooling and chilling)

Calories **210**
Protein **27g.**
Cholesterol **65mg.**
Total fat **9g.**
Saturated fat **4g.**
Sodium **210mg.**

1½ lb. eggplant (2 small), trimmed
4 garlic cloves, peeled and thinly sliced
1 tbsp. virgin olive oil
¼ lb. fresh grape leaves, stemmed, blanched for one minute in boiling water, rinsed, drained, and dried
1 oz. dry-packed sun-dried tomatoes (about 8), soaked in hot water to cover for 15 minutes, drained, squeezed dry, and coarsely chopped
1 tbsp. tomato paste
1 tsp. red wine vinegar
1 lb. lean lamb, ground or finely chopped
1 tsp. ground cumin
½ tsp. salt
freshly ground black pepper

Preheat the oven to 375° F. In the eggplant skins, make slits large enough to hold the garlic slices. Insert the garlic slivers into the skin. Roast the eggplants until they are soft—30 to 40 minutes. Set the eggplants aside to cool. Lower the oven temperature to 350° F.

Lightly brush a terrine or loaf pan 7½ by 3¾ by 2 inches with a little of the olive oil, and line it with the grape leaves, vein side out. Overlap the grape leaves so that there are no gaps, and allow some of the leaves to overhang the container's edges so that they can be folded over later to enclose the filling.

In a large bowl, mix the chopped sun-dried toma-toes with the tomato paste, most of the remaining oil, and the vinegar. Stir in the ground or chopped lamb.

Remove the garlic slivers from the cooked egg-plants, and press them through a small sieve or garlic press. Scrape the eggplant flesh away from the skin and purée the flesh in a food processor. Add the garlic pulp to the purée, together with the lamb mixture, cumin, salt, and some black pepper, and process these ingredients until they are well mixed. Spoon the mix-ture into the lined terrine or pan, pressing it down with the back of the spoon. Fold the overhanging grape leaves over the contents of the terrine. Brush the ex-posed side of the grape leaves with the remaining olive oil, and cover the terrine with a lid or foil.

Bake the terrine until it is firm to the touch and a skewer inserted in the middle is hot to the touch when removed—about 50 minutes. Weight the top of the terrine with a 1-pound weight (box, page 19) and allow it to cool to room temperature—about two hours. Chill the terrine for at least four hours. About 30 minutes before serving, remove the terrine from the refrigerator and allow it to come to room temperature. Drain off any excess juices, then turn out the terrine onto a board or flat serving plate and slice it.

SUGGESTED ACCOMPANIMENTS: spinach salad; cherry toma-toes and flat-leaf parsley.

EDITOR'S NOTE: Canned grape leaves may be used if fresh leaves are not available. Remove the stems, wash them in cold water to rid them of excess salt, then drain them thoroughly on a folded dishtowel. They do not require blanching. If sun-dried tomatoes are unavailable, increase the quantity of tomato paste to 2 tablespoons, and add to the minced lamb two ripe tomatoes, peeled, seeded, chopped, and drained.

Terrine of Rabbit with Mixed Lentils and Peas

Serves 8 as a main course
Working time: about 2 hours
Total time: about 1 day (includes
marinating and chilling)

Calories **285**
Protein **33g.**
Cholesterol **70mg.**
Total fat **9g.**
Saturated fat **4g.**
Sodium **75mg.**

1 large rabbit, legs removed, remainder boned whole, hind legs boned, bones reserved
1 tbsp. cognac, Armagnac, or brandy
2½ onions, two quartered, one-half finely chopped
2 celery stalks, sliced
1 carrot, sliced
3 tsp. fresh thyme, or ¾ tsp. dried thyme leaves
3½ garlic cloves, three unpeeled and crushed, one-half finely chopped
8 black peppercorns
1 bay leaf
2 tbsp. plain low-fat yogurt
¾ tsp. salt
freshly ground black pepper
⅛ tsp. powdered saffron or turmeric
8 dried morels, soaked in tepid water for 20 minutes, drained and rinsed well, stems removed
1 tsp. finely cut chives
1 tsp. finely chopped parsley
⅓ cup yellow split peas, picked over and rinsed
⅓ cup green or brown lentils, picked over and rinsed
1 tsp. virgin olive oil
1½ oz. mushrooms, wiped clean and finely chopped
¼ cup fresh breadcrumbs
1 piece of caul fat (about ⅓ oz.), softened in acidulated water for 10 minutes
4 spinach leaves, blanched and drained, central ribs removed
4 tsp. powdered gelatin
1 egg, white only, shell washed
1 tsp. red wine vinegar

Trim the boned whole rabbit to fit a terrine 7½ by 3¾ by 2 inches; the loins will line the bottom, and the rib cage flaps will line the sides and extend over the filling. Flatten the flaps slightly between two sheets of plastic wrap, using a meat mallet or rolling pin. Rub the cognac into the meat. Place the meat in a shallow dish, cover the dish, and leave it in the refrigerator for eight hours or overnight to allow the flavor to develop.

Meanwhile make a rabbit stock. Fill a pot half full with water and bring it to a boil. Reserve the meat from the two hind legs; add the remaining meat and bones to the water, and blanch them for two minutes to cleanse them. Drain the meat and bones in a colander, discarding the liquid. Rinse the meat and bones under cold running water and return them to the pot. Add the quartered onions, celery, and carrot. Pour in

enough water to cover the contents of the pot by about 2 inches, and bring the water to a boil over medium heat. Lower the heat to maintain a simmer, and skim any impurities from the surface. Add one-third of the thyme, the crushed garlic, peppercorns, and bay leaf, and simmer the stock very gently for four hours, skimming occasionally. Strain the stock into a large bowl; allow the solids to drain thoroughly before discarding them. Degrease the stock (box, page 11). Put ½ cup of the stock into a small saucepan and reduce it by half. Set it aside and reserve 1½ cups of the remaining stock separately.

Meanwhile, grind or finely chop the reserved leg meat. Wrap one-third of the ground meat in plastic wrap and place it in the refrigerator. Beat the yogurt, ¼ teaspoon of the salt, and some pepper into the remaining ground meat to form a paste. Place the paste in the refrigerator to chill for 10 minutes. Transfer 3 tablespoons of the chilled paste to a small bowl and blend in the saffron or turmeric to turn it a bright yellow color. Stuff the morels with this spiced paste. Mix the chives and parsley into the rest of the paste and spread it into a 6½-by-3-inch rectangle on a sheet of plastic wrap. Lay the stuffed morels along the center of the rectangle, and with the help of the plastic wrap, roll the herbed paste around the mushrooms to form a sausage. Wrap the sausage in the plastic wrap and place it in the refrigerator for at least 20 minutes to allow it to get firm.

Put the split peas into a large pan of water and bring them to a boil. Lower the heat and simmer the peas for five minutes; add the lentils and simmer them for 15 minutes more.

Drain the split peas and lentils in a sieve, refresh them under cold running water, and drain them again. In a heavy-bottomed skillet, heat the oil over medium heat and brown the chopped onion lightly. Add the chopped garlic and mushrooms, and cook them until the mixture is quite dry—7 to 10 minutes. Add the lentils and split peas, stir for one to two minutes to dry the mixture a little, then transfer it to a mixing bowl to cool slightly. Mix the reserved ground rabbit, the breadcrumbs, the remaining thyme, the reduced stock, ¼ teaspoon of the salt, and some freshly ground black pepper into the lentil and split pea mixture. Cover the bowl and set the filling aside.

Preheat the oven to 450° F.

Drain the caul fat and line the terrine with it, leaving enough overhanging to wrap over the filling. Place the boned rabbit in the terrine, placing the loins along the bottom and lining the sides with the flaps. Season them with the remaining salt and freshly ground black pepper. Spread half of the lentil and split pea mixture in the terrine. Remove the plastic wrap from the rabbit sausage and wrap the sausage in the blanched spinach leaves. Place the sausage along the center of the terrine, and cover it with the remaining lentil and split pea mixture. Fold the flaps over the filling, then wrap the excess caul fat over the flaps.

Bake the terrine for 20 minutes, then remove it from the oven and cover it with a double thickness of aluminum foil. Lower the oven temperature to 375° F. Set the terrine in a large roasting pan and add enough hot water to come two-thirds of the way up the side of the terrine; bake the terrine for 40 minutes more. Turn off the heat and leave the terrine in the oven for an additional 15 minutes.

Remove the terrine from the oven and discard the foil. Pour off and reserve any cooking juices. Turn out the stuffed rabbit onto a plate. Deglaze the terrine with some of the reserved rabbit stock; strain this back into the stock, along with the cooking juices, and set the stock aside. Clean the terrine and replace the rabbit in it, then cover it loosely with plastic wrap. Weight the terrine with a 4-pound weight (box, page 19). Put the terrine in the refrigerator to chill and press for 8 to 12 hours.

Meanwhile, using the powdered gelatin, the egg white and shell, and the vinegar, convert the reserved rabbit stock into aspic, following the method on page 12. Pour the aspic over the terrine and return it to the refrigerator for two to three hours, until it is set. Serve the terrine cut into slices.

SUGGESTED ACCOMPANIMENT: *baby leeks vinaigrette.*

Rabbit Mold with Peas and Asparagus

Serves 6 as a main course
Working time: about 1 hour and 30 minutes
Total time: about 24 hours (includes marinating and chilling)

Calories **245**
Protein **39g.**
Cholesterol **70mg.**
Total fat **8g.**
Saturated fat **3g.**
Sodium **190mg.**

one 2½-lb. rabbit, cut into pieces, trimmed of fat and membrane, viscera discarded
5 cups unsalted vegetable stock (recipe, page 10)
½ tsp. salt
6 tbsp. powdered gelatin
3 eggs, whites only, washed shells reserved
2 tbsp. vinegar
¾ cup fresh peas, shelled, or 2 oz. frozen peas, thawed
2 oz. thin asparagus tips (about 8)
3 young lavender sprigs (optional)
1 tbsp. lavender or thyme flowers (optional)
Wine and herb marinade
⅔ cup dry white wine
1 bay leaf
1 tbsp. fresh thyme
1 lavender sprig, including flowers (optional)

First prepare the marinade. Briefly warm the wine, bay leaf, thyme, and lavender sprig, if you are using it, in a small saucepan over low heat, then let the mixture cool. Place the rabbit in a large bowl and pour the cooled marinade over it. Cover the dish and let the rabbit marinate in the refrigerator for 12 to 24 hours, turning the pieces of rabbit occasionally.

Place the rabbit and the marinade in a large, non-reactive saucepan or heatproof casserole. Pour in half of the vegetable stock and bring it slowly to a boil,

skimming the surface. Lower the heat, cover the casserole, and gently simmer the rabbit until it is tender and falling off the bone—about two and a half hours. Check the level of the liquid occasionally during cooking and add more hot vegetable stock or boiling water to keep the rabbit covered by liquid.

Let the rabbit cool to room temperature in its cooking liquid—about one hour—then remove the meat with a slotted spoon. Bone the rabbit as neatly as possible, separating the chunks of meat from the smaller trimmings.

Strain the cooking liquid through a fine sieve into a large bowl; discard the bay leaf, thyme, and lavender. Add any remaining vegetable stock or enough water to the liquid to make 5 cups, and season it with the salt. Using the powdered gelatin, the egg whites and shells, and the vinegar, convert the stock into aspic following the method on page 12. Let the aspic cool to room temperature.

Meanwhile, blanch the peas and asparagus separately in rapidly boiling water until just tender—about one to two minutes each. Refresh them under cold running water and drain them. (If you are using frozen peas, do not blanch them.)

Pour a little of the cooled aspic into a 1½-quart, flat-bottomed charlotte mold to a depth of ½ inch. Chill this in the refrigerator until it is set—about 15 minutes. Arrange the peas in a single layer over the set aspic, reserving any left over, and spoon a little more aspic over them to cover. Chill the aspic as before. Arrange half of the rabbit chunks to form a layer in the mold, and encircle the meat with half of the lavender sprigs, adding half of the lavender or thyme flowers, if you are using them. Spoon over a little more liquid aspic to cover the rabbit and chill the mold again until the aspic is set—about 15 minutes. Pile half of the smaller pieces of rabbit in the center of the mold and surround them with half of the asparagus tips. Cover with a little more aspic and chill until set—about 15 minutes. Continue layering the remaining rabbit chunks and smaller pieces in this way, adding any remaining peas to the final layer. Chill the completed mold for at least four hours.

To serve the mold, dip the dish into hot water for about five seconds, then invert it onto a serving plate and shake free the contents.

SUGGESTED ACCOMPANIMENTS: *grainy mustard; whole-wheat bread; green salad.*

EDITOR'S NOTE: *Chicken may be substituted for the rabbit in this recipe. The bird should be cut into pieces and skinned, then cooked for one and a half hours. If asparagus is not available, very thin green beans may be used instead.*

Terrine of Rabbit with Prunes and Green Peppercorns

Serves 8 as a main course
Working time: about 1 hour
Total time: about 7 hours (includes cooling and chilling)

Calories **285**
Protein **25g.**
Cholesterol **70mg.**
Total fat **15g.**
Saturated fat **4g.**
Sodium **440mg.**

one 2-lb. rabbit, boned, loins left whole, liver reserved
½ tsp. salt
freshly ground black pepper
½ tsp. safflower oil
2 shallots, finely chopped
1 tbsp. raspberry vinegar
1 tbsp. green peppercorns, rinsed and dried
2 egg whites
3 tbsp. plain low-fat yogurt
1 tsp. fresh thyme, or ¼ tsp. dried thyme leaves
1 tsp. fresh marjoram, or ¼ tsp. dried marjoram
⅛ tsp. ground allspice
¼ cup walnuts, finely chopped
¼ cup large pitted prunes, soaked in hot water for 20 minutes
½ cup bulgur, soaked in ⅔ cup water for 10 minutes
5 oz. lean bacon slices
3 tbsp. pistachio nuts

Remove and discard the thin membrane that encloses each rabbit loin. Divide each loin lengthwise into one long and one short strip. (The loin tapers, so the division is a natural one.) Trim the two short strips to even thicknesses. Season the strips of meat with half of the salt and plenty of pepper.

Heat the oil in a heavy-bottomed skillet over high heat, add the two long and two short strips of rabbit, and cook them quickly, turning once, until evenly sealed—about 20 to 30 seconds. Transfer the strips to a plate and lower the heat to medium. Add the liver to the oil remaining in the pan and cook it for one minute, turning it once. Transfer the liver to the plate. Add the shallots to the pan and cook them gently until they are soft but not browned—about two minutes. Stir in the raspberry vinegar and peppercorns, then remove the pan from the heat and let the shallot mixture cool in the pan.

Using a food processor, grind the remaining raw rabbit meat into a smooth paste—about two to three minutes. Add the egg whites and yogurt, a little at a time, processing the ingredients between each addition. Add the cooked liver, thyme, marjoram, allspice, remaining salt, and some black pepper, and process for a few seconds more until the liver is finely chopped and the ingredients are well mixed.

Combine 1 tablespoon of the rabbit mixture with the chopped walnuts. Thoroughly drain the prunes and fill them with the walnut and rabbit mixture. Set the stuffed prunes aside. Stir the cooled shallot mixture and the soaked bulgur into the remaining rabbit mixture, and combine well.

Preheat the oven to 350° F. Lay the bacon slices flat on a cutting board and stretch them as thin as possible with the back of a knife. Line a terrine or loaf pan 8½ by 4½ by 2 inches with the bacon, laying the slices across the terrine with the ends overhanging the rim. Spoon a quarter of the rabbit mixture into the bottom ▶

of the bacon-lined terrine. Press the mixture down with the back of a spoon, hollowing a channel down the middle. Place one of the long rabbit strips in the channel and arrange a row of pistachio nuts on either side of it.

Top this layer with a third of the remaining rabbit mixture, spreading it evenly. Lay the stuffed prunes in a neat row down the middle of the terrine. Spoon half of the remaining rabbit mixture on top and spread it evenly. Lay the remaining long strip of rabbit on top, to one side of the terrine; lay the two short strips of rabbit, end to end, down the other side. Arrange a row of pistachios between them. Cover the rabbit strips with the remainder of the rabbit mixture, pressing it down lightly. Fold the loose ends of the bacon over the filling. Cover the terrine tightly and set it in a roasting pan or large, ovenproof dish. Pour enough boiling water into the roasting pan to come two-thirds of the way up the outside of the terrine. Cook the terrine until a skewer inserted in the middle feels hot to the touch when withdrawn—about one hour. When the terrine is cooked, remove the cover and weight the terrine down with a 1-pound weight *(box, page 19)*. Let the terrine cool for about one hour, then chill it for at least four hours.

To serve the terrine, turn it out onto a serving platter and cut it into slices.

SUGGESTED ACCOMPANIMENTS: *crusty bread; raw vegetables.*
EDITOR'S NOTE: *The cooked terrine will keep in the refrigerator for up to 10 days.*

Venison and Apricot Terrine

Serves 6 as a main course
Working time: about 1 hour
Total time: about 2 days (includes marinating)

Calories **495**
Protein **41g.**
Cholesterol **60mg.**
Total fat **13g.**
Saturated fat **3g.**
Sodium **505mg.**

1¾ lb. venison, sliced along the grain into ½-inch-thick slices
½ cup dried apricots
6 tbsp. red wine
1 cup short-grain brown rice, rinsed under cold water
8 large green cabbage leaves
1 tsp. virgin olive oil
1 onion, finely chopped
1 garlic clove, finely chopped
⅓ cup pine nuts
6 slices lean bacon (about 2 oz.)
½ tsp. salt
freshly ground black pepper
1 egg white
7 tbsp. fresh whole-wheat breadcrumbs
1 tbsp. fresh rosemary leaves, plus 6 sprigs fresh rosemary for garnish
Red wine marinade
1 tsp. virgin olive oil
1 celery stalk, chopped
1 small carrot, chopped
1 small onion, chopped
1 garlic clove, crushed
8 black peppercorns, crushed
4 cloves
1½ tsp. chopped fresh ginger
½ cup red wine
1½ tbsp. balsamic vinegar, or 1 tbsp. red wine vinegar mixed with ¼ tsp. honey
1 tbsp. brandy

To make the marinade, heat the oil in a heavy-bottomed saucepan over medium heat, then add the celery, carrot, onion, and garlic, and cook them until they are lightly browned—about 10 minutes. Add the peppercorns, cloves, ginger, wine, and vinegar, and bring the liquid to a boil. Remove the pan from the heat, cover it, and let the ingredients infuse and cool —about one hour. Put the venison in a large, nonreactive bowl. Stir the brandy into the cooled marinade and pour it over the meat. Let the meat marinate in the refrigerator for 48 hours, turning it several times.

Place the dried apricots in a flameproof bowl. Heat the red wine in a small pan. Pour the wine over the apricots. Cover the bowl and set it aside for at least one hour, until the apricots are plumped up.

Put the rice in a heavy-bottomed saucepan with 1¼ cups of water and bring the water to a boil. Boil the rice for two minutes, skimming the surface of the liquid several times. Lower the heat, cover the pan, and simmer the rice for 15 minutes. Remove the pan from the heat and let the rice steam, covered, for 15 minutes more, then remove the lid and set the rice aside to cool.

Meanwhile, cut each cabbage leaf in half and discard the tough center rib. Blanch the leaves in boiling water for one minute, refresh them under cold running water, and drain them on paper towels. Heat the oil in a frying pan over low heat, add the onion and garlic, and cook them for three minutes, until they start to color. Add the pine nuts and cook them until they and the onions are golden brown—about five minutes. Stir the contents of the pan into the rice.

Line a terrine or loaf pan 8½ by 4½ by 2½ inches with six of the cabbage leaves, using a double layer on the bottom and leaving a 2½-inch overhang at the top. Stretch the bacon with the back of a knife so that each slice is the length of the terrine. Drain the apricots and cut each one in half. Using a slotted spoon, remove the venison from the marinade, pat it dry on paper towels, and season it with ¼ teaspoon of the salt and some black pepper.

Lightly whisk the egg white together with the remaining ¼ teaspoon of salt, then stir it into the rice mixture. Add the breadcrumbs, rosemary leaves, and some pepper, and mix the ingredients together well.

Preheat the oven to 350° F. Lay one-third of the venison in the bottom of the terrine and place two bacon slices lengthwise on top. Spread one-quarter of the rice mixture over the bacon and venison. Arrange half of the apricots in two lengthwise rows on the rice, then add another quarter of the rice, spreading it evenly. Repeat this sequence of layers, finishing with a layer of venison topped with bacon. (The filling will be higher than the sides of the terrine or pan.) Cover the bacon with the remaining two cabbage leaves, and fold the overhanging cabbage leaves over these. Cover the terrine with a double layer of foil.

Place the terrine in a roasting pan or large, oven-proof dish, pour in boiling water to come two-thirds of the way up the sides of the terrine, and cover the

whole with a large sheet of foil. Bake the terrine in the oven until a skewer inserted in the middle of the terrine feels hot to the touch when withdrawn—about one hour and fifteen minutes.

Remove the terrine from the oven and discard the foil coverings. Invert the terrine, still in its mold, onto a jelly roll pan, propped up slightly at one end to allow the juices to drain out of the terrine. Cover the terrine with foil to help keep it warm. Place a 2-pound weight on top of the terrine's bottom and let the terrine firm and drain for 30 minutes.

Unmold the terrine onto a platter and serve it cut into slices, garnished with the sprigs of rosemary.

SUGGESTED ACCOMPANIMENTS: *red-currant jelly; warm salad of broccoli, cauliflower, and lettuce.*

EDITOR'S NOTE: *Round steak can be successfully substituted for venison in this recipe.*

Lining a Loaf Pan

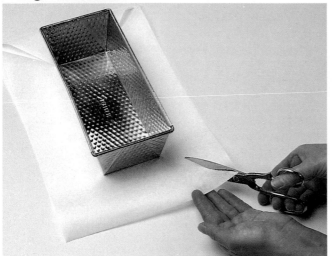

1 *CUTTING NEAT CORNERS. Cut a sheet of parchment paper large enough to cover the bottom and sides of the pan. Place the pan in the center of the sheet. Cut a straight diagonal line from each corner of the paper to the nearest corner of the pan (above).*

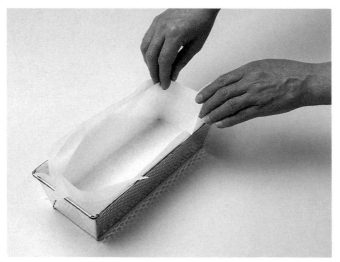

2 *FITTING THE PAPER. Grease the inside of the pan with melted fat. Position the paper in the pan, and press it firmly against the bottom and sides. Overlap the corner flaps, lightly greasing their undersides so that the pairs of flaps adhere and lie flat.*

Chicken and Rabbit Terrine with Grainy Mustard

Serves 20 as a first course
Working time: about 30 minutes
Total time: about 7 hours and 30 minutes
(includes chilling)

Calories **100**
Protein **17g.**
Cholesterol **45mg.**
Total fat **3g.**
Saturated fat **1g.**
Sodium **180mg.**

2 saddles of rabbit, meat removed from the bone to yield loins
2 tbsp. dry white wine
¼ cup grainy mustard
2 lb. boneless chicken breasts, skinned
4 shallots, or ½ small onion
2 tsp. salt
freshly ground black pepper
3 egg whites

Place the rabbit loins in a shallow, nonreactive dish. Mix the wine with 1½ teaspoons of the mustard and pour it over the rabbit. Turn the rabbit to coat it evenly and set it aside to marinate for 30 minutes. Meanwhile, finely chop the chicken, or grind it in a food processor, with the shallots or onion. Mix 4½ teaspoons of the remaining mustard, the salt, and some pepper into the chopped chicken.

Preheat the oven to 350° F. Drain the rabbit loins on paper towels. Pour the remaining marinade into the chicken mixture and mix it in well. Whisk the egg whites until they stand in very soft peaks, then lightly stir them into the chicken mixture.

Line a terrine or loaf pan measuring 7½ by 3¾ by 2 inches with parchment paper (technique, left).

Spoon half of the chicken mixture into the prepared pan and press it down evenly but lightly with the back of a spoon. Lay the rabbit loins on top of the chicken mixture. Cover the rabbit with the remaining chicken mixture, again pressing it down evenly with the back of a spoon. Spread the remaining 2 tablespoons of mustard on top.

Cover the terrine with a piece of parchment paper or foil. Set the terrine or pan in a large roasting pan or dish. Pour boiling water into the roasting pan to come two-thirds of the way up the outside of the terrine or pan. Bake the terrine until a skewer inserted in the middle of the terrine feels hot to the touch when removed—about one hour and 30 minutes. Allow the terrine to cool—about one hour—then chill it for at least four hours. Serve the terrine sliced.

SUGGESTED ACCOMPANIMENTS: *crusty French bread; cherry tomatoes.*

Terrine of Squab and Veal

Serves 20 as a first course
Working time: about 25 minutes
Total time: about 1 day
(includes marinating and chilling)

Calories **95**
Protein **14g.**
Cholesterol **40mg.**
Total fat **3g.**
Saturated fat **1g.**
Sodium **130mg.**

4 squab breasts, skinned
6 tbsp. dry Madeira
1 tbsp. balsamic vinegar, or 2 tsp. red wine vinegar mixed with ¼ tsp. honey
2 lb. ground veal
7 tbsp. fine fresh white breadcrumbs
1 tbsp. finely chopped parsley
1 tbsp. juniper berries
2 tsp. salt
freshly ground black pepper
4 egg whites
2 bay leaves

Place the squab breasts in a shallow, nonreactive dish, and pour 4 tablespoons of the Madeira and all of the vinegar over them. Cover the dish and let the breasts marinate overnight in the refrigerator.

Preheat the oven to 350° F. Combine the veal, breadcrumbs, parsley, and remaining Madeira in a bowl. Reserve a few of the juniper berries for garnish. Crush the rest and add them to the veal mixture. Season it with the salt and some black pepper. Whisk the egg whites until they stand in soft peaks, then lightly stir them into the veal mixture.

Place about a third of the veal mixture in a 1½-quart oval terrine and press it down evenly in the bottom of the dish. Lay two of the squab breasts on top of the veal mixture. Spoon another third of the veal mixture over the squab, spreading it in an even layer. Lay the remaining squab breasts in the dish and top them with a final layer of veal. Pour any remaining marinade from the squab breasts over the terrine.

Place the bay leaves and the reserved juniper berries on top of the veal mixture. Cover the terrine closely with foil and set it in a large roasting pan or dish. Pour boiling water into the roasting pan to come two-thirds of the way up the outside of the terrine. Bake the terrine until a skewer inserted in the middle of the terrine feels hot to the touch when removed—about two hours. Allow the terrine to cool at room temperature—about one hour—then chill it for at least two hours or overnight before serving.

Lining an Oval Mold with Pastry

1 *POSITIONING THE PASTRY. Roll up a pastry strip and carefully unroll it inside the mold to line the sides and the bottom. Keep the top pastry edge at least 1½ inches above the rim of the mold.*

2 *SEALING THE SEAMS. Press the dough against the sides and into the corners of the mold. Close and smooth out the seam in the bottom of the mold.*

Squab Pâté

THIS MODERN PÂTÉ IS MADE WITH A MINIMUM OF FAT WHILE RETAINING THE SHAPE, SATISFYING TEXTURE, AND FLAVOR OF TRADITIONAL FARE. MAKE THE PÂTÉ A DAY IN ADVANCE AND CHILL IT OVERNIGHT TO ALLOW THE FLAVORS TO BLEND AND IMPROVE.

Serves 12 as a main course
Working time: about 1 hour and 30 minutes
Total time: about 1 day (includes chilling)

Calories **365**
Protein **31g.**
Cholesterol **105mg.**
Total fat **16g.**
Saturated fat **5g.**
Sodium **330mg.**

3 squabs (about ½ lb. each)
2 onions, one quartered, one very finely chopped
2 garlic cloves, one unpeeled, one peeled and finely chopped
1 bay leaf
8 black peppercorns
1 sprig fresh thyme
1½ tsp. virgin olive oil
1½ lb. veal cutlets, trimmed of fat and connective tissue
2 tsp. dried mixed herbs
1 tsp. salt
freshly ground black pepper
ground allspice
½ lb. round steak, trimmed of all fat and connective tissue, cut into ½-inch-thick strips
4 tsp. powdered gelatin
Hot-water crust pastry
3 cups unbleached all-purpose flour
¼ tsp. salt
1 egg yolk
1 stick (¼ lb.) polyunsaturated margarine
1 egg, beaten, for glaze

Using a small, sharp knife, remove the breasts from each squab, then remove the skin from the breasts. Set the breasts aside. Put the bones into a large saucepan and pour in enough cold water to just cover them. Bring the liquid slowly to a boil; reduce the heat to low. Skim off the scum as it rises to the surface of the liquid, and add the quartered onion, unpeeled garlic clove, bay leaf, peppercorns, and thyme sprig. Partially cover the saucepan and simmer gently for two hours to make a stock.

Heat the olive oil in a skillet over medium heat, add the chopped onion, and cook gently until it is softened but not browned—about six to eight minutes. Remove the pan from the heat and allow the onion to cool.

Cut the veal into small pieces, put them in a food processor, and process them until the meat is very finely ground. Add the softened onion, chopped garlic, mixed herbs, ½ teaspoon of the salt, and some black pepper. Process until the ingredients are evenly blended. Set the veal mixture aside.

Preheat the oven to 425° F. Grease an oval pâté mold with collapsible sides 8½ by 5 by 4 inches.

To make the pastry, sift the flour and salt into a mixing bowl, and make a well in the center. Drop the egg yolk into the well. Put the margarine into a saucepan with ½ cup of cold water. Heat gently until the margarine melts. Bring the liquid to a boil. Immediately pour the boiling liquid into the well in the flour, stirring with a wooden spoon at the same time to incorporate the egg yolk and flour in a soft dough. Knead the dough on a lightly floured surface until smooth.

Cut off one-third of the pastry, cover it with plastic wrap, and set it aside. Roll the remaining pastry into a strip measuring roughly 21 by 6 inches and use it to line the greased pâté mold *(technique, left)*.

Spoon the veal mixture into the pastry-lined mold, pressing it against the bottom and sides of the pastry with the back of the spoon to leave a hollow center. Put two of the squab breasts in the bottom of the hollow. Season them with a little of the remaining salt, a few generous grindings of black pepper, and some allspice. Place half of the round-steak strips on top of the squab breasts and season as before. Repeat with the remaining squab breasts and steak strips, ending with squab breasts. Sprinkle 3 tablespoons of the stock over the filling.

Roll out the reserved pastry to an oval shape large enough to cover the pâté. Brush the overhanging pastry edges with water, then place the pastry lid in position on top of the pâté. Press the edges firmly together to seal them. Using kitchen scissors, trim the edge of the pastry to neaten it, then pinch the edge between forefinger and thumb all around the pâté to create a decorative rippled edge. Lightly knead and reroll the pastry trimmings, and cut out leaf shapes to decorate the top of the pâté.

Brush the top of the pastry with a little beaten egg. Make three evenly spaced holes in the pastry. Decorate the pâté with the pastry leaves and brush them with a little more of the egg; reserve the remaining egg.

Place the pâté on a baking sheet. Bake it for 20 minutes, then lower the oven temperature to 375° F. and continue cooking for one and a half hours. Check that the top of the pâté does not become too brown during cooking; if necessary, cover it loosely with a piece of foil. Remove the pâté from the oven and very carefully remove the outside of the mold. Brush the sides of the pâté with the reserved egg. Return it to the oven for 10 to 15 minutes until the sides are golden brown. Allow the pâté to cool for one hour, then chill it for about three hours.

Meanwhile, degrease the remaining squab stock *(box, page 11)*, and boil it until it is reduced to 2 cups—15 to 20 minutes. Dissolve the gelatin in 3 tablespoons of water, following the instructions on page 13. Add the dissolved gelatin to the reduced stock and stir well. Let the stock sit until cool but not set—about 40 minutes.

Using a funnel, carefully pour the stock through the three holes in the pastry into the pâté. Refrigerate the pâté overnight. Remove the pâté from the bottom of the mold before serving. Serve cut into slices.

EDITOR'S NOTE: *The pâté will keep well in the refrigerator for up to four days.*

Terrine of Pheasant, Squab, and Quail with Wild Mushrooms

Serves 8 as a first course
Working time: about 1 hour and 45 minutes
Total time: about 16 hours (includes marinating and chilling)

Calories **115**
Protein **14g.**
Cholesterol **25mg.**
Total fat **3g.**
Saturated fat **trace**
Sodium **190mg.**

2 pheasants (about 1 lb. each)
2 squabs (about ½ lb. each)
2 quails (about ½ lb. total weight)
1 oz. dried shiitake mushrooms
1 oz. dried morels
1 oz. dried cloud-ear mushrooms
¼ lb. fresh chanterelles, wiped clean
¼ lb. fresh oyster mushrooms, wiped clean
2 onions, quartered
2 celery stalks, chopped
2 carrots, sliced
3 unpeeled garlic cloves, crushed
8 black peppercorns
3 cloves
2 tsp. fresh thyme, or ½ tsp. dried thyme leaves
1 bay leaf
4 very ripe tomatoes, or 1 cup canned tomatoes
½ oz. dried ceps
¾ tsp. salt
3 tbsp. Madeira
1 scant cup dry white wine
⅔ cup unsalted chicken stock (recipe, page 10)
¾-inch piece fresh ginger, thinly sliced
1 egg, white only, shell washed and reserved
1 tbsp. red wine vinegar
4 tsp. powdered gelatin
8 small bunches of mustard cress or fresh herbs, for garnish

Madeira marinade

½ tsp. black peppercorns
2 bay leaves
¾-inch piece fresh ginger, peeled
1 garlic clove
3 tbsp. Madeira

Remove the breasts from the pheasants, squabs, and quails; reserve the bones. Skin the breasts, trimming away any fat and sinew, and flatten them a little with a mallet or rolling pin. Place the breasts in a single layer in a large, shallow, nonreactive dish.

To make the Madeira marinade, pound the peppercorns, bay leaves, ginger, and garlic together into a rough paste, using a mortar and pestle, then mix in the Madeira. Pour the marinade over the breasts, and cover the dish. Refrigerate the dish and allow the meat to marinate for about eight hours, turning it over several times.

Soak the dried shiitake mushrooms, morels, and cloud-ears in tepid water for 20 minutes, or until they are soft; soak the shiitake mushrooms separately, since the other mushrooms are usually very gritty. Squeeze the mushrooms dry over their soaking bowls, then rinse them in several changes of cold, fresh water. Strain the mushroom-soaking liquids through a cheesecloth-lined sieve into a small bowl; cover the bowl and set it aside. Trim away any tough stalks from the reconstituted dried mushrooms and the chanterelle and oyster mushrooms, reserving the trimmings. Cover the mushrooms and refrigerate them until they are needed.

Meanwhile, prepare the stock for the game aspic. Preheat the oven to 425° F. Remove and discard the skin and fat from the bones and reserve the legs from the pheasants for another use. Place the bones in a large roasting pan, together with the onions, celery, and carrots. Roast the bones and vegetables until they are well browned—about one hour. Turn off the oven. Transfer the contents of the roasting pan to a large pot. Pour 2 cups of water into the roasting pan; with a spatula, scrape the browned bits from the bottom of the pan. Pour the liquid into the pot. Add the garlic, peppercorns, cloves, thyme, and bay leaf. Pour in enough water to cover the contents of the pot by about 2 inches. Bring the liquid to a boil; lower the heat to maintain a simmer, and skim any impurities from the surface. Simmer the stock very gently for about 30 minutes. Add the tomatoes, dried ceps, and the reserved mushroom trimmings and soaking liquid. Simmer the stock for two hours and 30 minutes more, skimming it occasionally.

Strain the stock; allow the solids to drain thoroughly into the stock before discarding them. Degrease the stock (box, page 11).

Preheat the oven to 475° F.

Remove the breast fillets from their marinade and wipe them dry. Strain the marinade through a cheesecloth-lined sieve into the game stock. In a non-stick skillet, brown the breasts over medium heat, allowing two minutes on each side for the pheasant, two minutes on each side for the squab, and one minute on each side for the quail. Place the browned breasts in an ovenproof dish, season them with ¼ teaspoon of the salt, and sprinkle on 1 tablespoon of the Madeira. Cover the dish with foil and cook the breasts in the oven for three minutes, then turn off the heat. Set the oven door slightly ajar and let the meat rest in the warm oven for 10 minutes more. Remove the dish from the oven and set it aside for the breasts to cool. (The squab breasts should still be pink.)

Cut the pheasant and squab breasts into ½-inch strips along the grain; leave the quail breasts whole. Place the meat in a dish, cover it, and chill it in the refrigerator until required. Strain the cooking juices into the game stock. Bring the game stock to a simmer, add the reconstituted dried mushrooms, and poach them for 20 minutes.

Meanwhile, mix the white wine with the chicken stock in a small, nonreactive saucepan, add the ginger, and bring the liquid to a simmer. Add the fresh mushrooms and poach them for five minutes. (They would discolor if poached in the game stock.) Using a slotted spoon, remove the mushrooms from the stocks, drain them on paper towels, then place them in a dish, cover it, and place it in the refrigerator. Strain the chicken stock into the game stock.

Reduce the stock to about 1 quart, then convert it into aspic using the egg white, egg shell, vinegar, and gelatin, following the instructions on page 12. While the aspic is still hot, stir in the remaining salt and Madeira. Set the aspic aside to cool—about one hour.

Carefully ladle a thin layer of the cooled aspic into the bottom of a chilled terrine or loaf pan; refrigerate for 15 minutes, or until it is set. Set aside some of the better-looking mushrooms for garnish. Arrange the quail breasts centrally on the aspic along the length of the terrine and the morels on either side. Pour on sufficient aspic to half cover them and return the terrine to the refrigerator to partially set—about 15 minutes. Pour on more aspic to cover the quail breasts and morels completely. Repeat this process with the remaining ingredients in the following order: chanterelles, strips of squab, oyster mushrooms, cloud-ear mushrooms, strips of pheasant, and finally shiitake mushrooms. Chill the terrine for two to three hours.

Serve the terrine sliced, garnished with the reserved mushrooms and small bunches of mustard cress or fresh herbs.

EDITOR'S NOTE: *The bird breasts can be marinated overnight and the game stock prepared in advance.*

Potted Pheasant with Caramelized Apples

Serves 4 as a main course
Working time: about 1 hour and 15 minutes
Total time: about 30 hours (includes marinating and cooling)

Calories **325**
Protein **27g.**
Cholesterol **55mg.**
Total fat **10g.**
Saturated fat **3g.**
Sodium **275mg.**

2 pheasants (about 1 lb. each), or 4 squabs (about ½ lb. each)
¾ cup plus 1 tsp. Calvados
12 black peppercorns, crushed
1 shallot, halved
1 large garlic clove, finely chopped
1 leek, white part only, washed and split
1 carrot, sliced
1 celery stalk, sliced
1 fresh bouquet garni
2½ cups unsalted chicken stock (recipe, page 10) or water
2 firm cooking apples, peeled, cored, and halved horizontally
½ tsp. salt
¼ tsp. ground mace
5 tsp. honey
¼ cup peeled hazelnuts, toasted and coarsely chopped

Cut the pheasants or squabs into pieces, removing as much skin and fat as possible, and place them in a bowl. Sprinkle ½ cup of the Calvados and the crushed peppercorns over the pieces. Cover the dish and let the pheasants marinate in the refrigerator for 24 hours, occasionally turning the pieces.

At the end of this time, put the shallot, garlic, leek, carrot, celery, and bouquet garni in a large, heavy-bottomed saucepan or flameproof casserole. Pour in the stock or water, and bring it to a boil, skimming the liquid. Lower the heat and add the pheasant pieces together with the marinade. Bring the liquid back to a boil, skim it again, then simmer the pheasants, partly covered, for 15 minutes. Add the apples and simmer for 30 minutes more (15 minutes if you are using squabs); check the liquid from time to time, and if necessary, add more boiling stock or boiling water to just cover the fruit.

Remove the apples with a slotted spoon and set them aside. Check the pheasants: The meat should be almost falling off the bones. If any of the meat is not tender, simmer the pieces for 10 to 15 minutes more. Remove the pheasants from the pan or casserole, and place the pieces in a deep bowl. Strain the cooking liquid through a fine sieve over the pheasants, pressing down hard on the vegetables to extract all their juices. Let the meat cool in the liquid—about one hour.

When the pheasants have cooled, remove them from the liquid. Skim off and discard any fat from the surface of the cooking liquid, then pour the liquid into a saucepan and boil it hard until it is reduced to ¾ cup. Meanwhile, cut all the meat from the bones. Shred the tenderest meat with two forks and set it aside. Place the rest of the meat, the salt, the ground mace, the teaspoon of Calvados, 2 teaspoons of the honey, and all but ¼ cup of the reduced cooking liquid in a food processor, and blend until smooth. Stir the shredded meat and the chopped hazelnuts into the processed mixture, then pack it into a 3-cup serving dish and chill it for about 30 minutes.

Just before serving, caramelize the apples. Pour the reserved ¼ cup of cooking liquid into a nonreactive saucepan. Add the remaining ¼ cup of Calvados, the remaining honey, and the poached apples. Simmer gently, turning the apples once, until the liquid has turned into a golden caramel glaze coating the apples—about 10 minutes. Then remove the pan from the heat immediately; cooking the caramel any longer will darken it.

Serve the potted pheasant, scooped onto individual plates, with the hot caramelized apples.

SUGGESTED ACCOMPANIMENTS: *French bread; tossed salad.*

EDITOR'S NOTE: *To toast hazelnuts, place them on a baking sheet in a preheated 350° F. oven for about 10 minutes.*

Duck Pâté with Orange and Juniper

DRIED CITRUS PEEL HAS A UNIQUE, RICH FLAVOR AND IS OFTEN
USED IN DUCK AND BEEF DISHES. IT IS AVAILABLE
FROM ASIAN MARKETS.

Serves 10 as a first course
Working time: about 1 hour and 30 minutes
Total time: about 16 hours (includes marinating
and chilling)

Calories **155**
Protein **17g.**
Cholesterol **55mg.**
Total fat **6g.**
Saturated fat **2g.**
Sodium **95mg.**

½ tsp. coarse salt
¼ tsp. sugar
½ tsp. freshly ground black pepper
4 duck legs and thighs, skinned and boned
1 tbsp. virgin olive oil
10 oz. lean pork, trimmed of fat and connective tissue, cut into large cubes
1 large garlic clove, chopped
4 shallots, chopped
2 tbsp. brandy
1¼ cups red wine
1 orange, juice only
1 cup unsalted chicken stock (recipe, page 10)
¼ tsp. salt
10 juniper berries
10 black peppercorns
strip of fresh tangerine or dried citrus peel, 1 by 2 inches
3 bay leaves
⅓ cup vegetable aspic (recipe, page 13), melted (optional)

Combine the coarse salt, sugar, and some black pepper on a plate, and coat the duck meat evenly with this mixture. Cover the duck, and let it marinate in the refrigerator for at least eight hours, or up to 24 hours.

Wipe the duck clean with a damp cloth, pat it dry, and cut it into large cubes.

Preheat the oven to 300° F.

Heat the olive oil in a large skillet over medium heat, add the duck and pork cubes, and brown the meat in the oil for about five minutes. Using a slotted spoon, remove the meat from the pan and set it aside in an ovenproof dish. Cook the garlic and shallots in the pan until they are lightly browned. Warm the brandy in a small saucepan, add it to the shallots and garlic, and light it with a match. When the flame dies down, add the red wine, and cook, scraping the pan with a spatula, until the liquid has reduced slightly. Add the orange juice and continue to cook until the liquid has reduced by a quarter.

Add the chicken stock to the skillet. Bring the liquid to a boil and add the salt, then pour the contents of the pan over the duck and pork. Scatter the juniper berries and peppercorns over the meat, tuck the citrus peel into the middle, and cover the dish tightly. Cook the duck and pork in the oven for two and a half hours. ▶

Remove the dish from the oven and set it aside to cool, still covered, for about 30 minutes. Using a slotted spoon, remove the cooled meat from the cooking juices. Strain the juices through a sieve into a measuring cup. There should be about ¾ cup of liquid: If there is less, add a little stock; if there is more, reduce it by boiling. Reserve a few of the juniper berries for garnish and discard the rest of the spices in the sieve.

Separate the pork from the duck (the duck is the darker meat) and purée the pork in a food processor with the strained cooking juices. Transfer the purée to a mixing bowl. Using two forks, shred the duck and mix it into the pork purée. Pack the mixture into an earthenware pot and leave it in the refrigerator until set—about three hours.

Decorate the top of the pâté with the reserved juniper berries and the bay leaves. If desired, carefully spoon vegetable aspic over the top to a depth of about ¼ inch. Leave the pâté in the refrigerator until the aspic has set—at least 30 to 40 minutes.

SUGGESTED ACCOMPANIMENT: *fingers of thin whole-wheat toast.*

EDITOR'S NOTE: *The pâté will benefit from being left in the refrigerator for up to four days before serving so that the flavor can mature.*

Potted Pheasant with Chestnuts

Serves 6 as a first course
Working time: about 40 minutes
Total time: about 4 hours (includes cooling)

Calories **245**
Protein **25g.**
Cholesterol **55mg.**
Total fat **12g.**
Saturated fat **3g.**
Sodium **125mg.**

½ tsp. safflower oil
2 slices lean bacon, coarsely chopped
1 onion, sliced
2 garlic cloves, thinly sliced
2 celery stalks, sliced
1 small carrot, sliced
1 pheasant (about 1½ lb.)
6 juniper berries, crushed
1¼ cups red wine
1¼ cups unsalted vegetable or chicken stock (recipes, page 10)
½ cup unsweetened chestnut purée
½ orange, juice and grated zest
⅛ tsp. salt
freshly ground black pepper
2 tbsp. polyunsaturated margarine
fresh bay leaves for garnish (optional)
juniper berries for garnish (optional)
orange slices for garnish (optional)

Preheat the oven to 350° F.

Heat the oil in a heavy skillet, add the bacon, and sauté it for about two minutes. Add the onion, garlic, celery, and carrot, and sauté them until the onion is transparent—about five minutes more. Remove the pan from the heat and spoon half of the vegetable mixture into a casserole that will hold the pheasant snugly. Place the pheasant, breast downward, in the casserole, then spoon the remaining vegetable mixture over the top and around the sides of the pheasant. Sprinkle the crushed juniper berries into the casserole. Pour in the red wine and enough stock to come two-thirds of the way up the sides of the bird.

Cover the casserole, and bake it until the pheasant is tender and the juices run clear when a skewer is inserted in a thigh—about two hours. Allow the pheasant to cool in the cooking liquid. When the bird is cool enough to handle, lift it out of the casserole; reserve the cooking liquid. Remove the meat from the bones and chop it finely, discarding the skin.

Put the chestnut purée in a blender or food processor, together with the orange juice and zest, the salt, some black pepper, and ¼ cup of the pheasant-cooking liquid. (Save the remaining cooking liquid for a soup.) Blend the mixture until it is smooth. In a bowl, beat the margarine with a wooden spoon until it is soft and creamy. Gradually mix in the chestnut purée, together with the chopped pheasant.

Divide the mixture between six individual small pots or ramekins. Serve the potted pheasant at room temperature, garnished, if desired, with bay leaves, juniper berries, and a slice of orange.

SUGGESTED ACCOMPANIMENT: *whole-wheat bread.*

EDITOR'S NOTE: *To make the chestnut purée for this recipe from fresh chestnuts, slit about 4 ounces of chestnuts down one side, parboil them for about 10 minutes, then shell and peel them while they are warm. Simmer the chestnuts in water until they are tender—about 20 minutes. Drain them and put them through a sieve.*

Turkey and Pheasant Galantine

Serves 14 as a main course
Working time: about 2 hours and 20 minutes
Total time: about 1 day (includes chilling)

Calories **250**
Protein **40g.**
Cholesterol **105mg.**
Total fat **10g.**
Saturated fat **3g.**
Sodium **220mg.**

1 small turkey (about 7 lb.), boned (opposite), bones reserved	
1 pheasant (about 2½ lb.), boned (opposite), bones reserved	
1 onion, sliced	
½ lemon, sliced	
1 bay leaf	
5 sprigs parsley	
10 black peppercorns	
¾ cup plain low-fat yogurt	
3 cups vegetable aspic (recipe, page 13), melted	
cucumber peel, cut into strips and diamond shapes, for garnish	
½ sweet red pepper, peeled (technique, page 90), seeded, deribbed, and cut into petal shapes with an aspic cutter, for garnish	
1 black olive for garnish	
Mushroom stuffing	
1 tbsp. safflower oil	
1 onion, finely chopped	
1 garlic clove, finely chopped	
½ lb. mushrooms, wiped clean and chopped	
½ tsp. salt	
freshly ground black pepper	
¼ tsp. ground coriander	
1 tbsp. cut chives	
1 to 2 tbsp. chopped parsley	
1 cup fresh whole-wheat breadcrumbs	

1 egg, beaten

Put the turkey bones and pheasant bones into a large saucepan, pour in enough water to cover them, and bring the water to a boil, skimming off any scum that rises to the surface. Add the sliced onion to the pan. Lower the heat, cover the saucepan, and simmer for one hour, stirring the stock occasionally.

Meanwhile, prepare the mushroom stuffing. Heat the oil in a heavy skillet, add the chopped onion and garlic, and cook gently over medium heat until the onion is soft—about five minutes. Add the mushrooms and continue to cook until they too are soft—two to three minutes. Using a slotted spoon, transfer the onions, garlic, and mushrooms to a bowl. Mix in the salt, some black pepper, the coriander, chives, parsley, and breadcrumbs, then stir in the egg to bind the stuffing together.

Lay the pheasant flat on the work surface, skin side down, and spoon the mushroom stuffing along the center of the bird. Fold the sides of the pheasant over and around the stuffing.

Lay the turkey flat on the work surface, skin side down. Carefully place the stuffed pheasant in the center of the turkey, and bring the sides of the turkey over the pheasant to enclose it completely. Using a trussing needle, sew up the seam with butcher's twine, leaving long ends of twine for easy removal. Mold the turkey into an attractive shape; it will set in this shape when cooked. Wrap the galantine in a large piece of cheesecloth, tying it securely at both ends with twine.

Preheat the oven to 325° F.

Place the galantine on a long, double-thickness strip of foil and use the foil to lower it into a large, flameproof casserole. Add the sliced lemon, bay leaf, parsley sprigs, and peppercorns. Remove the bones from the stock and discard them, then strain sufficient stock into the casserole through a cheesecloth-lined sieve to cover the galantine. Bring the stock slowly to a boil over medium heat. Cover the casserole with a tight-fitting lid and cook it in the oven for two hours. Remove the casserole from the oven and let the galantine cool in the stock—about three hours. Using the strip of foil, carefully lift the cooled galantine out of the casserole, and let it drain well on a wire rack that has been set over a tray. Chill the galantine thoroughly overnight.

For the coating, combine the yogurt and 1¼ cups of the vegetable aspic, and chill the mixture until the sauce is well thickened but not quite set—about 30 minutes. Remove the cheesecloth and the twine from the galantine, and place it on a wire rack set over a tray or large plate. Spoon and brush a layer of the sauce all over the turkey, then chill it until the sauce has set—about 20 minutes.

Collect the sauce that has dripped on the tray, place it in a flameproof bowl, and set it over a saucepan of simmering water to melt. Stir the sauce to remove any lumps, then chill it until it begins to set. Coat the galantine with a second layer of sauce. Set the galantine on the rack over a clean tray, and chill it for 30 minutes more.

Dip the cucumber-peel and red-pepper shapes and the olive in the remaining vegetable aspic, and use them to decorate the sauce-coated galantine. Chill the galantine for 15 minutes, and chill the aspic until it is thick but not set. Pour the aspic over the galantine to glaze it. Return the galantine to the refrigerator and

chill until the aspic is completely set—about one hour.

Place the galantine on a large serving dish. Carefully scrape the aspic on the bottom of the tray onto a very clean, dampened cutting board and chop it into small cubes with a wet knife. Serve the galantine sliced straight downward to reveal the layers of turkey, pheasant, and stuffing, and garnished with the chopped vegetable aspic.

Boning a Bird for a Galantine

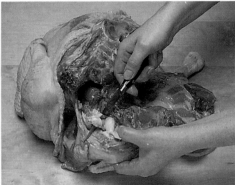

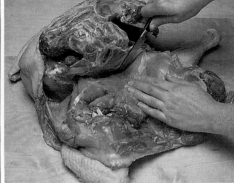

1 CUTTING THE BIRD OPEN. Place the chilled bird (here, a turkey) with its breast down on a wooden cutting board, drumsticks facing you. Using a boning knife or a small, strong, sharp knife, make a slit from the neck to the tail, cutting through the skin to expose the long upper ridge of the backbone. Cut off the tail if it is still attached. With the knife blade held firmly against one side of the backbone, begin freeing the meat from that side of the bird. Using your other hand to lift the skin and flesh, cut and scrape under the oyster-shaped piece of meat (above) and around and down the outside of the collarbone.

2 SEVERING THE WING AND THIGH JOINTS. Working on the same side of the bird, pull the wing away from the breast. Cut around the base of the wing and through the joint to dislocate the wing. Cut about one-third of the way down the rib bones, working along the length of the carcass until you encounter the thigh joint. To locate the thigh socket, grasp the end of the drumstick and pull the leg toward you. Cut away the meat and cartilage around the joint. Sever the joint by cutting around the ball where it joins the socket.

3 FREEING THE SIDES. Continue cutting downward to detach the leg, being careful not to slice through the bottom layer of breast skin. Cut the skin and flesh from around the neck and collarbone so that the back meat comes away from the carcass. Pressing the blade of the knife against the rib cage and then the breastbone, cut and scrape away the breast (above). Take care not to pierce the skin (that would allow filling to escape later), and stop cutting when you reach the ridge of the breastbone. Repeat Steps 1, 2, and 3 on the other side of the bird.

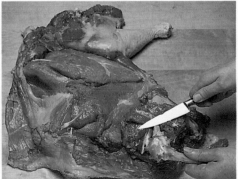

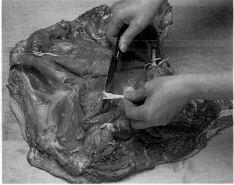

4 DETACHING THE CARCASS. Scrape away the flesh on either side of the breastbone to expose the ridge and tip of the breastbone. Lift the carcass with one hand. Then, starting at the tip of the breastbone, free the carcass by cutting just under the breastbone ridge and through the cartilage with the knife (above). Be careful not to puncture the skin; there is no flesh between skin and bone at this point. Cut off the wing tips at the first joint.

5 REMOVING THE LEG AND WING BONES. Starting at the detached end of one of the thighbones, cut into the flesh on either side of the bone along its length. Scrape away the flesh from the sides and detached end of the bone. Holding the bone with one hand, scrape down its length to expose the joint, and continue scraping down the length of the drumstick (above). Remove the leg. Repeat the process to remove the other thighbone and drumstick. Remove the wing bones in the same way.

6 OPENING OUT THE BONED BIRD. Remove the white tendon from the thick ends of the breast meat by slicing through the flesh on either side of the tendon. Remove the leg tendons in the same way. Carefully trim off any excess fat and membrane. Refrigerate the bird until it is required.

Chicken Galantine with an Herbed Veal and Vegetable Stuffing

THIS RECIPE FOR AN ELEGANT PARTY DISH USES FRESH
VEGETABLES COMBINED WITH VEAL FOR ITS STUFFING.

Serves 10 as a main course
Working time: about 2 hours
Total time: about 12 hours (includes chilling)

Calories **140**
Protein **22g.**
Cholesterol **50mg.**
Total fat **4g.**
Saturated fat **2g.**
Sodium **90mg.**

one 3-lb. chicken
½ tsp. salt
freshly ground black pepper
5 tbsp. Madeira
2 oz. baby carrots (about 3 to 4), cut into strips
2 oz. baby corn (about 3 to 4), trimmed if necessary
½ leek, cleaned thoroughly, cut into ½-inch chunks
2 oz. small turnip or kohlrabi, cut into matchstick-size pieces
2 oz. small parsnips (about 3 to 4), cut into strips
¾ lb. ground lean veal
3 tbsp. finely chopped parsley, plus 2 sprigs parsley
3 tbsp. finely chopped chervil
6 sprigs fresh tarragon, leaves of 4 sprigs finely chopped
9 cups unsalted veal stock (recipe, page 10)
3 tsp. powdered gelatin
½ cup plain low-fat yogurt
fresh herb leaves, such as chervil, parsley, chives, for garnish

Bone the chicken, leaving the legs and wings intact, but cutting off the wing tips with a sharp knife *(page 45, Steps 1, 2, 3, and 4).* Lay the boned chicken flat on the work surface, skin down, and sprinkle the flesh with half of the salt, plenty of black pepper, and 1 tablespoon of the Madeira.

Bring a large saucepan of water to a boil. Blanch the carrots and corn in the boiling water for three minutes, then add the leek, turnip or kohlrabi, and the parsnips, and boil the vegetables for 30 seconds more. Drain the vegetables, refresh them under cold running water, then drain them again.

Combine the veal with the finely chopped parsley, chervil, and tarragon, 1 tablespoon of the Madeira, the remaining salt, and some black pepper. Spread half of this mixture over the boned chicken. Place the cooked vegetables lengthwise down the middle of the chicken, arranging them so that they lie in four or five rows stacked on top of each other from neck to tail; the vegetables should be arranged so that each slice of the galantine will contain a variety. Pack the remaining veal mixture over and around the vegetables. Bring the sides of the bird over the stuffing, and using a trussing needle, sew up the seam with butcher's twine, leaving a long end to ensure easy removal when the galantine is cooked. Mold the chicken to resemble the original shape of the bird; it will set this way when cooked. Wrap the galantine in a large piece of cheesecloth measuring about 18 by 24 inches, tying it securely at both ends with twine. Pour the veal stock into a flame-proof casserole or saucepan large enough to hold the wrapped chicken. Add the tarragon and parsley sprigs to the stock, and bring it to a boil. Lower the chicken into the stock and bring it back to a boil, then lower the heat and simmer the chicken, partly covered, for 45 minutes. Carefully turn the chicken over in the stock and simmer it for 30 minutes more. Remove the casserole or pan from the heat, cover it with a tight-fitting lid, and leave the chicken in its hot liquid for 30 minutes more. Remove the chicken from the stock, allow it to cool to room temperature—one and a half to two hours—then place it, still wrapped in the cheesecloth, in a baking pan or dish. Cover it with plastic wrap and chill it for six hours.

Skim the fat off the surface of the stock. Pour the stock through a cheesecloth-lined sieve into a saucepan, bring it to a boil, and let it boil vigorously until it has reduced in volume to 3 cups. Set the stock aside to cool at room temperature.

Unwrap the chilled chicken and carefully remove all of its skin. Remove and discard the twine. Place a long, double-thickness strip of wax paper or foil about 4 inches wide on a wire rack set over a baking sheet, and place the skinned chicken on it.

Dissolve 2 teaspoons of the gelatin in 2 tablespoons of the remaining Madeira *(technique, page 13).* Stir the dissolved gelatin into ⅔ cup of the reduced cooking stock, then gradually stir the liquid into the yogurt, making sure the sauce is thoroughly blended. Chill the sauce until it is just beginning to set—about 10 minutes—then spoon it over the chicken to coat it evenly, including the leg and wing tip. Work quickly; the sauce sets rapidly. Garnish the chicken with the fresh herb leaves, pressing them lightly into the sauce coating.

Dissolve the remaining gelatin in the remaining Madeira *(technique, page 13)*, then stir it into 5 tablespoons of the remaining reduced stock, and chill the mixture until it is just beginning to set—about 10 minutes. Pour this aspic over the galantine. Transfer the galantine to a serving platter, using the strip of wax paper or foil to lift it, and chill it for at least one hour, or up to 24 hours, before carving. The leg and wing joints may be removed and served separately.

EDITOR'S NOTE: *The remaining reduced stock may be chilled until firm—at least one hour—chopped, and served as a garnish. Alternatively, the stock can be reserved for use in another recipe.*

Potted Turkey

Serves 4 as a first course
Working time: about 45 minutes
Total time: about 3 hours (includes chilling)

Calories **175**
Protein **19g.**
Cholesterol **65mg.**
Total fat **6g.**
Saturated fat **2g.**
Sodium **110mg.**

1 lb. boneless turkey breast, skinned and cut into 1-inch cubes
1 onion, one half coarsely chopped, the other half finely chopped
1 bay leaf
2 lemon slices
¼ tsp. salt
freshly ground black pepper
1 tbsp. unsalted butter
1 garlic clove, finely chopped
¼ tsp. ground allspice
2 tbsp. dry sherry
3 tbsp. plain low-fat yogurt
1 cup vegetable aspic (recipe, page 13), melted
dill sprig for garnish

Place the turkey with the coarsely chopped onion, bay leaf, lemon slices, half of the salt, and a little black pepper in a heavy-bottomed saucepan. Pour 1¼ cups of water into the pan and bring it to a boil. Lower the heat, cover the pan, and simmer until the turkey is tender—about 20 minutes. Let the turkey cool in its cooking liquid for about 20 minutes. Using a slotted spoon, remove the turkey from the cooking liquid and set it aside. Boil the liquid until it is reduced to about 1½ tablespoons, then strain it; discard the onion, bay leaf, and lemon slices.

Melt the butter in a small skillet over medium heat, add the finely chopped onion and garlic, and cook them until they are soft but not browned—about three minutes. Place the turkey, onion, and garlic in a food processor, and process them until they are smooth. Transfer the turkey mixture to a bowl. Add the strained cooking liquid together with the allspice, sherry, yogurt, the remaining salt, and plenty of black pepper. Mix well; the mixture should be stiff but spreadable.

Press the turkey mixture into a large serving bowl and chill it in the refrigerator for about one hour.

Allow the melted aspic to cool until it is just beginning to thicken, then spoon it over the turkey. Set the dill sprig into the aspic. Chill the turkey until the aspic has set—about 20 minutes.

SUGGESTED ACCOMPANIMENT: *toast, crackers, or crusty bread.*

Jellied Asparagus and Chicken Terrine

Serves 12 as a first course
Working time: about 60 minutes
Total time: about 7 hours (includes chilling)

Calories **72**
Protein **10g.**
Cholesterol **20mg.**
Total fat **3g.**
Saturated fat **1g.**
Sodium **40mg.**

2 boneless chicken breast halves (about 6 oz. each), skinned
1 tsp. grated lemon zest
1 small garlic clove, finely chopped
¼ cup dry white wine
2 sprigs fresh tarragon, plus 1 tbsp. chopped fresh tarragon
12 thin asparagus spears (about ¾ lb.), trimmed and peeled
6 cups vegetable aspic (recipe, page 13), melted
1 tbsp. cut chives
2 tbsp. chopped parsley
1 hard-boiled egg, finely chopped
red-leaf lettuce leaves for garnish
Lemon yogurt sauce
1 lemon, grated zest, plus 1 tbsp. juice
1 tsp. chopped fresh tarragon
2 tsp. chopped parsley
⅛ tsp. sugar
1¼ cups plain low-fat yogurt

Place the chicken breast halves in a shallow baking dish, and sprinkle them with the lemon zest and garlic. Set the chicken aside, covered, for 30 minutes to one hour, to marinate.

While the chicken is marinating, preheat the oven to 400° F. When the chicken is ready, pour the wine over the breasts, add the tarragon sprigs, and cover the dish. Bake the chicken until it is tender—25 to 30 minutes. Allow the chicken to cool, still covered, in its cooking liquid.

Place the asparagus in a steamer and steam it until it is tender—six to eight minutes. Drain the asparagus, refresh it under cold running water, and drain it again. Cut off a 2-inch tip from each spear and set the tips aside. Thinly slice the stalks and set them aside.

Ladle a little of the vegetable aspic into a loaf pan or terrine 11 by 3½ by 3½ inches to cover the bottom of the pan by ¼ inch. Arrange the asparagus tips in an even layer across the bottom of the pan, alternating the direction of the tips. Pour in enough vegetable aspic to just cover the asparagus tips and chill it until it is set—about 15 minutes.

Drain the chicken (reserve the cooking liquid for another use) and cut it into 2-by-¼-inch bâtonnets. Position a chicken bâtonnet on each asparagus tip. Mix the chopped tarragon, chives, and parsley together, and sprinkle a third of the mixed herbs over the chicken. Cover this layer with more of the vegetable aspic and chill until it is set. Sprinkle half of the sliced asparagus and half of the chopped egg in an even layer over the chilled aspic. Cover with more vegetable aspic and chill again until it is set. Continue layering the chicken and herbs, and the asparagus and egg in the pan to make three more layers, pouring aspic over each layer and letting it chill and set for about 15 minutes between layers. Pour the remaining vegetable aspic over the final layer and chill it until it is very firm—at least four hours, or overnight.

To make the lemon yogurt sauce, mix the lemon zest and juice with the chopped tarragon and parsley and the sugar. Stir in the yogurt and chill the sauce thoroughly before serving—about one hour.

To unmold the terrine, dip the pan in hot water for five seconds, then invert it onto a flat serving plate. Serve the terrine garnished with the lettuce leaves and accompanied by the sauce.

EDITOR'S NOTE: *If you are making the vegetable aspic especially for this recipe, the reserved chicken-cooking liquid can be incorporated into the aspic before it is clarified.*

Chicken and Asparagus Molds

Serves 4 as a first course
Working time: about 30 minutes
Total time: about 2 hours

Calories **145**
Protein **23g.**
Cholesterol **45mg.**
Total fat **5g.**
Saturated fat **2g.**
Sodium **150mg.**

2 boneless chicken breast halves (about 4 oz. each), skinned
1 large sprig fresh tarragon, plus ½ tsp. chopped fresh tarragon
1 strip lemon zest
¼ tsp. salt
freshly ground black pepper
8 thin asparagus spears (about 4 oz.)
2 tbsp. dry white wine
3 tsp. powdered gelatin
5 tbsp. plain low-fat yogurt
2 tsp. fresh lemon juice
1 tomato, cut into wedges, for garnish

Place the chicken breast halves in a saucepan together with the tarragon sprig, lemon zest, half of the salt, some black pepper, and ⅔ cup of water. Cover the pan, gently bring the water to a boil, then simmer the chicken for 20 minutes.

Meanwhile, cook the asparagus spears in a saucepan of simmering water until they are just tender—about two minutes. Drain the asparagus spears, re-fresh them under cold running water, and drain them again. Cut off a 2-inch tip from each spear and set the tips aside. Coarsely chop the stalks.

Drain the cooked chicken breasts on paper towels. Strain the stock through a cheesecloth-lined sieve and, if necessary, add enough cold water to make ⅔ cup. Stir the wine into the stock.

To make an aspic, dissolve ½ teaspoon of the gelatin in ¼ cup of the wine and stock mixture (technique, page 13). Pour 1 tablespoon of the aspic into each of four ½-cup molds. Let the aspic partially set in the refrigerator—about five minutes. Arrange two asparagus tips on the partially set jelly in each mold. Then return the molds to the refrigerator until the aspic is firmly set—about 10 minutes.

Meanwhile, coarsely chop the chicken and process it in a food processor to form a smooth paste. Dissolve the remaining 2½ teaspoons of gelatin in the rest of the stock, and add it to the chicken, together with the yogurt and the lemon juice. Process the ingredients briefly to blend them. Turn the chicken mousseline into a bowl, add the chopped asparagus stalks, the chopped tarragon, the remaining salt, and some black pepper, and mix well. Spoon the mousseline over the set jelly in the molds. Place the molds in the refrigerator until the mousseline has set—about one hour.

To serve the molds, dip them briefly in hot water and unmold them onto individual plates. Garnish with the tomato wedges.

Poached Chicken and Pistachio Sausage

IN THIS LOW-FAT ADAPTATION OF CLASSIC FRENCH *BOUDIN BLANC*, "WHITE PUDDING," A SPICED, CHOPPED CHICKEN MIXTURE IS POACHED AND SERVED IN THINLY SLICED ROUNDS.

Serves 6 as a main course
Working time: about 2 hours and 45 minutes
Total time: about 30 hours (includes chilling)

Calories **220**
Protein **25g.**
Cholesterol **55mg.**
Total fat **8g.**
Saturated fat **2g.**
Sodium **275mg.**

1 onion, chopped
¼ tsp. ground mace
5 tbsp. skim milk
3 tbsp. sour cream
7 tbsp. fresh white breadcrumbs
½ lb. skinned, boneless chicken breast, ground or finely chopped
½ lb. lean veal, ground or finely chopped
1 egg, shell washed and reserved
3 egg whites
¼ tsp. grated nutmeg
¼ tsp. ground allspice
¼ tsp. cinnamon
½ tsp. salt
ground white pepper
3 tbsp. pistachio nuts, peeled
1 quart unsalted brown stock (recipe, page 11)
½ cup dry Madeira
4 tsp. powdered gelatin
1 tsp. red wine vinegar

Place the onion, mace, and milk in a saucepan. Slowly

bring the milk to a boil, remove the pan from the heat, and let it infuse—15 to 30 minutes. Strain the liquid through a fine sieve into a small saucepan, pressing down hard on the onion to extract its juice. Stir the sour cream and then the breadcrumbs into the milk. Cook the mixture over low heat, stirring constantly, until it thickens and comes away cleanly from the sides of the pan—two to three minutes. Set it aside to cool.

Place the chicken and veal in a food processor, and process them until they form a smooth paste. Blend in the bread mixture, then the whole egg. With the processor running, gradually add two of the egg whites. Last, blend in the nutmeg, allspice, cinnamon, salt, and some pepper. Put the mixture into a bowl, fold in the pistachios, and chill the mixture for at least two hours.

Lay a 12-by-12-inch piece of plastic wrap on the work surface. Form the chicken and veal mixture into a 10-inch-long oblong on the wrap and use the plastic wrap to roll the mixture into a neat sausage. Rinse a square of cheesecloth, wring it out, lay it on the work surface, and brush it lightly with oil. Unroll the sausage onto one edge of the cheesecloth square, removing the plastic wrap, then roll up the sausage firmly in the cheesecloth. Tie one end of the roll with butcher's twine, ensure that the filling is packed firmly, then tie the other end tightly. Leave the sausage in the refrigerator for 24 hours to allow the flavors to develop.

To cook the sausage, bring the stock to a boil in a saucepan, then pour it into a terrine or loaf pan 11 by 3½ by 3½ inches. Add the Madeira and place the terrine in a deep roasting pan on the stove. Pour boiling water into the pan to come halfway up the sides of the terrine. Heat the water until the stock in the terrine is just simmering. Using twine, tie the two ends of the cheesecloth-wrapped sausage to the handle of a long wooden spoon. Lower the sausage into the stock, resting the spoon on the rim of the pan; the sausage must not touch the bottom of the pan. Add boiling water to the stock to cover the sausage by about 1 inch. Poach the sausage gently for 30 minutes, adding boiling water to the roasting pan if necessary.

At the end of this time, remove and drain the sausage, cut off the tied ends of the cheesecloth, unwrap the sausage, and place it on a wire rack set over a tray. Baste the sausage generously with its cooking liquid, then wrap it in foil and let it cool—about 30 minutes.

Meanwhile, convert the remaining stock into aspic. Strain the stock and reduce it over high heat to 1¼ cups. Follow the instructions on page 13 for making vegetable aspic, using the reduced stock, the powdered gelatin, the remaining egg white, reserved egg shell, and wine vinegar. When the stock has cooled, chill it until it sets to a firm jelly—about one hour.

Serve the sausage at room temperature, cut into thin slices and garnished with cubes of aspic.

SUGGESTED ACCOMPANIMENTS: *whole-wheat bread; carrot curls; cucumber strips.*

EDITOR'S NOTE: *To peel pistachios, simmer them in boiling water for one minute, then rub them briskly in a towel.*

Chicken and Spinach Timbales

Serves 10 as a first course
Working time: about 1 hour and 30 minutes
Total time: about 3 hours

Calories **195**
Protein **28g.**
Cholesterol **45mg.**
Total fat **7g.**
Saturated fat **2g.**
Sodium **175mg.**

5 tsp. safflower oil
2 carrots, finely chopped
1 onion, finely chopped
3 celery stalks, finely chopped
2 garlic cloves, finely chopped
3 tbsp. unbleached all-purpose flour
2 tbsp. curry powder
½ cup dry white wine
one 3½-lb. chicken, skinned, cut into pieces, and all fat removed
1 bouquet garni
2½ cups unsalted chicken stock (recipe, page 10)
1½ lb. spinach, washed and stemmed
⅛ tsp. salt
freshly ground black pepper
4 egg whites
10 fresh grape leaves for garnish (optional)
grapes for garnish (optional)

Heat 3 teaspoons of the oil in a flameproof casserole. Add the carrots, onion, celery, and garlic, and cook them over medium heat, stirring frequently, until they are lightly browned—about five minutes. Stir in the flour and curry powder, and cook for three minutes more. Pour in the wine, stirring continuously, and arrange the chicken pieces on top of the vegetables. Add the bouquet garni and pour in the chicken stock to cover the chicken pieces. Heat the stock slowly until it is just boiling, then lower the heat, cover the casserole, and simmer the chicken until cooked throughout—about 40 minutes.

Using a slotted spoon, remove the chicken pieces and discard the bouquet garni. Strain the cooking liquid through a cheesecloth-lined sieve into the casserole and reserve the vegetables. Skim any fat from the surface of the liquid, and if necessary, boil the liquid until it is reduced to 2 cups. Meanwhile, remove the chicken meat from the bones, discarding any fat and gristle, and cut it into chunks.

Preheat the oven to 375° F. Grease ten ½-cup ramekins with the remaining oil. Cut out circles of parchment paper to fit the bottoms of the ramekins and press a circle of paper into each ramekin.

Select the largest spinach leaves (about one-fourth of the total leaves). Dip them, a few at a time, into simmering water just until they become pliable, then drain them and lay them on paper towels to dry. Line the prepared ramekins with the leaves, overlapping them and allowing the edges to hang over the rims of the dishes. Blanch the remaining spinach leaves in the water for 20 seconds, drain them well in a fine sieve, and squeeze them dry by hand.

Purée the squeezed spinach in a food processor. Add the chicken meat and chop it finely. Transfer the mixture to a large bowl. Add the reserved vegetables and the reduced cooking liquid, mix well, and season with the salt and some black pepper. Beat the egg whites until they form stiff peaks. Gently fold the egg whites into the chicken mixture and divide it among the spinach-lined ramekins. Fold the edges of the spinach leaves over the filling, then cover each timbale with foil. Place the ramekins in a roasting pan or dish, and pour in boiling water to come halfway up the sides of the ramekins. Bake the timbales until they are firm to the touch—about 35 minutes.

When the timbales are cooked, invert them onto individual serving plates. Lift off the ramekins and remove the paper. If desired, garnish the timbales with grape leaves and grapes. Serve them immediately.

Chicken and Ham Mousses

Serves 4 as a first course
Working time: about 50 minutes
Total time: about 1 hour and 45 minutes

Calories **230**
Protein **27g.**
Cholesterol **60mg.**
Total fat **11g.**
Saturated fat **5g.**
Sodium **520mg.**

1 tbsp. unsalted butter
1 small onion, finely chopped
½ lb. boneless chicken breast, skinned and diced
¼ lb. lean cooked ham, coarsely diced
3 tbsp. sour cream
3 tbsp. plain low-fat yogurt
⅛ tsp. ground mace
freshly ground black pepper
2 egg whites
watercress sprigs for garnish
Green sauce
¼ cup sour cream
½ cup plain low-fat yogurt
2 oz. watercress (about ¼ bunch), washed, stemmed, and finely chopped
2 tsp. chopped parsley

Melt the butter in a nonstick skillet and cook the onion over low heat until it begins to soften—about three minutes. Add the chicken, and cook it gently, stirring frequently, until it is opaque, firm, and cooked through—five to six minutes. Remove the pan from the heat, let the chicken cool for a few minutes, then place it in a food processor. Process the chicken until it is finely chopped, add the ham, and process again until the ham, too, is finely chopped. Transfer the chicken and ham mixture to a bowl, add the sour cream and yogurt, the mace, and some black pepper, and mix very thoroughly.

Preheat the oven to 350° F. Lightly grease four ½-cup ramekins or ovenproof molds.

Beat the egg whites until they are stiff, then beat about 2 tablespoons of the stiffened whites into the chicken mixture. Fold in the remaining egg whites quickly and evenly. Divide the mixture among the prepared molds, giving each one a sharp tap on a flat surface to release any air bubbles. Place the molds in a roasting pan and add boiling water to come two-thirds of the way up the sides of the molds. Cook the mousses in the oven until they are firm to the touch—30 to 35 minutes.

Meanwhile, make the sauce: Place the sour cream, yogurt, chopped watercress, and chopped parsley in a food processor or blender, and process to make a smooth, pale green sauce—about one minute.

Let the cooked mousses cool slightly, then carefully turn each one out onto a small plate. Spoon a little green sauce over part of each mousse and onto the plate. Serve the mousses while they are still warm, garnished with watercress sprigs.

EDITOR'S NOTE: *The mousses can be served either as a first course or as the main course for a light lunch.*

Jellied Lemon Chicken

Serves 12 as a main course
Working time: about 45 minutes
Total time: about 15 hours (includes chilling)

Calories **140**
Protein **26g.**
Cholesterol **70mg.**
Total fat **4g.**
Saturated fat **2g.**
Sodium **170mg.**

one 6½-lb. chicken, giblets reserved except the liver
3 lemons, one quartered, grated zest only of two
1 onion, coarsely chopped
2 carrots, coarsely chopped
2 celery stalks, coarsely chopped
¼ cup finely chopped parsley, plus 1 parsley sprig
1 tsp. salt
8 black peppercorns
freshly ground black pepper
4 tsp. capers
parsley sprigs and cucumber slices for garnish

Rinse the chicken and the giblets well under cold running water, and pat them dry with paper towels. Put the lemon quarters inside the chicken. Place the chicken and giblets in a large saucepan, and pour in 2½ cups of cold water. Add the onion, carrots, celery, parsley sprig, ½ teaspoon of the salt, and the peppercorns. Bring the liquid to a boil over medium heat,

then reduce the heat to low. Partially cover the saucepan, and simmer until the chicken is cooked and the juices run clear when a thigh is pierced with a skewer—one and a half to two hours. Remove the chicken from the pan and set it aside, partially covered, to cool.

Strain the stock through a cheesecloth-lined sieve into a bowl. Allow the stock to cool for about one hour, then place it in the refrigerator until the fat rises to the surface and solidifies—three to four hours. Remove and discard all of the fat from the now-jellied stock, then place the bowl in hot water until the stock becomes liquid again.

Meanwhile, remove the meat from the chicken, discarding the skin and bones, and cut it into 1-inch cubes. Place one-third of the chicken in a large, round serving bowl, and season it with a little of the remaining salt and some black pepper. Sprinkle one-third each of the capers, chopped parsley, and grated lemon zest over the chicken. Repeat twice, ending with a layer of capers, parsley, and lemon zest. Carefully pour the stock into the bowl to cover the chicken completely. Cover the bowl and chill the chicken overnight. Serve garnished with herb sprigs and cucumber slices.

SUGGESTED ACCOMPANIMENTS: *salad; crusty garlic bread.*

2 *Raw marinated sea bass, rice, and shellfish feature in a Japanese-inspired terrine wrapped in dried nori seaweed (recipe, page 66).*

Lightness and Flavor from Fish

It is not surprising that fish plays a leading role in the new style of cooking. Low in calories and saturated fat, fish of all kinds is generously endowed with protein and other vital nutrients. Moreover, where terrines and pâtés are concerned, fish is infinitely versatile. Its delicate flesh is easily flaked for creamy, quickly prepared pâtés, or puréed to form the basis of a silk-smooth mousseline. Slender fillets of sole or pink-fleshed trout or salmon can be wrapped around a filling, or used as a colorful lining for a terrine. Chunks of lightly cooked rainbow trout and morsels of shellfish, held in suspension in a wine or lemon aspic, provide a refreshing first course for a summer lunch, while a whole fish, such as sea bass—boned, stuffed, poached, and presented as a galantine—makes a spectacular centerpiece for a formal buffet.

Some of the recipes on the following pages call for white-fleshed fish such as haddock, cod, or Dover sole; others require oily species such as mackerel or salmon. In all cases, substitutions can be made, so long as you keep to fish of the same basic type. A dish of delicately flavored elements, such as the three-fish pâté with shrimp on page 78, would not be improved by the inclusion of an assertive, oily-fleshed species such as mackerel. In turn, the robust flavorings in the curried shrimp pâté on page 77 would overpower the subtlety of sea bass or sole.

Indispensable to every successful fish terrine, pâté, or galantine is a first-class fish market. As well as supplying seafood of impeccable freshness, a good fish dealer will provide a fund of information and enough practical help to cut your working time virtually in half. If the day's catch does not include the species called for in a recipe, the fish dealer will suggest the best alternatives. A dealer will also free the cook from such necessary but time-consuming chores as gutting, filleting, or boning a fish. And if you intend to serve a raw fish preparation, such as the Terrine Mikado on page 66, a trusted source is essential. It is a cardinal rule that dishes containing uncooked fish should be made only with seafood that is absolutely fresh, and that they should be eaten on the day they are prepared.

Because freshness is such a vital factor, even those pâtés and terrines based on cooked fish or shellfish are better served on the day they are made. Those that are to be served well chilled should be prepared a few hours before they are needed and kept in the refrigerator, tightly covered with plastic wrap. Freezing is not advisable for fish terrines; it could mar both their flavor and their texture.

Mullet and Pasta Timbale Wrapped in Spinach

Serves 6 as a main course
Working time: about 1 hour
Total time: about 2 hours

Calories **360**
Protein **28g.**
Cholesterol **110mg.**
Total fat **9g.**
Saturated fat **3g.**
Sodium **250mg.**

½ lb. fresh fettuccine or linguine
1½ lb. red or gray mullet, or red snapper, cleaned and scaled
⅔ cup skim milk
1 onion, grated or finely chopped
1 celery stalk, cut into four pieces
4 black peppercorns
½ lb. large spinach leaves, stemmed and washed
2 tbsp. chopped parsley
2 tbsp. chopped cilantro
½ lemon, grated zest and juice only
freshly ground black pepper
2 tbsp. cornstarch
⅔ cup unsalted fish stock (recipe, page 11)
2 eggs, beaten
2 tbsp. freshly grated Parmesan cheese
Tomato sauce
1 tbsp. virgin olive oil
1 onion, finely chopped
1 garlic clove, finely chopped
2 lb. ripe tomatoes, peeled, seeded, and coarsely chopped
⅔ cup dry white wine
1 tbsp. white wine vinegar
1 tsp. sugar
2 tbsp. chopped fresh basil
¼ tsp. salt
freshly ground black pepper

Bring 3 quarts of lightly salted water to a boil in a large saucepan. Add the pasta, bring the water back to a

boil, and cook the pasta until it is *al dente*—about two minutes. Drain the pasta, rinse it under cold running water, and set it aside.

Place the mullet or red snapper in a large pan, add the milk, onion, celery, and peppercorns, and poach the fish over low heat until it is just tender and flakes—about seven minutes.

In the meantime, blanch the spinach leaves in a large saucepan of rapidly boiling water for 20 seconds. Drain the spinach leaves, refresh them under cold running water, and drain them again. Spread out the leaves on paper towels to dry.

Remove the cooked fish from the pan using a slotted spoon and set it aside in a bowl. Strain the cooking liquid into another bowl, discarding the vegetables and peppercorns, and set it aside. Remove the skin and bones from the fish, and then flake the fish. Mix the parsley, cilantro, lemon zest and juice, and some black pepper into the flaked fish.

Preheat the oven to 350° F.

Mix the cornstarch into the bowl of fish-cooking liquid to form a paste, then stir in the fish stock. Pour the liquid into a saucepan, slowly bring it to a boil, and cook it until the sauce thickens, stirring continuously. Remove the pan from the heat and mix in the beaten eggs. Add the sauce to the pasta with the Parmesan cheese and mix thoroughly.

Line a 1½-quart ovenproof bowl with most of the blanched spinach leaves, overlapping them to prevent any liquid from seeping through, and allowing their ends to overhang the sides of the bowl. Spoon half of the pasta mixture into the bowl, pressing it down lightly. Spoon the fish mixture over the pasta and cover it with the remaining pasta, again pressing down lightly. Cover the pasta layer with the reserved spinach leaves and fold the overhanging leaves over the top of the assembly. Place a small ovenproof plate, upside down, on the top to hold the leaves in place.

Place the bowl in a deep roasting pan and pour boiling water into the pan to come two-thirds of the way up the sides of the bowl. Bake the timbale until a skewer inserted in the center feels hot to the touch when removed—40 to 50 minutes.

While the timbale is baking, make the tomato sauce. Heat the oil in a nonreactive saucepan over medium heat, then cook the onion and garlic until the onion is transparent—about four minutes. Add the tomatoes and cook them for three minutes more, stirring; then add the wine, vinegar, sugar, basil, salt, and a few generous grindings of black pepper. Bring the liquid to a boil, then lower the heat and simmer for 10 minutes. Allow the mixture to cool slightly, then purée it in a food processor or blender.

Remove the roasting pan from the oven and allow the timbale to cool for five minutes. Take off the plate and turn out the timbale onto a serving dish. Serve the timbale hot, accompanied by the tomato sauce, gently reheated if necessary.

SUGGESTED ACCOMPANIMENT: *tossed salad.*

Smoked Salmon Parcels with a Chive and Salmon Trout Filling

Serves 8 as a first course
Working time: about 45 minutes
Total time: about 4 hours (includes chilling)

Calories **120**
Protein **19g.**
Cholesterol **40mg.**
Total fat **5g.**
Saturated fat **1g.**
Sodium **370mg.**

14 oz. salmon trout fillets or salmon fillets
¼ onion, chopped
2 lemon slices, plus extra lemon slices for garnish (optional)
1 bay leaf
6 black peppercorns
⅔ cup low-fat cottage cheese, sieved
⅛ tsp. salt
freshly ground black pepper
⅛ tsp. ground coriander
2 tsp. powdered gelatin
1 tbsp. fresh lemon juice
1 tbsp. thinly sliced chives, plus 16 long chives
1 egg white
¼ lb. smoked salmon, trimmed into eight rectangles 6½ by 2 inches
curly endive for garnish (optional)

Lay the trout or salmon fillets in a skillet. Add the onion, lemon slices, bay leaf, and peppercorns, then pour in 1 cup of water to barely cover the fish. Bring the water just to a boil, lower the heat, and cover the pan; then simmer the trout until it is cooked—four to five minutes. (If you are using salmon, you may need more water to cover the fish. Cook the salmon for six to seven minutes.) Let the fish cool in the cooking liquid. Meanwhile, line a loaf pan 8 by 4½ by 2 inches with parchment paper *(technique, page 34).*

Lift the cooled fillets from the pan and discard the cooking liquid. Flake the fish finely, discarding the skin and any bones. Place the flaked fish in a bowl, and beat in the cottage cheese, the salt, a little black pepper, and the ground coriander. Dissolve the gelatin in the lemon juice and 2 tablespoons of water, following the method on page 13; then stir it into the fish mixture together with the cut chives. Immediately beat the egg white until it is very stiff. Beat 2 tablespoons of the egg white into the fish, then fold in the remainder, making sure that it is evenly distributed. Turn the fish mousse into the prepared pan and chill it until it is firmly set—at least three hours.

Just before serving the mousse, turn it out of the pan and remove the paper. Cut the mousse into eight equal blocks whose lengths are the width of the smoked salmon rectangles. Wrap each portion of mousse in a piece of smoked salmon, leaving the ends of the mousse portion exposed. Wrap two chives around the long and short dimensions of the parcel, as if tying up a package, and lightly knot the ends of the chives together. Serve the parcels on individual plates, garnished with lemon slices and curly endive.

Two-Layered Herbed Fish Terrine

Serves 16 as a first course
Working time: about 45 minutes
Total time: about 4 hours (includes chilling)

Calories **50**
Protein **7g.**
Cholesterol **30mg.**
Total fat **2g.**
Saturated fat **1g.**
Sodium **85mg.**

1 lb. salmon trout fillets, skinned, or salmon fillets
1½ tsp. chopped fennel
1½ tsp. finely cut fresh dill
4 egg whites
½ tsp. salt
ground white pepper
1 tbsp. unsalted butter
¾ cup loosely packed parsley, stalks removed
1 lb. halibut or haddock fillets, skinned
1 tbsp. chopped fresh tarragon, or 1 tsp. dried tarragon
1 tbsp. dry sherry or vermouth

Line a terrine or loaf pan 7½ by 3¾ by 2 inches with parchment paper.

To make the first layer, coarsely chop the trout or salmon fillets, then purée them in a food processor or blender. Add the fennel, dill, two of the egg whites, ¼ teaspoon of the salt, and some white pepper, and blend again to form a smooth paste. Transfer this fish paste to the prepared pan, smoothing it down with the back of a spoon, then make a deep groove lengthwise down the center of the layer. Chill the paste while you prepare the second layer.

Preheat the oven to 375° F. Melt the butter in a small saucepan, add the parsley, and cook it over low heat until it is soft—about 10 minutes. Allow the parsley to cool, then place it in the food processor. Coarsely chop the white fish and add it to the parsley. Process the parsley and fish until they are well blended. Add the tarragon, the remaining egg whites, the sherry or vermouth, the remaining salt, and some white pepper. Process the mixture to a smooth purée. Transfer the purée to the terrine or pan and smooth it into an even layer with the back of a spoon.

Cover the terrine loosely with parchment paper, and place the terrine in a large roasting pan or ovenproof dish. Pour boiling water into the roasting pan to come two-thirds of the way up the sides of the terrine. Bake the terrine until the mixture is set and firm to the touch—about 35 minutes. Let the terrine cool, then chill it for at least two hours. To serve the terrine, turn it out and cut it into slices.

SUGGESTED ACCOMPANIMENTS: *curly endive and radish salad; Melba toast.*

Haddock Terrine with Dill

Serves 16 as a first course
Working time: about 45 minutes
Total time: about 5 hours (includes chilling)

Calories **70**
Protein **11g.**
Cholesterol **30mg.**
Total fat **2g.**
Saturated fat **trace**
Sodium **295mg.**

¾ cup fine fresh white breadcrumbs
1 cup skim milk
9 oz. boned and skinned smoked haddock or cod, cut into pieces
10 oz. boned and skinned fresh haddock or cod, cut into pieces
1 egg
3 egg whites
1 tbsp. dry white vermouth
½ tsp. finely grated lemon rind
1½ tbsp. fresh lemon juice
2½ tbsp. chopped parsley
3 tbsp. finely cut fresh dill
1¼ cups vegetable aspic (recipe, page 13), melted
3 quail eggs, hard-boiled (optional)

Preheat the oven to 350° F. Place ½ cup of the bread-crumbs in a bowl, pour the milk over them, and leave them until they have absorbed the milk—about five minutes. Place the smoked haddock or cod and two-thirds of the fresh haddock or cod in a food processor; then add the egg, two of the egg whites, the ver-mouth, lemon zest, and lemon juice, together with the milk-soaked breadcrumbs. Process the ingredients to a smooth purée. Set the purée aside.

Clean the food processor, then place in it the re-maining fresh fish, egg white, and breadcrumbs, the parsley, and 2 tablespoons of the dill. Process these ingredients until they form a smooth, thick purée.

Line a terrine or loaf pan 7½ by 3¾ by 2 inches with parchment paper (technique, page 34). Spoon half of the smoked haddock purée into the terrine, making sure that the corners of the dish are neatly filled. Lightly smooth the top of the mixture with the back of the spoon. Carefully place the herbed haddock mixture, a tablespoon at a time, down the center of the smoked haddock purée. (The herbed mixture will sink slightly into the smoked haddock purée.) Carefully spread the remaining smoked haddock purée on top, disturbing the herbed purée as little as possible.

Cover the terrine with a lid or aluminum foil, and place it in a large roasting pan or ovenproof dish. Pour in boiling water to come two-thirds of the way up the sides of the terrine.

Bake the terrine until a skewer inserted in the center is hot to the touch when withdrawn—one to one and a quarter hours. Pour off any excess cooking liquid. Let the terrine cool—about one hour—then chill it in the refrigerator for two hours.

Pour a thin layer of aspic over the surface of the terrine and chill it until it has almost set—about 10 minutes. Sprinkle the remaining dill over the aspic, pressing it in lightly, then chill the terrine again until the aspic has completely set—10 minutes more. If you are using quail eggs, cut them into thin, vertical slices and arrange the best slices on top of the terrine. Add the remaining aspic to the terrine and chill it until it has set—10 to 15 minutes.

Pink Trout Mousse

Serves 12 as a first course
Working time: about 30 minutes
Total time: about 4 hours (includes chilling)

Calories **75**
Protein **12g.**
Cholesterol **25mg.**
Total fat **2g.**
Saturated fat **trace**
Sodium **120mg.**

2 shallots, finely chopped
1¼ cups unsalted fish stock (recipe, page 11)
½ lime, juice only
2 tbsp. dry vermouth
1 lb. trout fillets
1 tbsp. tomato paste
2 tbsp. sour cream
2 tbsp. plain low-fat yogurt
½ tsp. salt
ground white pepper
1 tbsp. powdered gelatin
3 egg whites
¼ cucumber, sliced, for garnish (optional)

Place the shallots in a large, shallow, nonreactive pan with the fish stock, lime juice, and vermouth. Bring the liquid to a boil, lower the heat, and simmer for three minutes, until the shallots have softened. Lay the trout fillets in the stock, skin side down. Cover the pan and simmer for three minutes, then remove the pan from the heat and let the fish cool in the stock.

Drain and roughly flake the fish, discarding the skin and any bones. Strain the stock. Place the fish in a food processor or blender together with the strained stock, and blend the ingredients until they are smooth. Turn the mixture into a bowl and beat in the tomato paste, sour cream, yogurt, salt, and some white pepper.

Dissolve the gelatin in 3 tablespoons of cold water, following the instructions on page 13. Slowly pour the dissolved gelatin over the fish mixture, beating it well all the time. Chill the fish mixture until it just begins to set—15 to 20 minutes.

Beat the egg whites until they are stiff but not dry. Using a rubber spatula, stir one-third of the egg whites into the fish mixture to lighten it, then gently fold in the remaining egg whites; avoid overmixing. Turn the mousse into a dampened serving dish and chill it until it is set—about three hours.

Serve the mousse garnished, if desired, with the slices of cucumber.

SUGGESTED ACCOMPANIMENT: *whole-wheat toast; lime wedges.*

Salmon Coulibiac

THIS IS A VARIATION OF A CLASSIC RUSSIAN FISH PIE.
TRADITIONALLY, THE PIE IS LADEN WITH BUTTER AND EGGS;
HERE, A LOW-FAT COD MOUSSELINE PROVIDES MOISTNESS.

Serves 20 as a main course
Working time: about 1 hour and 40 minutes
Total time: about 8 hours (includes rising and cooling)

Calories **270**
Protein **16g.**
Cholesterol **75mg.**
Total fat **10g.**
Saturated fat **3g.**
Sodium **200mg.**

1 lb. cod fillet, boned and skinned
2 egg whites
1¼ tsp. salt
¾ cup sour cream
ground white pepper
1 tbsp. virgin olive oil
1 onion, finely chopped
1¼ cups short-grain rice
1 quart unsalted chicken stock (recipe, page 10)
2 tbsp. chopped fresh marjoram
2 tbsp. chopped fresh oregano
2 lb. center cut piece of fresh salmon, skinned and boned, cut into ½-inch slices
6 tbsp. chopped fresh dill
freshly ground black pepper
½ lemon, juice only
1 egg, beaten
Brioche dough
2 pkgs. (½ oz.) dried yeast
4 cups unbleached all-purpose flour
¼ tsp. salt
2 eggs, beaten
2 egg whites
4 tbsp. polyunsaturated margarine

Begin by preparing the brioche dough. Sprinkle the yeast over ¼ cup of tepid water and set it aside for five minutes. Sift the flour and salt into a mixing bowl and make a well in the center. Add the two beaten eggs, the egg whites, the margarine, and the yeast liquid to the well. Mix the ingredients together to form a firm dough. Knead the dough on a lightly floured surface for 10 minutes, until it is silky smooth and elastic. Place the dough in a clean, lightly floured bowl. Cover the bowl with plastic wrap and refrigerate it for at least

four hours, allowing the dough to rise slowly until it doubles in size.

Meanwhile, prepare the filling. Put the cod, egg whites, and ¼ teaspoon of the salt into a food processor, and process them to a smooth paste. Press the fish mixture through a fine sieve into a clean bowl, to remove all coarse fiber. Cover the bowl and refrigerate the cod mousseline for one hour.

Gradually beat the sour cream into the chilled cod, season it well with white pepper, then cover the bowl again and return it to the refrigerator until required.

To prepare the rice, first heat the oil in a large saucepan over medium-low heat, then add the onion and cook it for six to eight minutes, until it is softened but not browned. Add the rice and stir in the chicken stock, marjoram, oregano, and ¼ teaspoon of the salt. Bring the stock to a boil over high heat. Reduce the heat to low, cover the saucepan with a tightly fitting lid, and simmer for 20 to 25 minutes, until the rice is cooked and all the stock has been absorbed. Set the rice aside to cool.

Turn the risen brioche dough onto a lightly floured surface and knead it for one to two minutes, until it is smooth. Roll the dough out to a large oblong meas-

uring about 18 by 20 inches. Lift the dough carefully onto a large, clean dishtowel.

Spoon half of the rice down the center of the dough in a neat strip measuring about 6 by 14 inches. Cover the rice with half of the salmon slices. Sprinkle the salmon with half of the dill, then season it with ½ teaspoon of the remaining salt, some black pepper, and half of the lemon juice.

Spread the cod mousseline on top of the salmon, covering it completely. Place the remaining salmon on top of the mousseline, sprinkle it with the remaining dill, and season with the remaining salt, some more pepper, and the remaining lemon juice. Very carefully spoon the remaining rice over the salmon to cover it neatly and evenly.

Cut a 4-inch square from each corner of the pastry and set the squares aside. Bring the two short end pieces of pastry up and over the filling, then brush them with a little of the beaten egg. Bring one of the long sides of the pastry up and over the filling, and brush it with a little more of the beaten egg. Bring the remaining side of pastry up and over the top to enclose the filling completely. Gently press the pastry edges together to seal them.

▶

Grease a large baking sheet. With the aid of the dishtowel, very carefully turn the coulibiac onto the baking sheet so that the seams are underneath. Make three evenly spaced holes in the top of the coulibiac. Reknead and reroll the brioche trimmings until they are quite thin, then cut out some oval petal shapes. Brush the coulibiac with beaten egg and decorate it with the pastry petals. Brush the petals with the remaining beaten egg.

Cut a strip of foil about 48 inches long. Fold the foil into three or four sections lengthwise, so that its width is about the same as the coulibiac's depth. Butter the foil well on one side, then wrap it, buttered side inward, around the circumference of the coulibiac. Secure the ends of the strip together firmly with paper clips. (The foil will stop the coulibiac from spreading as it rises.) Set the wrapped coulibiac aside in a warm place for 30 minutes. Preheat the oven to 400° F.

Bake the coulibiac for 20 minutes; lower the oven temperature to 375° F., and continue cooking for 30 minutes more. Remove the foil and cook the coulibiac, uncovered, until the pastry is golden brown and a skewer inserted in the center of the coulibiac feels hot to the touch when removed—15 to 20 minutes.

Allow the coulibiac to cool to room temperature on the baking sheet—about one hour—then transfer it to a serving dish or board. Serve the coulibiac at room temperature, or chilled.

SUGGESTED ACCOMPANIMENTS: *green salad; lemon wedges; cucumber slices.*

EDITOR'S NOTE: *If the coulibiac is to be served chilled, it may be made the day before and stored overnight, covered, in the refrigerator.*

Jellied Bouillabaisse

THIS JELLIED TERRINE TAKES ITS INSPIRATION FROM BOUILLABAISSE, A SAFFRON-SCENTED SOUP MADE WITH AN ASSORTMENT OF MEDITERRANEAN FISH.

Serves 10 as a first course
Working time: about 1 hour
Total time: about 8 hours

Calories **45**
Protein **8g.**
Cholesterol **20mg.**
Total fat **trace**
Saturated fat **trace**
Sodium **30mg.**

¾ lb. sea bass fillets (or other nonoily, firm-textured white fish such as Dover sole, cod, or grouper), skinned

1½ quarts unsalted fish stock (recipe, page 11)

2 small fennel bulbs, bulbs finely chopped, stalks and feathery leaves reserved, plus sprigs for garnish

¼ tsp. saffron threads

4 leeks, trimmed, washed thoroughly to remove all grit, and chopped

½ onion, chopped

2 celery stalks, chopped

1 garlic clove, finely chopped

3 tbsp. powdered gelatin

3 eggs, whites and washed shells only

1 sweet green pepper, peeled (technique, page 90), seeded, and chopped

1 sweet red pepper, peeled (technique, page 90), seeded, and chopped

¾ lb. firm, ripe tomatoes (2 medium), peeled, seeded, and finely chopped, drained on paper towels

Place the fish fillets in a wide, shallow saucepan and pour in enough stock to cover them. Heat the stock gently until it is just simmering, then poach the fish for six to seven minutes, until it is just firm. Using a slotted spoon, carefully remove the fish from the pan. Cut the fillets into ¼-inch cubes and set them aside on paper towels to drain.

Add the chopped fennel bulbs to the fish-cooking liquid and simmer until they are tender—about three minutes. Drain the fennel and place it on paper towels to dry; reserve the cooking liquid.

Put the saffron, leeks, onion, celery, and garlic in a heavy-bottomed saucepan. Trim off the feathery leaves from the fennel stalks, chop them, and set them aside. Slice the stalks and add them to the pan. Pour in the remaining stock and the reserved fish-cooking liquid, bring the liquid slowly to a boil, then simmer it for 20 minutes. Strain the stock through a fine sieve into a large bowl; discard the vegetables. Add the gelatin, egg whites, and shells to the stock, and clarify it following the instructions on page 12. There should be about 1½ quarts of aspic: Pour off any extra or add a little water to make up the quantity, if necessary. Chill the aspic until it is cold and has just begun to set—about 40 minutes.

Ladle enough of the aspic into a loaf pan 11 by 4½ by 3½ inches to cover the bottom by a depth of about ¼ inch, and place the pan in the refrigerator until the aspic is set—about 10 minutes.

Arrange about a third of the cubed fish and some of the chopped green and red peppers in the bottom of the pan. Cover the fish and peppers with aspic and chill until it is set. Sprinkle about half of the chopped tomato and half of the cooked, chopped fennel evenly over the layer of fish and peppers, cover them with aspic, and chill again until it is set. Continue layering the ingredients in this way, chilling the aspic between each layer, and finishing with a layer of fish and peppers. Sprinkle the chopped fennel leaves over the top layer and cover them with the remaining aspic. Chill the terrine until it is completely set—at least four hours, or overnight.

To unmold the jellied bouillabaisse, dip the bottom and sides of the terrine in hot water for five seconds, then invert it onto a serving plate. Serve cut into slices, garnished with sprigs of fennel.

Terrine Niçoise

Serves 10 as a first course
Working time: about 1 hour
Total time: about 3 hours

Calories **155**
Protein **14g.**
Cholesterol **60mg.**
Total fat **7g.**
Saturated fat **2g.**
Sodium **280mg.**

½ lemon
3 large artichokes
6 oz. very small new potatoes (about 6 to 8)
3 oz. French beans or green beans, ends removed
8 to 10 large lettuce leaves
1 sweet red pepper, peeled (technique, page 90) and seeded
1 sweet yellow pepper, peeled (technique, page 90) and seeded
2 eggs
2 egg whites
1 tsp. salt
1¾ cups plain low-fat yogurt
¾ lb. fresh tuna, trimmed into five long strips, each about ¾-inch thick
ground white pepper
Anchovy vinaigrette
2 tbsp. virgin olive oil
2 tbsp. fresh lemon juice
1 tbsp. fresh apple or orange juice
¼ tsp. Dijon mustard
freshly ground black pepper
½ garlic clove, finely chopped (optional)
2 or 3 sprigs fresh thyme, leaves separated
2 or 3 sprigs fresh dill, finely chopped
1 tsp. finely cut chives
1 tsp. finely chopped parsley
2 black olives, finely diced
3 anchovy fillets, larger bones picked out, finely diced

Bring a large, nonreactive saucepan of water to a boil. Squeeze the lemon juice into the water and add the lemon half. Cook the artichokes in the water for 20 to 25 minutes, then drain them upside down. When they are cool, remove the leaves and the choke. Neaten the artichoke bottoms with a knife, and remove a slice from two opposite sides of each one so that they will lie closely side by side when arranged in the terrine.

Boil the potatoes for 8 to 10 minutes, until they are just tender but slightly underdone; refresh them under cold running water. Peel them or leave the skins on, as preferred. Cut a slice from both ends of each potato. Blanch the French beans in boiling water for about 40 seconds. (Blanch green beans for two to three minutes.) Refresh the beans under cold running water, drain them, and set them aside.

Remove the center rib from each lettuce leaf. Dip the leaves in boiling water for a few seconds, until they are soft. Refresh the leaves in cold water, drain them, and spread them out to dry on paper towels. Cut the red and yellow peppers into ⅜-inch strips.

Whisk the eggs and egg whites lightly with ¾ teaspoon of the salt, until they are blended but not frothy. Add the yogurt to the eggs and mix well.

Preheat the oven to 350° F. Line a 1½-quart terrine or loaf pan with the blanched lettuce leaves, leaving about 2½ inches overhanging at the top. Season the tuna and the artichoke bottoms with the remaining salt and some white pepper. Spread a thin layer of the egg and yogurt mixture in the bottom of the terrine, then lay the artichokes along the center with a strip of tuna on each side. Spread enough yogurt mixture over the artichokes and tuna to cover them, lay the strips of yellow pepper on top with a strip of tuna down the center, and cover with more egg and yogurt mixture. Continue layering, using first the beans and then the red pepper strips, and separating each layer with some of the egg and yogurt mixture. For the final layer, place two lines of potatoes on either side and two strips of tuna along the center, and cover these with the remaining egg and yogurt mixture.

Fold the lettuce leaves over the top, making sure that the terrine is completely enclosed by the leaves. (Patch any gaps with extra leaves.) Cover the terrine with foil, piercing a few holes in the foil to let out steam. Stand the terrine in a roasting pan or ovenproof dish, and pour in enough boiling water to come two-thirds of the way up the sides of the terrine. Bake the terrine for one hour; then remove the foil and bake the terrine until a skewer inserted into the center feels hot to the touch when removed—about 10 minutes more.

While the terrine is cooking, prepare the vinaigrette. Blend together the oil, fruit juices, mustard, some black pepper, and the garlic, if you are using it. Gently stir in the remaining ingredients, then set the dressing aside for 20 to 30 minutes at room temperature.

Let the terrine rest in the pan for 15 minutes, covered loosely with foil, then invert it onto a slightly inclined board and let it drain for five minutes. Serve the terrine warm, cut into slices, with the vinaigrette.

Sole and Watercress Terrine with Smoked Eel

Serves 6 as a main course
Working time: about 1 hour
Total time: about 9 hours (includes chilling)

Calories **120**
Protein **17g.**
Cholesterol **125mg.**
Total fat **5g.**
Saturated fat **2g.**
Sodium **250mg.**

1 lb. skinned lemon or Dover sole fillets
1 cup loosely packed watercress
½ cup loosely packed parsley
2 tbsp. chopped fresh chervil, plus sprigs for garnish
2 tbsp. chopped fresh dill or fennel tops
¾ lb. skinned haddock or halibut fillets
2 egg whites
6 tbsp. sour cream
2 tbsp. plain low-fat yogurt
⅛ tsp. ground cloves
⅛ tsp. ground cinnamon
¼ tsp. ground white pepper
½ tsp. salt
1½ oz. smoked eel fillet, cut into long, thin strips

Lightly oil a terrine or loaf pan 7½ by 3¾ by 2 inches. Flatten and stretch the sole fillets between two sheets of plastic wrap by beating them gently, then rolling them with a rolling pin. Make three light, diagonal cuts in the skinned side of each fillet to prevent shrinking and curling. Line the terrine with the fillets; place them skinned side upward across the terrine, overlapping them a little if possible. Press the fillets into the bottom of the terrine, allowing the ends to overhang its sides. Set the terrine aside.

Blanch the watercress and parsley in rapidly boiling water for 15 seconds; refresh them immediately under cold running water and squeeze them dry in a paper towel. Finely chop the watercress and parsley, then add the chervil and dill or fennel tops, and mix them together. Set the chopped herbs aside.

Preheat the oven to 350° F. Cut the haddock or halibut into chunks and process it finely in a food processor, scraping down the bowl from time to time. Add one egg white, process briefly, and scrape down the bowl, then add the second egg white and process to a smooth purée. If the mixture feels warm, chill it for 30 minutes before processing it with the sour cream and yogurt. Finally, add the chopped herbs, cloves, cinnamon, pepper, and salt, and process the mixture briefly to combine the ingredients.

Spoon half of the purée into the terrine, and using the back of the spoon, make a narrow channel in the center, running the length of the terrine. Arrange the eel fillets down the full length of this channel. Spoon the remaining purée over the eel, smoothing the surface with the back of the spoon, and fold the overhanging ends of sole over the purée.

Cover the terrine with a piece of foil and set it in a large roasting pan or ovenproof dish. Pour boiling water into the pan to come two-thirds of the way up the sides of the terrine. Bake the terrine until its surface is firm to the touch—about 40 minutes. Remove the terrine from the roasting pan and set it aside to cool.

When the terrine is cool, place a wire rack or similar flat drainer over it, then invert the terrine and rack together onto a tray. Let the terrine drain for about 20 minutes, then chill it for at least six hours. Serve the terrine sliced and garnished with chervil.

SUGGESTED ACCOMPANIMENTS: *rye bread; green salad.*

Terrine Mikado

THIS RECIPE COMBINES INTO A EUROPEAN-STYLE TERRINE THE ELEMENTS OF TWO QUINTESSENTIALLY JAPANESE HORS D'OEUVRE: SUSHI—SMALL MORSELS OF RICE AND SEAFOOD WRAPPED IN SEAWEED; AND SASHIMI—RAW FISH SERVED WITH SOY SAUCE AND WASABI (JAPANESE HORSERADISH).

Serves 10 as a first course
Working time: about 40 minutes
Total time: about 2 hours and 15 minutes
(includes marinating)

Calories **140**
Protein **11g.**
Cholesterol **40mg.**
Total fat **2g.**
Saturated fat **trace**
Sodium **75mg.**

1¼ lb. sea bass fillet, skinned
7 tbsp. rice vinegar
2 tsp. grated or finely chopped fresh ginger
¼ tsp. wasabi powder
1 generous cup sushi rice
2 tbsp. dried wakame seaweed, soaked for 10 minutes in cold water (optional)
¾ tsp. sugar
¼ tsp. salt
4 sheets nori seaweed
4 tsp. red salmon caviar (keta) for garnish (optional)

Cut the sea bass fillet diagonally into thin slices and lay them on a platter large enough to hold them in one layer without overlapping. Blend 3 tablespoons of the rice vinegar with the chopped ginger and wasabi powder, and pour the mixture over the fish. Cover the fish with plastic wrap and put it in the refrigerator to marinate for one and a half to three hours, turning it once during this time. The acidity of the marinade will turn the fish opaque.

Rinse the rice in cold water and drain it in a sieve. Put the rice into a pan with 1¼ cups of water, bring the water to a boil, cover the pan with a lid, and simmer the rice over very low heat for 10 minutes. Remove the pan from the heat and let the rice steam for 15 to 20 minutes more before you remove the lid.

Meanwhile, drain the wakame seaweed, if you are using it, in a square of cheesecloth; bring the corners of the cheesecloth together into a parcel and squeeze the wakame dry. Shred it fine and set it aside.

Scoop out the rice into a large, preferably shallow bowl. In a small bowl, mix the sugar and salt with 2½ tablespoons of the rice vinegar, stirring until they are dissolved, then pour the mixture evenly over the rice. Add the shredded wakame to the rice and toss the rice gently with a wooden spoon to mix it in well. With the other hand, fan the rice using a fan or a piece of cardboard, to cool it quickly so that the grains become glossy. Cover the rice with a damp cloth or with plastic wrap, and set it aside.

Remove the fish from the refrigerator. Drain it on layers of paper towels; wipe off the grated ginger, if you wish. Line a loaf pan 9 by 5 by 3 inches with plastic wrap, leaving enough overhanging to meet and wrap over at the top. Mix the remaining rice vinegar with 5 tablespoons of water and use this mixture to moisten your fingers when you are working with the rice, to prevent the grains from sticking to them. Wet a brush in the vinegared water, and use it to lightly moisten the inside of the lined pan. Toast the nori sheets by waving them 5 inches above a gas or electric burner for a few seconds, until they are fragrant.

To assemble the terrine, line the bottom and the long sides of the prepared pan with two of the nori sheets, overlapping them by about ½ inch along the bottom. Bend the nori sheets over the pan at the top to determine how much to trim away: They should cover the top of the pan and overlap by about ¾ inch. Trim off any excess with kitchen scissors. Tear the nori trimmings and the remaining nori sheets into strips. Arrange the pan so that one of the short sides is facing you. Moisten your fingers in the vinegared water and layer the fish, rice, and nori pieces in the terrine to create a random pattern, making sure that the final layer is level.

When all the rice and fish are used up, fold the overhanging nori over the terrine, and fold the plastic wrap over the nori. Weight the terrine with a 1-pound weight *(box, page 19);* let it firm in the refrigerator for at least 15 but no more than 30 minutes. If the terrine is left in the pan for longer than 30 minutes in total, the nori will absorb too much moisture and will tear easily when the terrine is turned out.

To serve the terrine, turn it out and remove the plastic wrap; cut the terrine into slices. Place a slice in the center of each plate and garnish with a little of the red salmon caviar, if you are using it.

EDITOR'S NOTE: *Other fine-flavored, firm white fish such as grouper or haddock can be used instead of sea bass; cooked, shelled mussels could be added for color and texture contrast. Sushi rice, wasabi powder, and the seaweed can be purchased from grocers and some health food shops. If sushi rice is unobtainable, another glutinous rice may be substituted.*

If you wish to prepare the terrine in advance, turn it out and slice it, then cover the slices with plastic wrap and leave them in the refrigerator until 5 to 10 minutes before serving.

Terrine of Salmon and Sole

Serves 6 as a main course
Working time: about 50 minutes
Total time: about 2 hours and 30 minutes
(includes cooling)

Calories **170**
Protein **21g.**
Cholesterol **55mg.**
Total fat **9g.**
Saturated fat **3g.**
Sodium **290mg.**

8 outer cabbage leaves, tough stems removed
½ lb. salmon tail fillet, skinned
3 oz. monkfish fillet
½ tsp. salt
ground white pepper
½ lb. lemon or Dover sole fillets, skinned
4 egg whites
2 slices stale white bread, crusts removed
2 tbsp. heavy cream
½ cup milk

Blanch the cabbage leaves in boiling water for two minutes. Drain them, refresh them under cold running water, then drain them again on paper towels. Line a loaf pan 7½ by 3¾ by 2 inches with all but two of the blanched cabbage leaves, arranging them so that they overhang the rim by at least 2 inches. Set the pan aside.

Cut a strip from the salmon fillet ½ inch wide and the same length as the pan. Trim the monkfish fillet to the same size as the salmon strip; reserve the trimmings. Season both strips of fish with a little of the salt and some pepper. Wrap each strip in one of the remaining cabbage leaves and set them aside.

Cut the sole into several pieces. Place them, with the monkfish trimmings, in a food processor, and process to a smooth purée. Add two of the egg whites and continue to process until evenly mixed. Moisten the slices of bread in cold water, then squeeze them dry; keep the slices separate. Add one moistened bread slice to the sole purée together with 1 tablespoon of

the cream and ¼ cup of the milk. Season the purée with half of the remaining salt and some pepper, and process it for 30 seconds more. Transfer the sole purée to a small bowl and place it in the refrigerater.

Cut the remaining salmon fillet into several pieces, and process them to a smooth purée in the food processor—about 30 seconds. Add the remaining egg whites and continue to process until they are well mixed with the salmon. Add the remaining moistened bread, cream, milk, salt, and some pepper, and process for 30 seconds more.

Preheat the oven to 350° F. To assemble the terrine, spread 3 tablespoons of the salmon purée against one side and along the bottom of the cabbage-lined pan. Lay the cabbage-leaf-wrapped strip of monkfish down the length of the salmon purée (see photograph, above, for placement), and cover it with the remaining salmon purée, spreading it evenly with a small spatula so that it fills exactly half of the mold diagonally. Gently spread about 5 tablespoons of the sole purée into the remaining space, lay the cabbage-leaf-wrapped strip of salmon on the mixture, and cover it with the remaining sole purée, smoothing the surface gently with the back of a spoon. Fold the overhanging cabbage leaves over the top of the terrine to cover it. Cover the terrine with foil.

Set the terrine in a large roasting pan or ovenproof dish. Pour boiling water into the roasting pan to come two-thirds of the way up the sides of the terrine. Bake the terrine until it is springy yet firm to the touch—about 35 minutes. Allow the terrine to cool completely before turning it out—about one hour. Cut it into slices to serve.

SUGGESTED ACCOMPANIMENT: *rice and vegetable salad.*

Fresh and Smoked Mackerel Pâté

Serves 10 as a first course
Working time: about 20 minutes
Total time: about 1 hour and 30 minutes (includes chilling)

Calories **145**
Protein **14g.**
Cholesterol **40mg.**
Total fat **10g.**
Saturated fat **3g.**
Sodium **265mg.**

¾ lb. fresh mackerel, filleted and skinned
½ lb. smoked mackerel fillets, skin and any bones removed
¾ cup plain low-fat yogurt
1 lemon, grated zest and juice only of one half, the other half cut into thin wedges
1 tbsp. cut fresh dill or chopped fennel tops, plus whole dill or fennel sprigs for garnish
freshly ground black pepper

Pour enough water into a saucepan to fill it 1 inch deep. Set a vegetable steamer in the pan and bring the water to a boil. Put the fresh mackerel in the steamer, cover the pan tightly, and steam the fish until it is cooked—about eight minutes.

Place the cooked fresh mackerel and the smoked mackerel into a food processor or blender, together with all but 1½ tablespoons of the yogurt, all of the lemon zest and juice, and the dill or fennel, and process the ingredients to a smooth paste. Season the pâté with some black pepper. Transfer the pâté to a bowl, cover it, and chill it for at least one hour.

Just before serving, stir the pâté and divide it among 10 individual ramekins. Spoon a little of the reserved yogurt onto each portion, and serve the pâté immediately, garnished with the wedges of lemon and the dill or fennel sprigs.

SUGGESTED ACCOMPANIMENT: *whole-wheat bread.*

Speckled Cod Timbales with Yellow-Pepper Sauce

Serves 6 as a first course
Working time: about 45 minutes
Total time: about 1 hour

Calories **90**	1 tsp. cornstarch
Protein **13g.**	1 scant cup skim milk
Cholesterol **10mg.**	1 lb. cod fillet, skinned
Total fat **1g.**	and cut into pieces
Saturated fat **trace**	1 tbsp. prepared horseradish
Sodium **295mg.**	¾ tsp. salt
	freshly ground black pepper
	1 large sweet yellow pepper
	2 egg whites
	½ tsp. white wine vinegar
	1 tbsp. black lumpfish roe for garnish (optional)
	flat-leaf parsley for garnish (optional)

Preheat the oven to 375° F.

Blend the cornstarch with a little of the milk in a small saucepan. Stir in the remaining milk and bring it to a boil over medium heat. Cook the sauce, stirring continuously, until it has thickened—about two minutes. Let it cool slightly—about 10 minutes.

Pour the thickened sauce into a food processor or blender, add the pieces of cod, and purée them until the mixture is completely smooth. Turn the purée into a bowl, and beat in the horseradish, ½ teaspoon of the salt, and some freshly ground black pepper.

Coarsely grate a quarter of the yellow pepper and add it to the bowl. Beat the egg whites until they are stiff. Using a rubber spatula, mix 2 tablespoons of the beaten egg white into the cod mixture, then fold in the remaining egg white.

Lightly grease six 3-inch ramekins and spoon in the cod mixture, smoothing the surface with the back of the spoon. Place the ramekins in a baking dish and pour in boiling water to fill the dish ½ inch deep. Cover the ramekins with lightly greased foil and bake the timbales until they have risen and feel just firm—20 to 25 minutes. Let them cool for 10 minutes.

Meanwhile, peel the remainder of the yellow pepper, following the instructions on page 90. Seed and derib the peeled pepper, then coarsely chop it, and purée it in a food processor or blender with 4 tablespoons of water. Using a spoon, push the pepper purée through a sieve into a small, nonreactive saucepan. Stir in the wine vinegar and the remaining salt, and heat the sauce over low heat for two minutes.

Loosen the edges of the timbales with a knife and turn them out onto paper towels to drain for one minute. Using a spatula, transfer them to warmed serving plates. Garnish each timbale with lumpfish roe and parsley, if desired; spoon a little of the pepper sauce around the bottom of each timbale.

Seafood Mosaic

Serves 12 as a first course
Working time: about 1 hour and 30 minutes
Total time: about 7 hours (includes chilling)

Calories **155**
Protein **25g.**
Cholesterol **120mg.**
Total fat **3g.**
Saturated fat **1g.**
Sodium **295mg.**

¼ lb. tomatoes (2 small), finely chopped
¼ lb. lean chicken, minced
2 leeks, white parts only, cleaned thoroughly and finely chopped
3 oz. mushrooms, finely chopped
2 celery stalks, finely chopped
1 tsp. finely chopped fresh ginger
1½ quarts unsalted fish stock (recipe, page 11)
2 tbsp. fresh lemon juice
7½ tbsp. powdered gelatin
4 large eggs, whites and shells only, shells washed and crushed into small pieces
1 tsp. salt
¼ lb. large cooked shrimp, peeled and deveined
½ lb. turbot or haddock fillet
6 oz. salmon or salmon trout fillet
8 oysters (optional)
15 to 20 small mussels
6 squid, with pouches measuring about 5 inches, cleaned (opposite)
2 lemons, grated zest only
5 tbsp. finely chopped mixed fresh herbs (tarragon, chervil, and parsley, or other mixture including parsley)
15 to 18 green peppercorns, finely crushed
5 shallots, finely chopped
Court-bouillon
1 cup dry white wine
1 carrot, sliced
1 leek, white part only, cleaned thoroughly and sliced
1 small onion, chopped
1½ celery stalks, sliced
1 small garlic clove, unpeeled
4 sprigs fresh parsley
3 sprigs fresh thyme
½ bay leaf
4 peppercorns
4 coriander seeds

First prepare the court-bouillon. Put the wine in a nonreactive pan with 1 quart of water. Bring the liquid to a boil, then lower the heat, add the rest of the ingredients, and simmer for 15 minutes. Allow the contents of the pan to cool and infuse for one hour at room temperature, or for no more than 24 hours in the refrigerator. Strain the court-bouillon and set it aside.

To make the aspic, first put the tomatoes, chicken, leeks, mushrooms, celery, and ginger in a saucepan with 1 pint of the fish stock. Bring to a boil, simmer for about 15 minutes, then strain the liquid and discard the solids. Add the lemon juice, gelatin, and the strained liquid to the remaining stock, and using the egg whites and crushed shells, clarify the combined liquids as described on page 12. Add ¾ teaspoon of the salt to the clarified stock, and set it aside in a cool place, stirring every now and then to prevent it from setting too firmly. (It must be kept in a syrupy state until you are ready to use it.)

Cut the shrimp in half crosswise. Slice the narrower ends into little rounds, and set them aside; leave the other halves intact. Cut the turbot and salmon, along the grain, into ¾-inch-wide strips. If using oysters, open them carefully; collect the juice and strain it into the court-bouillon. Detach the oysters from their shells. Scrub and debeard the mussels.

Bring the court-bouillon to a boil, then reduce the heat to a low simmer. Put in the squid pouches. As soon as they start to shrink and float to the surface, remove them with a slotted spoon and refresh them immediately in cold water. Let them drain in a colander, open ends down. Meanwhile, poach the tentacles, removing them from the court-bouillon as soon as they curl. Refresh them in cold water and drain. Stand the pouches with their open ends up in a bowl just large enough to hold them without crowding. Cover the bowl with plastic wrap and refrigerate it.

Maintaining the court-bouillon at a low simmer, carefully slip the turbot and salmon into the pan. Cook the fish for one and a half minutes, then remove them from the pan using a slotted spoon. Plunge them briefly into cold water to prevent further cooking. Remove the fish from the water, drain, then season with the remaining ¼ teaspoon salt and set aside.

Repeat this procedure with the oysters, if you are using them, poaching them for 30 seconds only, or until they are firm to the touch. Bring the court-bouillon to a boil again and drop in the cleaned mussels. Remove them from the pan with the slotted spoon as soon as they open, then refresh them as above and drain. Detach the mussels from their shells. Cover the poached seafood and refrigerate it.

Chop the tentacles into small dice and mix them with the shrimp rounds. Pour about ⅓ cup of the unset aspic into a small bowl and put it in the refrigerator until it thickens slightly—about 30 minutes—then stir in the shrimp rounds and the squid. (The jelly should be set just enough to keep the solids in suspension, but no more.) Using a small spoon, fill the squid pouches with this jelly; cover the bowl again and return the squid to the refrigerator until the jelly has firmly set.

Blanch the grated lemon zest in boiling water for 10 seconds. Drain it in a fine strainer, refresh it under cold running water, and dry it on paper towels. Mix the lemon zest into the remaining unset aspic with the chopped herbs, green peppercorns, and shallots. Pour a thin layer of aspic into the bottom of a terrine 11 by 3½ by 3½ inches, then put it into the refrigerator to set—about 15 minutes. When the jelly inside the squid pouches has set, trim about ¾ inch from the pointed ends of the body sacs.

Arrange a layer of seafood in the terrine in a random fashion, using some of each variety and packing the gaps with the halved shrimp and the mussels. Spoon a generous layer of aspic over the seafood and return the terrine to the refrigerator to set. Continue layering in the same way, making sure that the arrangement varies between layers. Leave the terrine in the refrigerator for three to four hours to set completely.

To unmold the terrine, dip the bottom and sides in hot water for five seconds and turn it out onto a platter. Cut it into ¾-inch slices to serve.

Preparing a Squid for Cooking

1 SEPARATING THE POUCH AND TENTACLES. Working over a bowl of water or a sink, hold the squid's pouch in one hand and its tentacles in the other. Gently pull the tentacles until the viscera separate from the pouch. Place the tentacles, with the head and viscera still attached, in the bowl.

2 REMOVING THE PEN. Feel inside the pouch with your fingers to locate the pen, or quill—a cartilaginous structure running nearly the length of the pouch. Pull out the pen and discard it. Reach inside the pouch again and scrape out any remaining gelatinous material; wash the pouch thoroughly.

3 SKINNING THE POUCH. Carefully pull off the edible triangular fins on either side of the pouch and skin them. Starting at the open end of the pouch, use your fingers to pull the mottled purplish skin away from the pale flesh. Continue peeling off the skin from the pouch; discard the skin. Rinse the pouch and fins, then set them aside in a bowl of fresh cold water.

4 CUTTING OFF THE TENTACLES. Lay the viscera, head, and tentacles on a cutting board. Sever the tentacles from the head below the eyes; the tentacles should remain joined together by a narrow band of flesh. Discard the head and viscera. If any of the bony beak remains in the tentacle section, squeeze it out.

Terrine of Bass, Salmon, and Squid

Serves 12 as a first course
Working time: about 1 hour
Total time: about 3 hours and 30 minutes
(includes cooling)

Calories **135**
Protein **14g.**
Cholesterol **95mg.**
Total fat **6g.**
Saturated fat **3g.**
Sodium **130mg.**

2 large leeks, measuring at least 12 inches when trimmed, 3 cleaned outer layers from each leek only
6 oz. French beans or green beans, ends removed
¾ lb. bass or haddock fillets, skinned, cut into pieces
4 egg whites
2 slices stale white bread, crusts removed
¼ cup heavy cream
½ cup milk
½ tsp. salt
ground white pepper
¾ lb. salmon fillet, skinned, cut into pieces
1 tbsp. finely cut fresh dill
4 small squid, pouches only, cleaned and skinned (technique, page 71)
flat-leaf parsley for garnish

Blanch the outer layers of the leeks in boiling water until they are soft—about three minutes. Remove them with a slotted spoon, reserving the cooking water. Refresh the layers under cold running water, drain them, and set them aside on paper towels to dry. Blanch the French beans in the leek-cooking water for one minute, drain them, refresh them under cold running water, drain them again, and set them aside. (Blanch green beans for two to three minutes.)

Line a terrine or nonreactive loaf pan 11 by 3½ by 3½ inches with the leek layers. Open them out flat and place them, overlapping, across the terrine so that they overhang the sides; they will be folded over the filling to enclose it. Set the lined terrine aside.

Place the bass or haddock in a food processor and process it until it is smooth. Lightly beat two of the egg whites and add them to the fish, one-third at a time, while the processor is running. Moisten the two slices of bread in cold water and squeeze them dry. Add one of the moistened bread slices to the fish, together with 2 tablespoons of the heavy cream, ¼ cup of the milk, ¼ teaspoon of salt, and some white pepper, and process the mixture for 30 seconds. Transfer the fish mixture to a small bowl and place it in the refrigerator.

Place the salmon in the food processor and process it until it is smooth. Lightly beat the remaining egg whites, and add them to the salmon in three additions, as above. Add the remaining moistened bread slice, heavy cream, milk, and salt, together with some more white pepper and the dill, and process for 30 seconds.

Preheat the oven to 350° F.

Put one-quarter of the salmon mixture into a pastry bag fitted with a ½-inch plain tip and fill each of the squid pouches with the mixture. Using the back of a spoon, spread the remainder of the salmon mixture evenly over the bottom and sides of the terrine. Place half of the bass or haddock mixture in the bottom of the terrine. With the spoon, create a channel slightly wider than the stuffed squid pouches along the center of the terrine. Line the channel with a single layer of beans, then place the stuffed squid pouches in the bean-lined hollow. Carefully cover the pouches with the remaining beans, to create a ring of beans around the pouches along the length of the terrine. Cover the beans and fill the terrine with the remaining fish mixture. Fold the overhanging leeks over the top of the terrine, to completely enclose the filling.

Cover the terrine with foil, place it in a roasting pan or ovenproof dish, and pour enough boiling water into the pan to come two-thirds of the way up the sides of the terrine. Bake the terrine for 40 minutes. Let it cool for about two hours before turning it out onto a serving dish. Serve cut into slices, garnished with parsley.

EDITOR'S NOTE: *The unused squid pieces can be incorporated into a seafood salad or a fish soup or stew.*

Layered Seafood in Wine Jelly

Serves 6 as a first course
Working time: about 45 minutes
Total time: about 4 hours and 30 minutes
(includes chilling)

Calories **110**
Protein **18g.**
Cholesterol **110mg.**
Total fat **2g.**
Saturated fat **1g.**
Sodium **100mg.**

½ lb. whole rainbow trout, cleaned, filleted, and skinned, bones and head washed and reserved
10 oz. whole lemon or Dover sole, cleaned, filleted, and skinned, bones and head reserved
2 long celery stalks, one coarsely chopped, one finely sliced
1 carrot, coarsely chopped
½ leek, trimmed, washed thoroughly, and coarsely chopped
1 bay leaf
1 sprig parsley
1 small onion, sliced
⅛ tsp. salt
3 white peppercorns
⅔ cup dry white wine
2 tsp. powdered gelatin
1 tsp. fresh lemon juice
1 tbsp. finely cut fresh dill, plus a few whole dill sprigs
2 oz. peeled cooked shrimp
2 tsp. red lumpfish roe

Place the trout and sole bones and heads in a nonreactive saucepan, and add the chopped celery, the carrot, leek, bay leaf, parsley, onion, and salt. Pour 1 cup of water into the pan and bring it to a boil; cover the pan and simmer the ingredients for 15 minutes.

Add the peppercorns and wine to the stock, and bring it back to a simmer. Place a sheet of parchment paper in the bottom of a steamer. Arrange the trout and sole fillets in layers in the steamer, with parchment paper between the layers. Set the steamer over the saucepan, and continue to simmer the stock until the fish is just firm—8 to 10 minutes. Remove the fish fillets from the steamer and let them cool. Line a sieve with a double thickness of cheesecloth or with two paper coffee filters, and strain the stock, discarding the fish trimmings; the stock will take between 30 minutes and one hour to filter. If necessary, add water to the strained stock to make 1¼ cups.

Place the sliced celery in a small saucepan, add water to cover, and bring it to a boil. Lower the heat and simmer the celery until it is just tender—about three minutes. Drain the celery and set it aside. Following the method on page 13, dissolve the gelatin in 3 tablespoons of the fish stock. Stir the gelatin mixture into the remaining stock, then stir in the lemon juice. Cover the bottom of a nonreactive loaf pan 8½ by 4½ by 2 inches with a very thin layer of the jelly. Arrange some whole dill sprigs in the jelly and let it set in the refrigerator—about 15 minutes.

Arrange the trout fillets and half of the cooked, sliced celery over the set jelly, and sprinkle them with half of the cut dill. Spoon in enough jelly to just cover the fish and chill again until the jelly has set—15 minutes more. Arrange the shrimp and fish roe in layers over the set jelly. Add enough jelly to cover, and chill again until set—about 15 minutes.

Last, arrange the sole fillets and remaining cooked, sliced celery over the shrimp, sprinkle them with the remaining cut dill, and gently add the remaining jelly. Chill in the refrigerator for at least two hours.

To turn the terrine out, dip the sides and bottom of the pan in hot water for five seconds. Invert it onto a serving plate and lift off the pan. If you like, garnish the terrine with a few more whole dill sprigs.

EDITOR'S NOTE: *Jellied terrines of this type can be difficult to slice without breaking up the main ingredients. For the best results, use a wet serrated knife to cut the terrine, and hold a spatula against the piece being cut as you slice; use a gentle sawing motion.*

Sea Bass Galantine Orientale

Serves 12 as a first course
Working time: about 2 hours
Total time: about 7 hours (includes marinating
and chilling)

Calories **150**
Protein **14g.**
Cholesterol **80mg.**
Total fat **5g.**
Saturated fat **1g.**
Sodium **160mg.**

2½ lb. sea bass, boned and gutted through the back, head and tail left intact, bones and trimmings reserved
1 tbsp. low-sodium soy sauce
1 tbsp. light sesame oil
3 tbsp. rice vinegar
2-inch piece fresh ginger, peeled
1 small carrot, sliced
1 leek, white part only, slit and cleaned thoroughly to remove all grit
1 small shallot, sliced
1 garlic clove
1 sprig parsley
1 sprig fresh tarragon
4 black peppercorns
2 cups dry white wine
1 tsp. powdered gelatin
2 tsp. white sesame seeds, toasted
2 tsp. black sesame seeds
1 black olive, halved and pitted
whole cooked shrimp for garnish (optional)

Shrimp and shiitake stuffing

5 tbsp. short-grain rice
1 tbsp. light sesame oil
2½ oz. fresh shiitake mushrooms, very finely sliced
¾ lb. raw jumbo shrimp, shells removed and reserved, shrimp deveined
2 garlic cloves
1-inch piece fresh ginger, peeled
¼ tsp. salt
1 tsp. arrowroot
1 egg white
5 oz. cooked jumbo shrimp, shells removed and reserved, shrimp deveined and finely diced

Rinse the bass thoroughly and pat it dry on paper towels. Pour the soy sauce, light sesame oil, and 1 tablespoon of the rice vinegar into a bowl. Using a garlic press, squeeze the juice from the ginger into the bowl. Whisk these ingredients together to make a marinade. Place the fish belly down on a dish, pour the marinade inside the fish, and let it marinate in the refrigerator for about one hour.

While the bass is marinating, prepare the stuffing. Put the rice and ¾ cup of water in a small saucepan, and bring them to a boil over medium-high heat. Lower the heat, tightly cover the saucepan, and simmer the rice until all of the liquid has been absorbed and the rice is just tender—approximately 20 minutes. Set the rice aside to cool.

Heat the oil in a small skillet and gently cook the

mushrooms, covered, for about 10 minutes. Remove the cover and drain off any liquid. Set the mushrooms aside to cool.

Reduce the raw shrimp and the cooled rice to a paste, using a food processor or a mortar and pestle. With a garlic press, squeeze the juices of the garlic and ginger into the shrimp mixture. Blend the ingredients well, then beat in the salt, arrowroot, and egg white until the mixture is fluffy.

Fold the diced cooked shrimp into the raw shrimp mixture, together with the shiitake mushrooms.

Pour off any unabsorbed marinade from the sea bass, and pack the shrimp and mushroom stuffing into the cavity of the fish. Wrap the fish in a 12-inch square of cheesecloth and secure it with butcher's twine. Place the fish on its belly on the rack of a fish poacher. Pour 1 inch of boiling water into the poacher, taking care to keep the water level below the belly of the fish. Cover the poacher and steam the fish over medium heat until the flesh in the middle of the back is

opaque—25 to 35 minutes. Remove the bass from the poacher and allow it to rest on its belly for five minutes, then invert it onto its back to drain and cool. When the fish is cool enough to handle, turn it back onto its belly, unwrap it, and carefully remove the skin. Place the bass in the refrigerator and allow it to chill thoroughly—about one hour.

While the fish is chilling, make the stock. Put all reserved bones and trimmings, the shrimp shells, carrot, leek, shallot, garlic clove, parsley, tarragon, peppercorns, wine, and the remaining rice vinegar in a large, nonreactive saucepan. Add 1¼ cups of water and simmer the liquid for 20 minutes. Strain the stock through cheesecloth, then return it to the pan and simmer it until it has reduced to about 6 tablespoons. Make an aspic by dissolving the gelatin in the reduced stock (technique, page 13), and set the aspic aside until it cools and begins to set—about 20 minutes.

Place the fish on a serving platter. As soon as the aspic has just begun to set, brush some of it all over

the fish. Place the fish in the refrigerator for five minutes, then garnish it with rows of white and black sesame seeds. Spoon the remaining aspic over the fish. Place the olive halves in the fish's eye sockets. Chill the bass for at least two hours before serving it, garnished with whole cooked shrimp, if desired.

EDITOR'S NOTE: *To bone and gut a bass through the back, slit it from head to tail on either side of the dorsal fin, and work the blade of a small, flexible knife around the rib cage of the fish. Cut the backbone at the head and tail ends with kitchen scissors, leaving both head and tail in position. Pull out and discard the backbone, viscera, and gills, then rinse the fish. Alternatively, ask your fish dealer to bone the fish for you.*

If you do not have a fish poacher or steamer pan of suitable size, wrap the fish in a double layer of oiled aluminum foil instead of cheesecloth. Place the fish on a rack in a roasting pan, pour in 1 inch of boiling water, and steam it for 25 minutes. Let the fish cool in the foil.

Black sesame seeds are available in Asian grocery stores.

Sea Bass Stuffed with Spinach and Mushrooms

Serves 6 as a main course
Working time: about 45 minutes
Total time: about 5 hours (includes chilling)

Calories **140**
Protein **21g.**
Cholesterol **65mg.**
Total fat **4g.**
Saturated fat **2g.**
Sodium **435mg.**

7 oz. spinach (about 3 cups, loosely packed), washed and stemmed
4 large raw shrimp, peeled
1 tbsp. unsalted butter
1 shallot, finely chopped
2 oz. mushrooms, chopped
½ tsp. chopped fresh thyme
2 egg whites
1 tsp. salt
ground white pepper
3 oz. grouper or haddock fillet, skinned, cut into pieces
1 tbsp. heavy cream
1½ lb. sea bass, boned and gutted through the back, head and tail left intact
2 tbsp. white wine vinegar
1 small carrot, finely sliced
1 small onion, sliced
2 parsley stalks
1 sprig thyme
½ bay leaf

To blanch the spinach, plunge it into a large pan of boiling water for 20 seconds. Drain the spinach, refresh it under cold running water, and drain it again. Set five of the leaves aside on paper towels to dry; squeeze the remaining spinach dry, then chop it finely. Arrange the reserved leaves flat on a work surface side by side, overlapping their edges. Place the peeled shrimp, end to end, in a row across the spinach leaves, and tightly roll the leaves around the shrimp into a cigar shape. Set the roll aside.

Melt the butter in a small saucepan, add the shallots, cover the pan, and soften the shallots over medium heat for two minutes. Add the mushrooms and thyme, and cook, uncovered, to evaporate the moisture—about five minutes. Remove the pan from the heat, stir in the chopped spinach and one egg white, and season with ¼ teaspoon of the salt and some white pepper. Allow the mixture to cool.

Place the grouper or haddock in a food processor, and process it until it is smooth. Add the remaining egg white a little at a time while the processor is running. Add the cream, ¼ teaspoon of the salt, and some white pepper, and process the ingredients until they are smooth. Allow the mixture to cool.

Moisten a 12-inch square of cheesecloth and stretch it out on the work surface. Rinse the sea bass thoroughly and pat it dry with paper towels. Place the fish upright on its belly and spoon the spinach mixture into the cavity, smoothing it with the back of the spoon. Spoon the fish mixture over the spinach mixture and form a channel along the center. Place the spinach-shrimp roll in the channel. Push the sides of the fish together to enclose the stuffing, wrap the fish tightly in the cheesecloth, and secure the cheesecloth with butcher's twine. Set the wrapped fish aside.

Place the white wine vinegar, carrot, onion, parsley stalks, thyme, bay leaf, and the remaining salt in a small fish poacher with 2 quarts of water. Bring the liquid to a boil and simmer it for three to four minutes. Lower the sea bass into the bouillon, place it on the rack, and simmer it gently for 15 minutes. Remove the fish poacher from the heat and allow the fish to cool in its cooking liquid—about one hour. Unwrap the sea bass carefully and chill it in the refrigerator for about three hours before serving.

SUGGESTED ACCOMPANIMENTS: *wild rice and mushrooms; parslied carrots.*

EDITOR'S NOTE: *To bone and gut a bass through the back, slit it from head to tail on either side of the dorsal fin, and work the blade of a small, flexible knife around the rib cage of the fish. Cut the backbone at the head and tail ends with kitchen scissors, leaving both head and tail in position. Pull out and discard the backbone, viscera, and gills, then rinse the fish. Alternatively, ask your dealer to bone the fish for you.*

If you do not have a fish poacher, wrap the fish and the carrot, onion, parsley, thyme, bay leaf, and salt (omit the vinegar) tightly in a double layer of oiled aluminum foil, instead of cheesecloth. Place the fish on a rack in a roasting pan, pour in 1 inch of boiling water, and steam it for 20 minutes. Let the fish cool in the foil.

Curried Shrimp Pâté

MAKE THIS PÂTÉ THE DAY BEFORE SERVING TO ALLOW
THE FLAVORS TO DEVELOP.

Serves 8 as an appetizer
Working time: about 45 minutes
Total time: about 12 hours (includes chilling)

Calories **125**
Protein **17g.**
Cholesterol **100mg.**
Total fat **4g.**
Saturated fat **1g.**
Sodium **265mg.**

6 oz. unpeeled cooked shrimp
1 tbsp. virgin olive oil
1 onion, finely chopped
1 garlic clove, finely chopped
1 tbsp. paprika
½ tsp. cayenne pepper
½ tsp. ground turmeric
4½ tsp. coriander seeds, ground
1 tsp. peppercorns, ground
½ tsp. fenugreek seeds, ground
½ tsp. fennel seeds, ground
1 tsp. finely chopped fresh ginger
1 tbsp. tomato paste
1 tsp. sugar
1½ tbsp. unsweetened shredded coconut
½ lb. haddock fillets, skinned and cut into 1-inch chunks
1 lemon, juice only
¼ cup fresh breadcrumbs
1 egg
freshly ground black pepper
cilantro for garnish (optional)

Peel the shrimp. Place the shells in a small saucepan; cover the shrimp and refrigerate them until required. Pour 1 cup of water over the shrimp shells, then heat them until the liquid is just boiling. Cover the pan, lower the heat, and simmer the shells for 15 minutes. Strain the shell stock and discard the shells. Pour the stock back into the saucepan and boil it, uncovered, until it has reduced to ¼ cup.

Preheat the oven to 350° F. Line a loaf pan 7½ by 3¾ by 2 inches with parchment paper *(technique, page 34)* and set it aside.

Heat the oil in a saucepan. Add the onion and garlic, and cook them over low heat until they are just soft—about three minutes. Stir in the paprika, cayenne pepper, turmeric, coriander seeds, peppercorns, fenugreek seeds, fennel seeds, and ginger. Cook for one minute more, then stir in the tomato paste, sugar, coconut, and reduced stock. Gently mix in the haddock. Cover the pan and simmer the fish until it is cooked but still firm—about 10 minutes. Remove the pan from the heat and let the haddock cool slightly.

Place the cooled fish with all the cooking juices and spices in a food processor or blender, and add the lemon juice, breadcrumbs, and egg. Process the ingredients to a smooth purée, then transfer the purée to a bowl. Reserve a few peeled shrimp for garnish; coarsely chop the remainder and mix them into the haddock purée. Season the purée with some freshly ground black pepper.

Spoon the pâté into the prepared loaf pan, smooth- ▶

ing the surface with the back of the spoon. Cover the pan loosely with aluminum foil, place it in a large roasting pan or ovenproof dish, and pour boiling water into the roasting pan to come two-thirds of the way up the sides of the loaf pan. Bake the pâté until it is firm to the touch—about one and a quarter hours. Weight the pâté with a 1-pound weight *(box, page 19)*

and allow it to cool—about two hours—then refrigerate it overnight.

To serve the pâté, turn it out onto a board or serving platter, and garnish it with the reserved whole shrimp and some cilantro.

SUGGESTED ACCOMPANIMENT: *poppadoms.*

Three-Fish Pâté with Shrimp

MAKE THIS PÂTÉ THE DAY BEFORE YOU WISH TO SERVE IT.

Serves 20 as a first course
Working time: about 1 hour and 15 minutes
Total time: about 12 hours (includes chilling)

Calories **235**
Protein **21g.**
Cholesterol **75mg.**
Total fat **9g.**
Saturated fat **2g.**
Sodium **250mg.**

one 1-lb. whole lemon or Dover sole
2 lb. haddock fillets, skinned
1 lb. center cut piece of fresh salmon, or 1½ lb. salmon trout
6 large raw shrimp
1 lemon
1 onion, sliced
4 large sprigs parsley
1 sprig fresh thyme
1 sprig fresh rosemary
1 tsp. salt
1¼ cups dry white wine
ground white pepper
1 egg, beaten
3 tsp. powdered gelatin
Hot-water crust pastry
3 cups unbleached all-purpose flour
¼ tsp. salt
1 egg yolk
1 stick (¼ lb.) polyunsaturated margarine

Using a very sharp filleting knife, remove the four fillets from the sole, then carefully remove and discard the skin. Set the fillets aside. Put the bones and head into a large, nonreactive saucepan. Cut the haddock flesh into long strips about 1½ inches wide, and set them aside. Cut the salmon flesh away from the bones, discarding the skin and any small bones; add the larger bones to the saucepan. Cut the salmon into long strips about 1½ inches wide, and set them aside.

Remove the shells from the shrimp and add the shells to the saucepan. Make a long slit along the back of each shrimp and remove the black intestinal tract. Rinse the shrimp well under cold water, then set them aside with the other fish. Cover all of the fish and refrigerate it while you make the stock and pastry.

Pour 2 quarts of cold water into the saucepan to cover the fish trimmings. Cut half of the lemon into slices and add these to the saucepan with the onion, parsley, thyme, rosemary, half of the salt, and the white wine. Set the saucepan over medium heat and bring the liquid almost to a boil. (Do not allow it to boil; this would make the stock cloudy.) Reduce the heat to

low and simmer the stock for 20 minutes, skimming off the scum as it rises to the surface.

Meanwhile, preheat the oven to 425° F. Grease an oblong hinged pâté mold 12 by 3 by 3 inches.

To make the hot-water crust pastry, sift the flour and salt into a mixing bowl and make a well in the center; drop the egg yolk into the well. Put the margarine in a saucepan with ½ cup of cold water. Heat until the margarine melts, then bring the liquid to a boil. Immediately pour the hot liquid into the well in the flour, stirring with a wooden spoon at the same time to form a soft dough. Knead the dough on a lightly floured surface until it is smooth.

Cut off one-third of the pastry, cover it with plastic wrap, and set it aside. Roll the remaining pastry out to an oblong measuring about 9 by 18 inches. Carefully line the pâté mold with the pastry, pressing it firmly into position across the bottom and up the sides, leaving a little excess overhanging the edge of the mold.

Fill the lined mold with the fish: Place half of the haddock strips in the bottom, then add the shrimp, sole fillets, salmon strips, and finally the remaining haddock strips. Season each layer with a little of the remaining salt, some white pepper, and some juice squeezed from the remaining lemon half.

Roll out the reserved pastry to an oblong large enough to cover the top of the pâté. Brush the overhanging pastry with a little cold water to moisten it, then place the pastry lid in position; press the edges of the pastry firmly together to make a seal. Using kitchen scissors, trim the edges of the pastry to neaten them. Reknead and reroll the pastry trimmings to an oblong measuring about 4 by 6 inches. Cut eight strips from the pastry, each one about ½ inch wide. Brush the top of the pâté with some of the beaten egg. Decorate the top with the pastry strips, arranging them in a lattice pattern. Trim the ends of the strips, then brush the top of the pâté once again with egg. Reserve the remaining egg. Make three evenly spaced holes in the top of the pâté.

Place the pâté on a baking sheet and bake it for 20 minutes, then lower the oven temperature to 375° F. and continue cooking for 40 minutes more. Remove the pâté from the oven and carefully remove the sides of the mold. Brush the sides of the pâté with the remaining beaten egg and return it to the oven for about 10 minutes more, until it is golden brown all over. Remove the pâté from the oven and allow it to cool for one hour, then refrigerate it until it is cold—three to four hours.

Strain the fish stock through a fine sieve lined with a double thickness of cheesecloth. Return the stock to the saucepan. Bring it to a boil over medium heat and allow it to simmer gently until it is reduced to 1 cup —about 20 minutes. Meanwhile, put ¼ cup of cold water into a small bowl. Sprinkle the gelatin evenly over the surface and set it aside to soften. When the stock is reduced, add the softened gelatin and stir until it is completely dissolved. Allow the stock to become quite cold but not set.

Using a small funnel, carefully pour the fish stock into the pâté through the holes in the top. Refrigerate the pâté overnight.

EDITOR'S NOTE: *If preferred, sole, haddock, and salmon, already filleted, may be used in the recipe, with 2 cups of unsalted fish stock (page 11) reduced to 1 cup, as above.*

Layered Crab Terrine
with Mushrooms

Serves 8 as a first course
Working time: about 45 minutes
Total time: about 5 hours and 30 minutes
(includes chilling)

Calories **120**
Protein **15g.**
Cholesterol **55mg.**
Total fat **5g.**
Saturated fat **1g.**
Sodium **340mg.**

1 lb. jumbo lump or backfin crabmeat, picked over
2½ cups unsalted vegetable stock (recipe, page 10)
4 tsp. unsalted butter
2 tsp. Dijon mustard
6 oz. mushrooms, wiped clean and finely chopped
1 tsp. fresh lemon juice
6 tbsp. dry sherry
½ tsp. salt
3½ tsp. powdered gelatin
2 oz. celery heart, finely sliced (about ½ cup)
2 tbsp. sour cream
1 tbsp. tomato paste
½ tsp. ground coriander
freshly ground black pepper

Break up any large pieces of crabmeat so that all the pieces are more or less the same size. Chill the crabmeat until it is required.

In a wide, shallow saucepan, bring the vegetable stock to a boil over high heat. Lower the heat and boil the stock gently until it is reduced to one-third of its volume—about 15 minutes.

Meanwhile, melt the butter in a nonstick frying pan over medium heat and stir in the mustard. Add the mushrooms, lemon juice, 1 tablespoon of the sherry, and ¼ teaspoon of the salt, and stir lightly. Cover the pan and cook the mushrooms until they give up their juice—one to two minutes. Remove the lid and continue to cook over medium heat, stirring continuously, until the mushroom mixture is soft and all excess moisture has evaporated—about 10 minutes. Set the mixture aside to cool.

If the reduced stock is cloudy, pass it through a sieve lined with a double layer of cheesecloth, or through a paper coffee filter. Following the method on page 13, dissolve 2 teaspoons of the gelatin in 3 tablespoons of the reduced stock. Add the dissolved gelatin to the remaining stock, together with 3 tablespoons of the remaining sherry and the remaining salt. Set the jelly aside to cool.

Rinse a loaf pan 9 by 5 by 3 inches with cold water. Pour just enough of the cooled jelly into the pan to coat the bottom. Chill the pan until the jelly has set—10 to 15 minutes. Stir half of the crabmeat and all of the sliced celery heart into the remaining jelly. Spoon this mixture into the pan to form an even layer. Return the pan to the refrigerator to chill until the crabmeat layer is set—about 30 minutes.

Process the remaining crabmeat in a food processor or blender until smooth. Add the mushroom mixture and blend again. Blend in the sour cream, the tomato paste, the ground coriander, and some black pepper.

Dissolve the remaining gelatin in the remaining sherry, again following the method on page 13. Then, with the processor or blender motor running, gradually pour the gelatin solution into the crab and mushroom mixture, to produce a mousse.

Spoon the crab and mushroom mousse into the mold, smoothing the surface with the back of the spoon. Chill the terrine until it is thoroughly set—about three hours.

To unmold the terrine, dip its bottom and sides in hot water for five seconds, then invert it onto a flat plate or board. Serve the terrine cut into slices.

Deviled Crab

Serves 4 as a first course
Working (and total) time: about 20 minutes

Calories **125**
Protein **17g.**
Cholesterol **85mg.**
Total fat **5g.**
Saturated fat **1g.**
Sodium **390mg.**

10 oz. backfin crabmeat, picked over
3 tbsp. plain low-fat yogurt
3 tbsp. fine fresh whole-wheat breadcrumbs
½ lemon, finely grated zest and juice only
1 tsp. Dijon mustard
2 tsp. Worcestershire sauce
½ tsp. paprika
⅛ tsp. salt
½ hard-boiled egg

Mash one-half of the crabmeat with the back of a fork to break it into separate strands, then set it aside. Place the remaining crabmeat in the bowl of a food processor. Add the yogurt, breadcrumbs, lemon zest and juice, mustard, Worcestershire sauce, paprika, and salt, and process the ingredients until they form a smooth purée. Transfer the purée to a bowl, and stir in the mashed crabmeat. Turn the deviled crab into a serving dish.

Separate the egg white and yolk, and chop the white finely. Press the yolk through a sieve, keeping it separate from the white. Sprinkle the yolk and white over the deviled crab and serve it at room temperature.

SUGGESTED ACCOMPANIMENT: *Melba toast.*

Scallop Timbales with Grated Orange Zest

Serves 6 as a first course
Working time: about 40 minutes
Total time: about 3 hours (includes marinating)

Calories **90**
Protein **12g.**
Cholesterol **20mg.**
Total fat **3g.**
Saturated fat **2g.**
Sodium **290mg.**

¾ lb. sea scallops, bright white connective tissue removed
½ tsp. coriander seeds
1 tbsp. vodka
1 orange, juice and ¼ tsp. grated zest
1 carrot, peeled and diced
¼ cup sour cream
2 tbsp. plain low-fat yogurt
¼ tsp. salt
ground white pepper
1 egg white

Select two of the most attractive, equally sized scallops and slice each one horizontally into three round sections; place the six scallop rounds in a small, nonreactive dish. Put the remaining scallops into the refrigerator to chill.

In a small, heavy-bottomed skillet, toast the coriander seeds over medium heat, shaking the pan continuously until the seeds become aromatic—about 30 seconds. Remove the pan from the heat and immediately stir the seeds into the vodka. Allow the vodka to infuse for 10 minutes. Strain the flavored vodka and mix it with 1 tablespoon of the orange juice. Spoon this marinade over the scallop rounds, coating them evenly. Cover the dish and refrigerate it for at least two hours to marinate the scallop rounds.

Meanwhile, cook the carrot dice in a pan of rapidly boiling water until they are almost tender—about four minutes. Drain, return to the pan, and mix in the remaining orange juice. Cook the mixture over high heat, stirring constantly, until the juice evaporates, then set it aside in the refrigerator.

Purée the chilled whole scallops in a food processor. Add the sour cream and yogurt, and blend well. Transfer the purée to a bowl, cover it, and chill it for 30 minutes. Stir in the salt, some white pepper, and the grated orange zest, then chill the scallop mixture again, covered, until the sliced scallops are ready.

Preheat the oven to 350° F.

Remove the scallop slices from their marinade and drain them on paper towels. Beat the egg white until it forms soft peaks, then gently fold it into the chilled scallop mixture together with the diced carrot. Spoon half of the resulting mousseline into six very lightly greased ⅓-cup timbale molds or ramekins. Place a scallop slice on top of the mousseline in each mold, then spoon in the remaining mousseline. Tap the molds on the work surface to even out the mousseline. Set the timbales in a large roasting pan or ovenproof dish, and pour boiling water into the pan to come two-thirds of the way up the sides of the timbales. Cover them with a piece of parchment paper or foil, and bake them in the oven until they are firm to the touch in the center—about 35 minutes.

Let the timbales rest for about five minutes. Gently loosen the edges with a knife and invert the timbales onto a double thickness of paper towels, to absorb any excess liquid. Serve the timbales warm.

SUGGESTED ACCOMPANIMENT: *mixed green salad.*

EDITOR'S NOTE: *The timbales may also be served chilled; unmold them just before serving.*

Spinach and Crab Terrine

Serves 8 as a first course
Working time: about 40 minutes
Total time: about 3 hours (includes chilling)

Calories **150**
Protein **16g.**
Cholesterol **50mg.**
Total fat **7g.**
Saturated fat **1g.**
Sodium **300mg.**

½ lb. spinach, washed and stemmed
2 tbsp. polyunsaturated margarine
¼ cup unbleached all-purpose flour
1¼ cups low-fat milk
¼ tsp. salt
ground white pepper
1 lb. jumbo lump or backfin crabmeat, picked over
2 tbsp. fresh lemon juice
3 tsp. powdered gelatin
lemon wedges for garnish
cucumber slices for garnish
lettuce leaves for garnish

To blanch the spinach, plunge it into a large saucepan of boiling water for one minute, then drain it and refresh it under cold running water. Drain the spinach thoroughly in a colander, pressing it with the back of a spoon to remove all the water. Chop the spinach in a blender or food processor.

Melt the margarine in a saucepan. Add the flour and cook it over low heat for one minute, stirring contin-uously. Gradually pour in the milk, still stirring con-tinuously, and cook over medium heat until the sauce boils. Lower the heat and simmer the sauce for two minutes. Stir in the salt and some ground white pep-per, then divide the sauce equally between two bowls. Add half of the crabmeat, the spinach, and 1 table-spoon of the lemon juice to one bowl of sauce, and mix thoroughly. Add the remaining crabmeat, the remain-ing lemon juice, and the tomato paste to the second bowl, and combine well.

Dissolve the gelatin in ¼ cup of cold water, follow-ing the instructions on page 13. Divide the gelatin mixture between the two bowls of crab mixture, and mix it in thoroughly.

Spoon half of the crabmeat and spinach mixture into a greased loaf pan 7½ by 3¾ by 2 inches, leveling it with the back of the spoon, and chill it until it just begins to set—about 15 minutes. Spoon the pink crab-meat mixture into the pan and level the surface, then gently spoon the remaining crabmeat and spinach mixture over the pink crabmeat mixture. Chill the ter-rine until it is firm—about two hours.

To unmold the terrine, dip its bottom and sides in hot water for five seconds, then invert it onto a flat serving plate. Serve the terrine garnished with lemon wedges, cucumber slices, and lettuce leaves.

3 *Blanched vegetable morsels and poached quail eggs, set in a golden vegetable aspic, make a picture-perfect first course (recipe, page 92).*

Vegetables in Novel Guises

Few dishes express the new style of cooking as well as the vegetable pâtés and terrines on the following pages. Light, fresh, colorful, and healthful, they are based on ingredients that are rich in valuable nutrients, low in calories, and virtually devoid of fat.

Delicate timbales of fresh green peas and snow peas *(page 90)*, an aromatic terrine of wild and cultivated mushrooms set in a creamy mushroom mousse *(page 100)*, or individual red-pepper ramekins *(page 99)* would make an elegant and intriguing prelude to a sophisticated dinner party menu; a vibrantly spiced black-eyed pea pâté *(page 109)*, or puréed carrots spiked with balsamic vinegar, fresh herbs, and cumin *(page 89)*, provide a simple, quickly prepared picnic treat or snack. Some vegetable terrines and pâtés are substantial enough to form a main course for a lunch or supper; many could serve either as a separate vegetable course or as an accompaniment to a main dish of poultry or meat.

The few recipes in this chapter that incorporate meat or poultry do so in only modest quantities. A little bacon, for instance, lends its distinctive flavor to the mushroom and chestnut pâté on page 93 and to the stuffed cabbage terrine on page 96, which is further enriched by a wrapping of caul fat. The mushroom and parsley mousselines on page 91 are based on pounded chicken breast, although similar mousselines could be made with haddock or other lean white fish.

Since vegetables take center stage, their quality is all-important. Use only vegetables in the peak of condition, and take advantage of those at their seasonal best. The molded pasta terrine on page 103, for instance, is an ideal dish for the hot days of summer, when sun-ripened tomatoes and the finest fresh basil are available. In winter, when a wide selection of genuinely first-rate produce is harder to come by, pâtés based on dried beans, or the potatoes layered with Gruyère and onions *(page 102)*, are inspired and inviting ways to begin a meal.

To take full advantage of their fresh color and flavor, vegetable terrines and pâtés are best prepared on the day they are to be served. Those intended to be eaten cold should be covered tightly with plastic wrap and kept in the refrigerator until shortly before serving time. Large pâtés should be removed from the refrigerator about 30 minutes before they are served; smaller items will come to an ideal serving temperature in about half that time.

Spicy Cauliflower Pâté

Serves 10 as a first course
Working time: about 30 minutes
Total time: about 1 hour and 15 minutes

Calories **70**
Protein **1g.**
Cholesterol **0mg.**
Total fat **5g.**
Saturated fat **1g.**
Sodium **200mg.**

4 tbsp. polyunsaturated margarine
1 onion, finely chopped
2 tsp. tomato paste
2 large tomatoes, peeled, seeded, and chopped
1 garlic clove, finely chopped
¼ tsp. ground cumin
¼ tsp. ground turmeric
¼ tsp. paprika, plus a little extra for garnish
¼ tsp. garam masala
⅛ tsp. chili powder
½ tsp. salt
1 large cauliflower (about 1½ lb.), broken into small florets
2 tsp. chopped fresh ginger
freshly ground black pepper

Melt the margarine in a large, heavy-bottomed saucepan over medium heat, then add the onion and sauté it for about one minute. Add the tomato paste, chopped tomatoes, garlic, cumin, turmeric, paprika, garam masala, chili powder, and salt. Cook the mixture, stirring it frequently, until the tomatoes have broken down—about five minutes. Add the cauliflower florets and mix them in thoroughly. Cover the pan and cook the florets gently until they soften and begin to break up—15 to 20 minutes; stir them regularly during this time to ensure they do not stick to the bottom of the pan, adding a tablespoon of water if necessary. Add the chopped ginger to the pan for the last few minutes of the cooking time.

Allow the mixture to cool slightly, then blend it until smooth in a food processor or blender. Season the purée with freshly ground black pepper. Turn it into a serving bowl, smooth the top, and let it cool; then put it in the refrigerator for about 15 minutes.

Just before serving, place a few strips of parchment paper over the top of the pâté in a decorative pattern. Sift a little paprika over the exposed surfaces as a garnish, then remove the paper strips and serve.

SUGGESTED ACCOMPANIMENT: *warm nan or pita bread.*

EDITOR'S NOTE: *The pâté may be kept in the refrigerator for a few hours, if necessary, although it should be served on the same day that it is prepared. Remove it from the refrigerator half an hour before serving, since it is best eaten at about room temperature.*

Cauliflower Terrine with a Spinach-Herb Sauce

Serves 8 as a first course
Working time: about 30 minutes
Total time: about 4 hours (includes cooling)

Calories **115**
Protein **10g.**
Cholesterol **70mg.**
Total fat **7g.**
Saturated fat **6g.**
Sodium **200mg.**

2 lemon slices
¾ lb. small cauliflower florets (about 4 cups)
2 eggs
1 egg white
1½ cups skim milk
freshly ground black pepper
½ tsp. dry mustard
¼ tsp. grated nutmeg or ground nutmeg
3 oz. white Cheddar cheese, finely grated (about ¾ cup)
assorted fresh salad leaves for garnish
Spinach-herb sauce
1½ cups loosely packed spinach, washed and stemmed
1½ cups loosely packed watercress, washed and stemmed
2 tsp. chopped parsley
1 tsp. chopped fresh tarragon
1 tbsp. finely cut chives
1 tbsp. fresh lemon juice
½ cup sour cream
½ cup plain low-fat yogurt
¼ tsp. salt
freshly ground black pepper
cayenne pepper

Lightly grease a nonstick loaf pan 9 by 5 by 3 inches. Preheat the oven to 350° F.

Put the lemon slices in a saucepan of water, bring the water to a boil, and add the cauliflower florets. Cover the pan, lower the heat, and simmer the florets for three minutes. Drain them well, discard the lemon slices, and spread the florets out on paper towels to drain and cool.

Meanwhile, whisk the eggs, egg white, milk, a few grindings of black pepper, the mustard, and the nutmeg together in a bowl. Layer the cauliflower florets in the prepared pan alternately with the grated cheese, then pour the egg and milk mixture over them. Lightly cover the pan with aluminum foil and place it in a baking dish. Pour enough boiling water into the dish to come two-thirds of the way up the sides of the pan and bake the terrine for about 50 minutes, or until it is set. Remove the terrine from the baking dish and allow it to cool completely.

Shortly before serving, prepare the sauce. Blanch the spinach and watercress together in a saucepan of boiling water for one minute. Drain them very well, then squeeze them in a clean dishtowel to remove excess liquid. Using a sharp knife, chop the spinach and watercress very fine. Place them in a mixing bowl, and add the parsley, tarragon, chives, lemon juice, sour cream, yogurt, salt, and some black pepper and cayenne. Mix the ingredients together well. Transfer the sauce to a serving bowl.

Turn the terrine out onto a flat serving platter. Serve it sliced, garnished with the fresh salad leaves and accompanied by the sauce.

Broccoli and Blue Cheese Pâté

Serves 10 as a first course
Working time: about 30 minutes
Total time: about 1 hour

Calories **150**	¾ lb. broccoli
Protein **6g.**	4 tbsp. polyunsaturated margarine
Cholesterol **10mg.**	1 leek, cleaned thoroughly to remove all grit, finely sliced
Total fat **8g.**	¼ tsp. grated nutmeg or ground nutmeg
Saturated fat **5g.**	¼ tsp. salt
Sodium **240mg.**	freshly ground black pepper
	2 oz. blue cheese
	1½ cups part-skim ricotta cheese
	3 tbsp. plain low-fat yogurt
	¼ cup vegetable aspic (recipe, page 13)

Trim six florets from the broccoli and blanch them for 30 seconds in boiling water. Drain the florets and refresh them under cold running water. Set them aside for garnish. Coarsely chop the remaining broccoli.

Melt the margarine in a heavy-bottomed saucepan over medium heat and add the chopped broccoli, the leek, nutmeg, salt, some black pepper, and 1 table-spoon of water. Cover the pan and cook the vegeta-bles until they soften—five to six minutes; stir them occasionally as they cook to keep them from burning.

Meanwhile, mash the blue cheese in a bowl. Grad-ually incorporate the ricotta cheese until the two cheeses are well mixed. Set the bowl aside.

Purée the cooked vegetables in a food processor until smooth, then transfer the purée to a large bowl and allow it to cool until it is tepid. Using a large fork, beat the cheese mixture into the vegetable purée. Transfer the pâté to a 1½-quart oval mold, smooth the surface, and chill it in the refrigerator for 30 minutes.

Combine the yogurt and vegetable aspic in a bowl, and chill the mixture until it is well thickened but not quite set—about 30 minutes. Remove the pâté from the refrigerator and pour the aspic mixture over the surface in a thin layer. Chill the pâté for 5 to 10 minutes more, to set the aspic topping. In the meantime, cut the reserved broccoli florets in half lengthwise, so that they will lie flat.

Arrange the broccoli florets on top of the pâté in the form of a tree. Serve the pâté on the day it is prepared.

SUGGESTED ACCOMPANIMENT: *Melba toast or whole-wheat rolls.*

Carrot and Herb Ramekins

Serves 4 as a first course
Working time: about 30 minutes
Total time: about 1 hour

Calories **120**
Protein **2g.**
Cholesterol **0mg.**
Total fat **9g.**
Saturated fat **2g.**
Sodium **410mg.**

1 cup loosely packed parsley
1 bunch chives
3 tbsp. polyunsaturated margarine
1 lb. carrots (5 to 6 medium), thinly sliced
1 garlic clove, finely chopped
2 tsp. balsamic or sherry vinegar
½ tsp. grated lemon zest
1 tbsp. fresh lemon juice
½ tsp. ground cumin
½ tsp. salt
freshly ground black pepper

Set aside four small sprigs of parsley and a few chives for garnish. Chop the remaining parsley and chives.

Melt the margarine in a heavy-bottomed saucepan over medium heat. Add the carrots and cook them, covered, until they soften—about six minutes—stirring them occasionally to prevent them from burning. When they are almost cooked, add the garlic, vinegar, lemon zest and juice, and the cumin. Stir the contents of the pan well and continue cooking for two minutes more. Add the chopped parsley and chives to the pan, stirring them in well.

Empty the mixture into a food processor or blender, and add the salt and some freshly ground black pepper. Process the ingredients to a purée. Spoon the purée into four individual ramekins and chill them in the refrigerator until the pâté has set—at least 30 minutes. Decorate the pâté with the reserved herbs before serving.

SUGGESTED ACCOMPANIMENT: *whole-wheat toast fingers.*

Pea and Tomato Timbales

Serves 6 as a first course
Working time: about 30 minutes
Total time: about 1 hour

Calories **65**
Protein **4g.**
Cholesterol **0mg.**
Total fat **4g.**
Saturated fat **1g.**
Sodium **140mg.**

7 oz. snow peas, strings removed
1 tbsp. safflower oil
1 small onion, finely chopped
1½ tsp. chopped fresh oregano, or ½ tsp. dried oregano
½ lb. tomatoes (about 2 medium), peeled, seeded, and chopped
5 tbsp. tomato juice
½ tsp. salt
freshly ground black pepper
1 tsp. red wine vinegar
1 sprig fresh mint
3½ cups fresh peas, shelled, or 1¼ cups frozen peas
1 tbsp. powdered gelatin
¼ cup plain low-fat yogurt
1 egg white
¼ tsp. fresh lemon juice

Lightly oil six ⅔-cup timbale molds or ramekins.

Bring a saucepan of water to a boil, add the snow peas, cover the pan, and cook them for three minutes. Drain the snow peas, refresh them under cold running water, and pat them dry on paper towels. Line the insides of the prepared molds with overlapping snow peas, ensuring they all face the same way and that their tips just touch the bottoms of the molds. Set the molds aside.

Heat the oil in a small, heavy-bottomed saucepan, and add the onion and oregano. Cover the pan and cook over low heat for three to four minutes, until the onion is soft but not colored. Add the tomatoes and stir them briefly. Remove the pan from the heat.

Put a teaspoon of the tomato mixture in the bottom of each mold. Add the tomato juice to the remaining mixture in the saucepan and simmer it for three min-

utes. Transfer the mixture to a food processor and purée it to form a smooth sauce. Season the sauce with ¼ teaspoon of the salt and some black pepper, and add the vinegar. Set the sauce aside until required.

Put the mint sprig in a saucepan of water and bring the water to a boil. Add the peas and cook them, covered, until they are tender—about five minutes for fresh peas and 30 seconds for frozen peas. Drain the peas and refresh them under cold running water. Transfer them to a food processor and blend them to a smooth purée.

Dissolve the gelatin in 3 tablespoons of water *(technique, page 13)*. Add the gelatin solution and 2 tablespoons of the yogurt to the pea purée. Blend the mixture well, and season it with the remaining ¼ teaspoon of salt and some black pepper.

Beat the egg white until it is stiff but not dry, and fold it into the pea purée. Spoon the mixture into the molds and refrigerate them for 30 minutes, or until the timbales are set.

Turn the timbales out onto individual plates and serve them with a little of the tomato sauce spooned around them. To feather the sauce, mix together the remaining yogurt and the lemon juice. Divide 1 teaspoon of this mixture into a line of eight or nine small mounds positioned in the tomato sauce near the edge of each plate. Use the tip of a skewer to link each line of mounds in a decorative, scrolled pattern.

EDITOR'S NOTE: *Although feathering a sauce is not difficult, it is a good idea to practice it a few times before attempting it for guests.*

Peeling Sweet Peppers

LOOSENING AND REMOVING THE SKIN. Place the pepper about 2 inches below a preheated broiler. Turn the pepper as its sides become slightly scorched; continue until the skin has blistered on all sides. Transfer the pepper to a bowl and cover it with plastic wrap, or put the pepper into a paper bag and fold it shut; the trapped steam will make the pepper limp and loosen its skin. With a knife, peel off the skin in sections, from top to bottom. The pepper may then be seeded and deribbed.

Vegetables in a Chicken Mousseline

Serves 12 as a first course
Working time: about 2 hours
Total time: about 12 hours (includes chilling)

Calories **150**
Protein **19g.**
Cholesterol **10mg.**
Total fat **6g.**
Saturated fat **3g.**
Sodium **200mg.**

2 tbsp. unsalted butter
1 large onion, finely chopped
½ lb. mushrooms, wiped clean, coarsely chopped
2½ lb. long carrots, cut lengthwise into ¼-inch-wide strips
6 oz. very small baby corn, fresh or frozen, trimmed if necessary
3 long asparagus spears, trimmed and peeled
6 oz. thin French or green beans, ends removed
1½ lb. skinless boned chicken breasts
3 egg whites
¾ tsp. salt
ground white pepper
¾ cup sour cream
½ cup plain low-fat yogurt
3 tbsp. chopped parsley
1 large sweet red pepper, peeled (technique, opposite), seeded, and cut into ¼-inch-wide strips

Melt the butter in a large, heavy skillet over medium heat. Add the onion and cook it until it is soft but not brown—about five minutes. Add the mushrooms to the pan and cook them for six to eight minutes, until they are soft and all the excess moisture has evaporated. Remove the pan from the heat and allow the

mushroom mixture to cool while you prepare the remaining vegetables.

Steam the carrot strips and the baby corn for six to eight minutes, until they are just tender. If you are using frozen corn, add it for the last minute only. Transfer the vegetables from the steamer to paper towels to drain and cool. Steam the asparagus spears for four to five minutes, until they are just tender, then drain them on paper towels. Meanwhile, cook the beans in boiling water for two to three minutes until they, too, are just tender. Pour them into a colander and refresh them under cold running water. Drain them well on paper towels.

Preheat the oven to 375° F.

Line a loaf pan 9 by 5 by 3 inches with parchment paper (technique, page 34).

Halve three of the baby corn lengthwise. Arrange the asparagus spears, the halved baby corn, and some of the carrot strips diagonally across the bottom of the loaf pan; alternate carrot strips and beans lengthwise in the spaces that remain. Do not leave any gaps.

Remove all sinew from the chicken breasts and cut the meat into large cubes. Place them in a food processor with the egg whites, the salt, and some white pepper. Process for about one minute, until a smooth paste is formed. Add the sour cream and yogurt, and process for another minute, until the mixture is very smooth. Divide the resulting chicken mousseline into two equal portions; blend the mushroom mixture into one half and the parsley into the other.

Carefully spoon half of the parsley mousseline into the prepared loaf pan and spread it evenly. Cover it with a layer of alternating lines, arranged lengthwise, of red-pepper strips and beans. Spoon half of the mushroom mousseline on top of the pepper strips and beans, and spread it evenly. Arrange alternating lines of carrot strips and baby corn lengthwise on top of the mousseline. Spoon the remaining parsley mousseline into the pan and spread it evenly. Cover it with the remaining beans. Finally, spoon in the remaining mushroom mousseline and level the top.

Cover the terrine with a sheet of greased parchment paper. Set it in a large, deep roasting pan or ovenproof dish and pour in boiling water to come two-thirds of the way up the sides of the loaf pan. Cook the terrine for 30 to 40 minutes, until the surface is firm and a skewer inserted into the center feels hot to the touch when it is removed.

Remove the terrine from the water bath and allow it to cool for about one hour. Refrigerate it overnight, until it is completely cold and firm.

Turn the terrine out onto a flat serving plate and remove the parchment paper. Use a sharp knife to cut the terrine into slices for serving.

Spring Vegetables and Quail Eggs in an Aspic Valentine

Serves 4 as a first course
Working time: about 45 minutes
Total time: about 3 hours (includes chilling)

Calories **55**
Protein **4g.**
Cholesterol **55mg.**
Total fat **2g.**
Saturated fat **1g.**
Sodium **315mg.**

½ tsp. cider vinegar
4 quail eggs
8 thin asparagus tips, trimmed to a length of 3 inches
8 very small baby corn, fresh or frozen
4 very small baby carrots, halved lengthwise
4 small broccoli florets
1½ tsp. powdered gelatin
1½ cups vegetable aspic (recipe, page 13)
6 tbsp. rosé or white wine
4 to 6 small mushrooms, halved, tossed in ½ tbsp. fresh lemon juice
4 small sprigs of chervil, plus chervil sprigs for garnish

Bring a shallow saucepan of water to a boil, add the vinegar, and reduce the heat to a low simmer. Carefully break the quail eggs into the water and poach them gently for about two minutes, or until the whites are just firm and the yolks are still creamy.

Using a slotted spoon, transfer the poached eggs to a bowl of cold water to arrest the cooking. Neaten the edges of the whites with a pair of scissors. Refrigerate the eggs, still in the water, until you are ready to assemble the aspic valentines.

Blanch the asparagus tips, corn, and carrots in a saucepan of boiling, salted water for two minutes. (If you are using frozen corn, add it for the second minute only.) Blanch the broccoli florets for one minute. Refresh the vegetables under cold running water and let them drain on paper towels.

Lightly wet with water the insides of four ½-cup heart-shaped molds. Dissolve the gelatin in 1 tablespoon of water *(technique, page 13)*. Mix the gelatin solution into the vegetable aspic, then stir in the wine. Pour a ¼-inch layer of wine aspic into the bottom of each mold. Place the molds in the refrigerator for 15 minutes to set the aspic.

Using a slotted spoon, transfer the eggs to paper towels to drain. Pat the mushroom halves dry on paper towels. Arrange the vegetables, the eggs, and the four small sprigs of chervil decoratively in the prepared molds, bearing in mind that the bottom of the mold will be the top of the valentine when it is turned out. Fill the molds halfway to the top with aspic, taking care not to disturb the position of the eggs and vegetables. Chill the molds in the refrigerator for 15 minutes, then fill the molds with the rest of the aspic and chill them for two hours, or until they are firmly set.

To serve, turn the valentines out onto individual plates and garnish them with chervil sprigs.

Mushroom and Chestnut Pâté with Madeira

Serves 10 as a first course
Working time: about 30 minutes
Total time: about 11 hours (includes soaking and chilling)

Calories **130**
Protein **4g.**
Cholesterol **5mg.**
Total fat **5g.**
Saturated fat **1g.**
Sodium **100mg.**

1 lb. fresh chestnuts, peeled, or ½ lb. dried chestnuts, soaked overnight and drained
1 oz. dried porcini (optional)
¼ cup Madeira
1 tbsp. safflower oil
1½ lb. fresh mushrooms, sliced
1 tbsp. sherry vinegar
1 tsp. fresh thyme
4½ tsp. low-sodium soy sauce
freshly ground black pepper
2 slices bacon (about 1½ oz.)
1 tbsp. chopped fresh parsley

To peel fresh chestnuts, cut a cross in the hull of each one, and drop them into boiling water. Parboil the nuts for about 10 minutes. Using a slotted spoon, lift the chestnuts, a few at a time, from the boiling water. Peel off the hulls and inner skins while the nuts are still warm. Place the chestnuts in a saucepan and cover them with fresh water. Bring the water to a boil and simmer the chestnuts, covered, until they are soft—30 to 45 minutes. Meanwhile, soak the porcini, if you are using them, in 1 tablespoon of the Madeira and 4 tablespoons of tepid water for 20 minutes.

Drain the chestnuts and purée them in a food processor. Squeeze out as much moisture as possible from the porcini; strain the soaking liquid through a double layer of cheesecloth or a paper coffee filter, and set it aside. Rinse the porcini thoroughly in a bowl of fresh water; squeeze them gently under water to expel grit. Pat the porcini dry on paper towels.

Heat the oil in a large, heavy, nonreactive skillet. Add the fresh mushrooms and cook them over medium heat until they are soft—about five minutes. Add the sherry vinegar, together with the dried mushrooms and their soaking liquid. Stir the mixture and cook it over medium heat for one minute. Pour in the remaining Madeira, increase the heat to high, and cook the mixture for three minutes to burn off the alcohol.

Add the mushroom mixture and the thyme to the chestnut purée in the food processor. Process until a smooth paste is formed. Add the soy sauce and some black pepper, and process again briefly. Transfer the pâté to a serving bowl and chill it for two hours.

Cook the bacon under a broiler until it is crisp, turning it once. Drain it on paper towels and let it cool, then crumble it over the top of the pâté. Sprinkle on the parsley and serve.

SUGGESTED ACCOMPANIMENTS: *celery sticks; French bread.*

Zucchini, Spinach, and Carrot Terrine

Serves 8 as a main course
Working time: about 45 minutes
Total time: about 13 hours (includes chilling)

Calories **145**
Protein **7g.**
Cholesterol **0mg.**
Total fat **4g.**
Saturated fat **1g.**
Sodium **220mg.**

2 large carrots, cut into ½-inch dice
2 tbsp. virgin olive oil
2½ lb. zucchini, grated
½ lb. scallions, chopped (about 1½ cups)
3 garlic cloves, finely chopped
1½ lb. fresh spinach, washed and stemmed
¼ cup chopped fresh dill
½ tsp. cayenne pepper
2 tsp. low-sodium soy sauce
1¼ cups dry breadcrumbs
4 egg whites, lightly beaten

Place the carrots in a saucepan and pour in enough cold water to cover them. Bring the water to a boil, lower the heat, and simmer the carrots until they are tender—about five minutes. Drain the carrots and refresh them under cold running water. Drain them again and set them aside on paper towels.

Heat the oil in a large, heavy skillet. Add the zucchini and scallions to the pan, and stir. Cover the pan and cook the vegetables over medium-low heat until they are tender—about 10 minutes; stir them occasionally during this time. Add the garlic, increase the heat slightly, and continue cooking the vegetables, uncovered, until most of the moisture has evaporated—8 to 10 minutes. Let the mixture cool a little, then transfer half of it to a food processor. Set the other half aside until it is required.

Preheat the oven to 325° F. Line a loaf pan 9 by 5 by 3 inches with parchment paper *(technique, page 34)*. Blanch the spinach for 30 seconds in a large pan of boiling water. Drain the spinach and squeeze out as much moisture as possible. Chop the spinach coarsely and add it to the zucchini mixture in the food processor. Add the dill, cayenne pepper, and soy sauce, and process the mixture briefly. Add the breadcrumbs and process again, just enough to mix the ingredients. Transfer the purée to a bowl and stir in the reserved zucchini mixture. Mix the egg whites in well.

Spread one-third of the spinach mixture in the bottom of the prepared pan. Arrange half of the carrots on top. Spread another third of the spinach mixture in the pan and top it with the remaining carrots. Finally, add the remaining spinach mixture and level the top with a spatula. Lightly press a piece of parchment paper onto the surface of the mixture and cover the pan with aluminum foil.

Set the loaf pan in a large roasting pan or ovenproof dish, and pour in enough boiling water to come two-thirds of the way up the sides of the pan. Bake the terrine until the mixture is set and firm to the touch—about one and a half hours. Uncover the mold, turn off the heat, and allow the terrine to cool in the oven. When the terrine is cold, cover it with plastic wrap and chill it overnight.

To unmold the terrine, turn it out onto a flat serving plate and peel off the lining paper. Cut the terrine into slices for serving.

SUGGESTED ACCOMPANIMENTS: *crusty bread; bean salad.*

Watercress and Broccoli Timbales

Serves 4 as a first course
Working time: about 40 minutes
Total time: about 4 hours (includes chilling)

Calories **65**
Protein **6g.**
Cholesterol **60mg.**
Total fat **4g.**
Saturated fat **2g.**
Sodium **75mg.**

⅔ cup vegetable aspic (recipe, page 13)
1 egg, hard-boiled
½ lb. broccoli, trimmed
2 small scallions, trimmed and sliced
1 bunch watercress, coarse stems removed
6 tbsp. plain low-fat yogurt
2 tbsp. half-and-half
⅛ tsp. salt
freshly ground black pepper
2 tsp. powdered gelatin
1 tsp. fresh lemon juice

Rinse out four ⅔-cup timbale molds with water; select molds that measure about 2½ inches in diameter at the rim. Spoon a thin layer of vegetable aspic into the bottom of each damp mold, and chill the molds until the aspic is set—about 15 minutes. Cut four thin slices, crosswise, from the widest part of the hard-boiled egg. Place one slice in the bottom of each mold. Divide the remaining aspic among the molds, spooning it over the egg slices. Chill the molds for 15 minutes more.

Meanwhile, cook the broccoli in a saucepan of boiling water until it is just tender—three to four minutes. Drain the broccoli, refresh it under cold running water, and drain it again very thoroughly.

Put the broccoli in a food processor with the scallions and three-quarters of the watercress, and process until smooth. Add the yogurt, half-and-half, salt, and some freshly ground black pepper, and process again. Transfer the purée to a mixing bowl. Finely chop the remaining hard-boiled egg, and stir it into the broccoli and watercress purée.

Dissolve the gelatin in 2 tablespoons of cold water and the lemon juice *(technique, page 13),* and stir the dissolved gelatin thoroughly into the broccoli mixture. Spoon the mixture into the molds and chill them for three to four hours, until the mixture is firmly set.

To serve, dip the bottom and sides of each mold in hot water for two or three seconds, and invert the timbales onto individual serving plates. Garnish the timbales with the remaining watercress.

Cabbage Stuffed with Chestnuts, Chard, and Bacon

Serves 6 as a main course
Working time: about 45 minutes
Total time: about 3 hours

Calories **165**
Protein **10g.**
Cholesterol **75mg.**
Total fat **8g.**
Saturated fat **2g.**
Sodium **235mg.**

8 fresh chestnuts
2 lb. firm cabbage
1 tbsp. virgin olive oil
2 small shallots, chopped
8 oz. Swiss chard, washed, stemmed, and chopped
3½ oz. spinach, washed, stemmed, and chopped
8 large sorrel leaves, washed, stemmed, and shredded
½ cup chopped parsley
1 tbsp. chopped fresh tarragon, or 1 tsp. dried tarragon
1 sprig summer savory (optional)
1 garlic clove, crushed
5 oz. pork caul fat, soaked for 15 minutes in warm water mixed with 1 tsp. of malt or white vinegar
2 oz. bacon, finely chopped
7 tbsp. fresh breadcrumbs
½ tsp. quatre épices, optional (glossary)
freshly ground black pepper
2 small eggs, lightly beaten

First, peel and cook the chestnuts. Cut a cross in the hull of each chestnut and drop them into boiling water. Parboil the nuts for about 10 minutes, to loosen their hulls. Using a slotted spoon, lift the chestnuts, a few at a time, from the boiling water. Peel off the hulls and inner skins while the nuts are still warm. Discard the cooking water, return the peeled nuts to the pan, pour in water to cover them, and simmer them for 30 minutes more, to cook them through. Drain the chestnuts and break them into large pieces.

Meanwhile, remove six outer leaves from the cabbage and blanch them for one to two minutes in boiling water, to make them supple. Drain the leaves thoroughly and lay them out on paper towels. Quarter the remaining cabbage; discard the hard stem and chop the leaves coarsely. Put the chopped cabbage into a large, heavy-bottomed saucepan with 2 tablespoons of water. Cook the cabbage, tightly covered, over low heat until it begins to soften—about 20 minutes. While the cabbage is cooking, heat the oil in a heavy skillet and cook the shallots over low heat in the oil until they are transparent—about five minutes.

Add the chard and spinach to the cabbage, and cook for five minutes more, to soften them. Remove the pan from the heat, and stir in the sorrel, parsley, tarragon, savory, if you are using it, shallots, garlic, and chestnuts. Transfer the mixture to a large bowl and set it aside.

Preheat the oven to 325° F. Remove the caul fat from its soaking water and pat it dry on paper towels. Stretch it out as thin as possible and drape it over a round terrine or soufflé dish measuring about 7 inches in diameter. Press the caul fat gently into the terrine to line the bottom and sides, and leave the edges of it overhanging the rim of the dish. Arrange the reserved cabbage leaves inside the terrine, overlapping them to line the dish completely; again, allow the edges of the leaves to overhang the rim of the dish.

Using a wooden spoon, mix the bacon into the

cabbage mixture with the breadcrumbs, *quatre épices*, if you are using it, and some freshly ground black pepper. Thoroughly mix in the beaten eggs. Turn the filling into the prepared terrine, packing it down tightly and mounding it slightly in the center. Fold the over-hanging cabbage leaves over the filling, pressing them down well, then drape and fold the edges of the caul fat over the top, tucking them down inside the edges of the terrine.

Place the terrine in a large, deep roasting pan or ovenproof dish, and pour in enough boiling water to come two-thirds of the way up the sides of the terrine.

Bake the terrine until a skewer inserted in the middle meets with little resistance—about one and a half hours. Increase the oven temperature to 425° F. and continue to bake the terrine until it is lightly browned on top—about 30 minutes.

Carefully pour off and discard all the fat at the top of the terrine. Invert the terrine first onto a flat plate, then back onto a chopping board so that it is the right way up. Serve the terrine sliced or cut into wedges.

EDITOR'S NOTE: *If sorrel is unavailable, increase the quantity of spinach to 4 ounces.*

Red-Pepper, Spinach, and Mushroom Loaf

Serves 6 as a main course
Working time: about 1 hour and 30 minutes
Total time: about 14 hours (includes chilling)

Calories **115**
Protein **8g.**
Cholesterol **0mg.**
Total fat **4g.**
Saturated fat **1g.**
Sodium **220mg.**

2 lb. sweet red peppers, peeled (technique, page 90) and seeded
1 tbsp. virgin olive oil
4 egg whites
½ cup dry breadcrumbs
1½ lb. mushrooms, sliced
1 tsp. chopped fresh basil
1 tsp. chopped fresh marjoram, or ¼ tsp. dried marjoram
1 tsp. chopped fresh oregano, or ¼ tsp. dried oregano
¼ tsp. salt
¾ lb. fresh spinach leaves, stemmed

Select one large red pepper, cut it into dice, and set the dice aside. Coarsely chop the remaining peppers. Heat ½ tablespoon of the olive oil in a heavy-bottomed saucepan over low heat. Add the coarsely chopped peppers and cook them, stirring occasionally, until they are tender—about 10 minutes. Cool the peppers slightly, then purée them in a food processor. Add two of the egg whites and 2 tablespoons of the bread-crumbs, and process again until the ingredients are thoroughly combined. Transfer the mixture to a bowl and set it aside.

Rinse out the saucepan and heat the remaining olive oil in it. Add the mushrooms and cook them over medium heat, stirring occasionally, until they are ten-der—about five minutes. Increase the heat and con-tinue to cook until all the moisture has evaporated—about 10 minutes. Stir the mushrooms occasionally, to prevent them from sticking to the pan. Allow them to cool a little, then purée them in the food processor. Add the remaining egg whites and breadcrumbs, and process again, then add the basil, marjoram, oregano, and salt, and process briefly to mix these into the purée. Set the mixture aside.

Blanch the spinach leaves in a large pan of boiling water for 30 seconds. Drain the spinach, refresh it under cold running water, and drain it again. Open out the leaves and lay them on paper towels to allow the remaining moisture to be absorbed.

Preheat the oven to 425° F. Line a loaf pan 7½ by 3¾ by 2 inches with parchment paper (*technique, page 34*). Sprinkle half of the reserved diced pepper over the bottom of the pan. Spoon in half of the pepper purée and spread it evenly, then lay a third of the spinach leaves over the top. Spread the mushroom mixture over the spinach. Lay another third of the spinach leaves over the mushroom mixture and sprin-kle on the remaining diced pepper. Pour in the rest of the pepper purée, smooth it level, and lay the last of the spinach leaves over the top. Cover the terrine with parchment paper.

Bake the terrine until a knife inserted in the center comes out clean—about 50 minutes. Let the terrine cool, then chill it for several hours or overnight.

Turn the terrine out onto a flat serving dish and peel off the lining paper. Serve the terrine cut into slices.

SUGGESTED ACCOMPANIMENT: *crisp young lettuce leaves dressed with a light vinaigrette.*

Asparagus and Red-Pepper Mousse

Serves 12 as a first course
Working time: about 1 hour and 10 minutes
Total time: about 8 hours (includes chilling)

Calories **65**
Protein **6g.**
Cholesterol **5mg.**
Total fat **3g.**
Saturated fat **2g.**
Sodium **105mg.**

2 lb. long asparagus spears, trimmed and peeled
2 tbsp. unsalted butter
¼ cup unbleached all-purpose flour
1¼ cups unsalted chicken stock (recipe, page 10)
2 tbsp. plain low-fat yogurt
¾ tsp. salt
ground white pepper
1 sweet red pepper, peeled (technique, page 90) and seeded
⅓ cup part-skim ricotta, pressed through a sieve
2 tbsp. cut chives
8 tsp. powdered gelatin
1 egg white

Place the asparagus in a steamer, and steam it until it is tender—six to eight minutes. Select eight of the best spears and set them aside. Purée the remaining asparagus in a food processor or blender. Trim the reserved asparagus spears so they will fit exactly, lengthwise, in the bottom of a nonreactive loaf pan 9 by 5 by 3 inches. Arrange the spears side by side in the bottom of the pan, alternating the orientation.

Melt the butter in a small, heavy-bottomed saucepan over medium heat. Stir in the flour, then stir in the stock. Bring the sauce to a boil, stirring continuously. Reduce the heat to low and allow the sauce to simmer until the flour is cooked—five to six minutes. Remove the pan from the heat, and stir in the asparagus purée and yogurt. Season the mixture with ½ teaspoon of the salt and some white pepper. Allow it to cool for about one hour at room temperature, stirring frequently to prevent a skin from forming.

Meanwhile, purée the red pepper in a food processor. Turn the purée into a small bowl, and season it with ⅛ teaspoon of the salt and some white pepper. Put the ricotta into another small bowl, and stir in the chives, the remaining salt, and a little white pepper.

Dissolve the gelatin in 6 tablespoons of cold water (technique, page 13). Stir 1 teaspoon of the gelatin solution into the pepper purée, and 1 teaspoon into the ricotta. Stir the remainder into the asparagus mixture. Beat the egg white until it will hold soft peaks and fold it gently into the asparagus mixture; refrigerate the mixture until it begins to thicken—20 to 30 minutes. Keep the pepper purée and ricotta at room temperature, to prevent them from setting.

Pour one-third of the asparagus mixture into the prepared pan. Spoon half of the pepper purée and the ricotta over the asparagus mixture, in random dollops. Pour in another third of the asparagus mixture, add the remaining pepper purée and ricotta as before, and finally pour in the remaining asparagus mixture. Level the top and chill the terrine until it has set firmly—four to five hours.

To unmold the terrine, quickly dip the bottom and sides of the pan in hot water, and invert it onto a flat serving plate. Serve the terrine in slices.

SUGGESTED ACCOMPANIMENT: *toast fingers.*

Red-Pepper Ramekins

Serves 8 as a first course
Working time: about 1 hour
Total time: about 5 hours and 30 minutes
(includes chilling)

Calories **50**
Protein **5g.**
Cholesterol **0mg.**
Total fat **1g.**
Saturated fat **trace**
Sodium **25mg.**

2 lb. sweet red peppers, seeded, deribbed, and sliced
3 oz. shallots, sliced
¼ lb. young leeks, trimmed, cleaned thoroughly to remove all grit, and chopped
1 cup unsalted vegetable stock (recipe, page 10)
1 bouquet garni
2 tbsp. powdered gelatin
⅔ cup plain low-fat yogurt
tomato juice (about ¾ cup)
10 drops hot red-pepper sauce
½ tsp. fresh lime juice
basil sprigs for garnish
lettuce leaves for garnish

Pepper salad

1 sweet red pepper, peeled (technique, page 90), seeded, and cut into thin strips
1 sweet yellow pepper, peeled (technique, page 90), seeded, and cut into thin strips
½ tsp. fresh lime juice
freshly ground black pepper

Place the red peppers, shallots, and leeks in a saucepan. Pour in the stock and add the bouquet garni. Bring the stock to a boil over low heat, then cover the pan and cook the vegetables until they are very soft—30 to 40 minutes. Drain the vegetables and reserve the cooking liquid; discard the bouquet garni. Purée the vegetables in a food processor and strain the purée to remove any coarse fibers.

Pour ½ cup of the reserved cooking liquid into a small bowl and set it aside to cool. Dissolve the gelatin in the cooled liquid (technique, page 13). Combine the remaining cooking liquid with the vegetable purée in a large measuring container; stir in the yogurt and enough tomato juice to make 1 quart. Stir the gelatin solution into this mixture, followed by the hot red-pepper sauce and the lime juice. Beat well, to ensure that the yogurt is thoroughly incorporated. Divide the mixture among eight ½-cup molds. Chill the molds for at least four hours, or overnight, until the mixture is completely set.

For the pepper salad, toss the strips of red and yellow pepper with the lime juice. Season the salad with freshly ground black pepper.

To serve the ramekins, dip the bottoms and sides of the molds in hot water for two or three seconds, and turn the ramekins out onto individual serving plates. Spoon a small portion of the pepper salad onto each plate, and garnish each plate with sprigs of basil and a few lettuce leaves.

Layered Mushroom Terrine

Serves 10 as a first course
Working time: about 2 hours
Total time: about 6 hours (includes chilling)

Calories **75**
Protein **4g.**
Cholesterol **25mg.**
Total fat **3g.**
Saturated fat **1g.**
Sodium **150mg.**

½ oz. dried ceps
¼ oz. dried chanterelles
1 oz. dried morels
2 cups unsalted brown stock (recipe, page 11)
¼ lb. button mushrooms, finely chopped
¼ lb. gray oyster mushrooms, finely chopped
2 garlic cloves
2 tbsp. chopped parsley
4 tbsp. Madeira
¾ tsp. salt
freshly ground black pepper
1 tbsp. unsalted butter
1 tsp. Dijon mustard
1 tsp. fresh lemon juice
6 oz. button mushrooms, finely chopped
¼ lb. golden oyster mushrooms, finely chopped
ground white pepper
3 tbsp. fresh breadcrumbs
1 small egg, lightly beaten
⅓ cup plain low-fat yogurt
1 tsp. cornstarch, sifted
1 egg white
1½ tsp. powdered gelatin

Place the dried ceps, dried chanterelles, and dried morels in three separate bowls. Add ⅓ cup of stock to both the ceps and the chanterelles, and add ⅔ cup to the morels. Let the mushrooms soak for about 30 minutes. At the end of this time, remove the mushrooms from their soaking liquids and squeeze them out, reserving the soaking liquids. Strain the soaking liquids through a paper coffee filter into one bowl, and set it aside. Keeping them separate, rinse the mushrooms in a bowl of fresh water and squeeze them gently to rid them of all their grit.

Place the ceps in a small, heavy-bottomed saucepan with the ¼ pound of button mushrooms, the gray oyster mushrooms, the garlic, the parsley, the remaining stock, 2 tablespoons of the Madeira, ¼ teaspoon of the salt, and some black pepper. Cover the pan and simmer the ingredients over low heat until the mushrooms are soft—about 20 minutes. Uncover the pan, increase the heat, and continue cooking until all the moisture has evaporated. Remove the garlic cloves if you wish, or crush them into the mixture. Turn the cep mixture into a bowl and let it cool.

Pat the chanterelles dry on paper towels. Chop them fine and set them aside.

Melt the butter in a small, heavy skillet, and stir in the mustard and lemon juice. Add the 6 ounces of button mushrooms, the golden oyster mushrooms, ¼ teaspoon of the salt, and some white pepper. Cover the pan and cook the mushrooms until they are tender—15 to 20 minutes. Uncover the pan, increase the heat, and continue to cook, stirring constantly, until all the moisture has evaporated. Transfer the mixture to a bowl and let it cool.

Preheat the oven to 350° F. Line a baking pan 8 by 8 by 3 inches with a double thickness of parchment paper (technique, page 34).

Stir the breadcrumbs and lightly beaten egg into the cooled cep mixture, and press the mixture into the bottom of the pan. Purée the second mushroom mixture in a food processor until it is smooth. Beat in the yogurt, cornstarch, and egg white, then fold in the finely chopped chanterelles. Spoon this mixture into the pan and level the surface.

Cover the terrine with a piece of lightly oiled aluminum foil and place it in a roasting pan or ovenproof dish. Pour in boiling water to come two-thirds of the way up the sides of the terrine, and bake the terrine in the oven until the center is firm to the touch—40 to 50 minutes. Remove the terrine from the water bath and allow it to cool.

Meanwhile, steam the morels in a steamer set over a saucepan of boiling water for five minutes. Dissolve the gelatin in 2 tablespoons of the reserved mushroom-soaking liquid (technique, page 13) and stir the gelatin solution into ⅔ cup of the remaining soaking liquid. Stir in the remaining 2 tablespoons of Madeira and the remaining ¼ teaspoon of salt. Set the liquid aspic aside in the refrigerator until it is on the point of setting—about 20 to 30 minutes.

Arrange the steamed morels on the surface of the terrine and press them down lightly. Spoon the partially set aspic over the morels and chill the terrine for at least two hours, or until the aspic layer is firmly set.

To unmold the terrine, run a sharp knife gently around all four sides of the pan to loosen the aspic, then use the lining paper to lift the terrine out of the pan. Fold down the paper, and use a large spatula to slide the terrine off its paper base and onto a serving plate. Neaten the edges if necessary. Serve the terrine cut into slices.

SUGGESTED ACCOMPANIMENTS: *crusty bread; lettuce leaves.*

EDITOR'S NOTE: *Any combination of dried and fresh mushrooms could be used in this terrine.*

Potatoes Layered with Gruyère and Onions

Serves 6 as a main course
Working time: about 35 minutes
Total time: about 2 hours

Calories **250**
Protein **9g.**
Cholesterol **25mg.**
Total fat **9g.**
Saturated fat **4g.**
Sodium **210mg.**

2½ lb. large potatoes, scrubbed
1 tbsp. virgin olive oil
1 cup thinly sliced scallions
1 garlic clove, crushed
1 large sweet red pepper, seeded, deribbed, and thinly sliced
½ tsp. salt
freshly ground black pepper
¼ lb. Gruyère cheese, coarsely grated
6 tbsp. unsalted chicken stock (recipe, page 10)
1 tbsp. chopped fresh parsley

Put the potatoes into a large saucepan and cover them with cold water. Put on the lid and bring the water to a boil, then lower the heat and simmer the potatoes until they are almost tender—about 30 minutes.

Meanwhile, heat the olive oil in a heavy skillet over medium heat. Add the scallions and crushed garlic, and cook them gently until they are soft but not browned—two to three minutes. Using a slotted spoon, remove the scallions and garlic from the pan, and set them aside. Add the pepper slices to the oil remaining in the skillet. Cover the skillet and cook the peppers over low heat until they are soft—15 to 20 minutes. Remove the pan from the heat.

Preheat the oven to 425° F. Grease a loaf pan 11 by 3½ by 3½ inches. Line the bottom with parchment paper *(technique, page 34)*.

Drain the potatoes, and holding each one in turn in a clean dishtowel, carefully peel off the skins while the potatoes are still hot. Allow the peeled potatoes to cool for 15 to 20 minutes, then cut them into slices a little less than ¼ inch thick.

Arrange the largest and best-looking potato slices in two neatly overlapping rows in the bottom of the loaf pan. Season them with a little of the salt and some black pepper. Cover the potato slices with half of the onions and garlic, and scatter on a quarter of the cheese. Sprinkle 1½ tablespoons of the stock over the top. Add another layer of potato slices, season them with a little more of the salt and some more pepper, and cover them with the slices of red pepper. Sprinkle on another quarter of the cheese and 1½ tablespoons of the stock. Arrange another layer of potato slices in the pan, season them as before, and add the remaining onions and garlic, another quarter of the cheese, and 1½ tablespoons of the stock. Finally, layer the remaining potato slices in the pan, add the remaining salt and a few more grindings of black pepper, and sprinkle on the remaining cheese and stock.

Bake the vegetables until the topmost layer of potatoes is golden brown and all the potatoes are cooked through—30 to 40 minutes. Remove the pan from the oven and let it stand for five minutes. Loosen the sides with a spatula, then turn the vegetables out onto a flat serving dish. Peel off the paper, scatter the parsley over the dish, and serve it hot, cut into slices.

SUGGESTED ACCOMPANIMENT: *salad of red-leaf lettuce and mixed greens.*

Spinach and Pasta Terrine

Serves 16 as a first course
Working time: about 40 minutes
Total time: about 3 hours (includes chilling)

Calories **135**
Protein **7g.**
Cholesterol **0mg.**
Total fat **5g.**
Saturated fat **1g.**
Sodium **200mg.**

3 lb. fresh spinach, washed and stemmed, 20 large leaves set aside, the remainder chopped
½ lb. penne or other large tubular pasta
¼ cup plus 1 tsp. virgin olive oil
2 lb. tomatoes (about 6 medium), peeled and seeded
2 tsp. tomato paste
1½ tsp. salt
freshly ground black pepper
2 tbsp. powdered gelatin
2 tsp. pesto
4 tsp. chopped fresh basil
2 tbsp. white wine vinegar

Blanch the whole spinach leaves in a saucepan of boiling water for 30 seconds, then drain them and plunge them into ice water. Drain them thoroughly and pat them dry on paper towels. Line a terrine 11 by 3½ by 3½ inches with plastic wrap, pulling the wrap as tight as possible and pressing it into the corners. Arrange the blanched leaves in the terrine, allowing them to overhang its sides.

Add the pasta to 3 quarts of boiling water with 1½ teaspoons of salt. Start testing the pasta after eight minutes and continue to cook until it is *al dente*. Drain the pasta and toss it in the teaspoon of olive oil. Set the pasta aside.

Place the tomatoes in a food processor or blender with the tomato paste, ½ teaspoon of the salt, and some black pepper. Purée the ingredients, then pass the purée through a fine sieve into a bowl. Dissolve the gelatin in 6 tablespoons of water (*technique, page 13*) and whisk the gelatin solution into the tomato purée. Set the tomato mixture aside.

Blanch the chopped spinach in a large pan of boiling water for one minute. Drain it well, then squeeze it very thoroughly in a clean dishtowel or a piece of cheesecloth to remove all excess liquid. Put the spinach in a bowl and mix in the pesto, the basil, ½ teaspoon of the salt, and some black pepper.

Place half of the pasta in the bottom of the terrine and pour half of the tomato mixture over it. Add the spinach mixture and gently smooth the surface to cover the pasta and tomatoes, then add the remaining pasta and the rest of the tomato mixture. Cover the terrine with the overhanging spinach leaves and place it in the refrigerator to chill for two to three hours.

Just before unmolding the terrine, make a vinaigrette. In a small bowl, stir the remaining ½ teaspoon of salt and the vinegar together until the salt dissolves. Beat in the 4 tablespoons of olive oil, beating until the oil and vinegar are thoroughly blended. Add some black pepper and set the vinaigrette aside.

To serve the terrine, unmold it onto a large platter or board, remove the plastic wrap, and cut it into slices using a sharp knife. Pass the vinaigrette separately.

Potted Chili Beans

Serves 8 as a main course
Working time: about 35 minutes
Total time: about 5 hours (includes soaking)

Calories **200**
Protein **15g.**
Cholesterol **0mg.**
Total fat **1g.**
Saturated fat **trace**
Sodium **370mg.**

1¼ cups dried red kidney beans, picked over
⅔ cup dried pinto beans, picked over
⅔ cup dried green or yellow peas, picked over
2 bay leaves
2 large onions, chopped
3 carrots, finely diced
2 celery stalks, finely diced
6 garlic cloves, finely chopped
3 fresh green chili peppers, seeded and chopped (cautionary note, page 9)
4 tsp. chopped fresh oregano, or 1 tsp. dried oregano
2 lemons, grated zest and juice only
2 tsp. sugar
1 tbsp. paprika
1½ tsp. salt
freshly ground black pepper
5 tbsp. chopped cilantro
cilantro sprigs for garnish

Rinse the kidney beans, pinto beans, and peas under cold running water, and put them into a large saucepan with enough cold water to cover them by about 3 inches. Discard any that float to the surface. Cover the saucepan, leaving the lid ajar, and slowly bring the liquid to a boil. Boil the beans and peas for two minutes, then turn off the heat and let them soak, covered, for at least an hour. (Alternatively, soak them overnight in cold water.)

Rinse the beans and peas, and place them in a clean saucepan with enough cold water to cover them by about 3 inches. Add the bay leaves. Bring the water to a boil, cover the pan, and reduce the heat to low. Simmer the beans and peas for one hour.

Add the onions, carrots, celery, garlic, chilies, and oregano to the pan, and stir them in. Continue to cook, uncovered, for 20 to 30 minutes more, stirring frequently, until the vegetables and the beans and peas are completely tender and all the cooking liquid has been absorbed.

Remove the pan from the heat and discard the bay leaves. Stir in the lemon zest and juice, the sugar, paprika, salt, and some freshly ground black pepper. Use a food processor to reduce the mixture to a coarse purée. Do this in batches, transferring the processed pâté to a mixing bowl. Stir in the chopped cilantro and let the pâté cool completely.

Divide the bean pâté among eight individual bowls and garnish each portion with a sprig of cilantro, if desired, before serving.

SUGGESTED ACCOMPANIMENTS: *tomato and onion salad; corn muffins or johnnycake.*

Two-Lentil Terrine

Serves 6 as a main course
Working time: about 45 minutes
Total time: about 6 hours (includes cooling)

Calories **230**
Protein **17g.**
Cholesterol **75mg.**
Total fat **5g.**
Saturated fat **2g.**
Sodium **210mg.**

1 cup red lentils, picked over and rinsed
1½ cups carrots (about 3 medium), finely sliced
1 orange
½ cup green lentils, picked over and rinsed
⅔ oz. dried ceps, rinsed thoroughly to remove all grit
2 tbsp. low-sodium soy sauce
1 bay leaf, broken in half
1 tbsp. cider vinegar
1 tsp. ground cumin
½ tsp. salt
ground white pepper
2 eggs
⅔ cup plain low-fat yogurt
2 tbsp. finely chopped parsley
1 tsp. finely chopped fresh thyme, or ½ tsp. dried thyme leaves
8 mint leaves, finely chopped
lettuce leaves for garnish

Place the red lentils and finely sliced carrots in a heavy-bottomed, nonreactive saucepan, and pour in enough water to cover them. Grate the zest from half the orange and set it aside. Squeeze the juice from the whole fruit, and add the juice to the pan with the lentils and carrots. Bring the liquid to a boil, cover the pan, and lower the heat. Simmer gently until the carrots are tender and the lentils are very soft—about 30 minutes. Stir the contents of the pan from time to time, to prevent burning, and add a little more water if necessary; all the liquid should have been absorbed by the end of the cooking time.

Meanwhile, place the green lentils and ceps in a second heavy-bottomed saucepan. Pour in 1 cup of water, add the soy sauce and bay leaf, and bring the liquid to a boil. Cover the pan and lower the heat. Simmer the lentils gently until they are completely tender—about 50 minutes. Uncover the saucepan toward the end of the cooking time to allow the moisture to evaporate, but do not allow the lentils to burn on the bottom of the pan. Place the lentils in a sieve over a bowl to cool and drain.

Lightly oil a terrine or loaf pan 9 by 5 by 3 inches and line it with parchment paper (technique, page 34). Lightly oil the lining paper. Preheat the oven to 350° F.

Purée the red lentils and carrots by pressing them through a sieve into a mixing bowl; a food processor may be used to do this, but take care not to overprocess, or the purée will be too runny. Add the reserved orange zest, the vinegar, the cumin, ¼ teaspoon of the salt, and some white pepper. Lightly beat one of the eggs, then add it to the mixture with ¼ cup of the yogurt and stir well. Spoon half of this mixture into the prepared terrine and level the surface.

Lightly beat the remaining egg. Discard the bay leaf halves from the cooked green lentils. Stir in the parsley, thyme, chopped mint, the remaining yogurt, the beaten egg, and the remaining salt. Spoon the mixture into the terrine, spreading it gently over the red lentil layer. Spoon the remaining red lentil mixture over the green lentils and level the surface. Cover the terrine with lightly oiled foil, tented slightly to ensure that it does not touch the contents of the terrine.

Place the terrine in a roasting pan or ovenproof dish, and pour in enough boiling water to come two-thirds of the way up the sides of the terrine. Bake the terrine until the center of the lentil mixture is firm to the touch—about one hour. Remove the terrine from the water bath and allow it to cool completely.

Invert the terrine onto a cutting board or other flat surface and peel off the lining paper. Use a sharp, long-bladed knife to cut the terrine into slices, and serve it on a bed of lettuce leaves.

EDITOR'S NOTE: To make this terrine easier to slice, chill it first in the refrigerator for at least two hours.

Fennel and Lentil Pâté

Serves 10 as a first course
Working time: about 50 minutes
Total time: about 5 hours

Calories **100**
Protein **9g.**
Cholesterol **0mg.**
Total fat **1g.**
Saturated fat **trace**
Sodium **225mg.**

1¼ cups green lentils, picked over and rinsed
1 large onion, chopped
2 garlic cloves, crushed
½ lb. fennel, trimmed and chopped, feathery tops reserved and chopped
1 tsp. safflower oil
¼ cup plain low-fat yogurt
1 tsp. mild chili powder
2 tsp. fresh lemon juice
1 tsp. salt
3 tbsp. chopped parsley
freshly ground black pepper
1 tsp. dry mustard
4 tsp. powdered gelatin
4 egg whites
lime slices for garnish
fennel tops for garnish

Put the lentils into a heavy-bottomed saucepan with 2½ cups of water. Bring the liquid to a boil, add half of the onion and garlic, cover the pan, and lower the heat. Simmer the lentils until they are tender—about 40 minutes. Turn them into a sieve set over a bowl, and let them drain and cool.

Meanwhile, put the fennel into another saucepan with water to cover, put the lid on the pan, and bring the water to a boil. Lower the heat, and simmer the fennel until it is tender—about eight minutes. Drain the fennel, reserving 2 tablespoons of the cooking liquid. Let the fennel cool. Heat the oil in a small, heavy-bottomed skillet, and sauté the remaining onion and garlic until they are soft—about five minutes.

Purée the drained lentils in a food processor until they are smooth. Turn the lentil purée into a bowl, and add the yogurt, chili powder, chopped fennel tops, half of the lemon juice and salt, 2 tablespoons of the chopped parsley, and a generous grinding of black pepper. Mix the ingredients together well.

Rinse out the food processor bowl, and process the drained fennel and the sautéed onion and garlic until

the mixture is smooth. Transfer the purée to a bowl, and mix in the dry mustard, the remaining salt and lemon juice, and some freshly ground black pepper.

Dissolve the gelatin in the reserved fennel-cooking water *(technique, page 13)*. Thoroughly mix half of the gelatin solution into the lentil mixture and the other half, equally thoroughly, into the fennel mixture.

Beat the egg whites until they stand in stiff peaks. Using a rubber spatula, stir 2 tablespoons of the beaten egg whites into each purée, to lighten the mixtures. Divide the remaining egg whites between the bowls and fold them in gently.

Line a loaf pan 7½ by 3¾ by 2 inches with parch-ment paper *(technique, page 34)*. Sprinkle the remaining chopped parsley evenly over the bottom of the pan. Pour in half of the lentil mixture and level the surface. Place the pan in the refrigerator for 10 minutes, to firm up the lentil layer. Add the fennel mixture to the pan and spread it evenly over the lentil layer. Place the pan in the refrigerator for 10 minutes more, to partially set the fennel mixture. Finally, pour in the rest of the lentil mixture and level the top. Chill until the pâté is firmly set—about three hours.

Turn out the pâté onto a flat serving plate and peel off the lining paper. Serve the pâté sliced, garnished with lime slices and fennel tops.

Anchovy and Lentil Dip

Serves 6 as a first course
Working time: about 15 minutes
Total time: about 1 hour

Calories **180**
Protein **13g.**
Cholesterol **10mg.**
Total fat **2g.**
Saturated fat **trace**
Sodium **450mg.**

1¼ cups red lentils, picked over and rinsed
1 or 2 garlic cloves, finely chopped
1 large onion, chopped
2½ cups unsalted vegetable stock (recipe, page 10)
2 oz. anchovy fillets, soaked in a little skim milk for 15 minutes to reduce their saltiness
2 tbsp. fresh lemon juice
5 tbsp. dry breadcrumbs
cut chives for garnish
lemon slices, cut into pieces, for garnish

Put the lentils, garlic, onion, and stock into a heavy-bottomed saucepan. Bring the stock to a boil, and skim off any scum that rises to the surface of the liquid. Lower the heat, cover the pan, and cook the lentils until they are soft and have absorbed all the stock—about 30 minutes. If any stock remains at the end of this time, cook the lentils uncovered over medium heat, stirring constantly, until all the moisture has evaporated.

Pat the anchovies dry on paper towels, and place them in a food processor or blender with the cooked lentils, lemon juice, and breadcrumbs. Process these ingredients until they are smooth. Divide the mixture among six individual ramekins and let it cool. Just before serving, garnish each portion with a few chives and pieces of lemon.

SUGGESTED ACCOMPANIMENT: *breadsticks.*

Terrine of Carrots and Black Beans

Serves 6 as a main course
Working time: about 45 minutes
Total time: about 5 hours (includes soaking)

Calories **155**
Protein **15g.**
Cholesterol **0mg.**
Total fat **4g.**
Saturated fat **2g.**
Sodium **490mg.**

½ cup dried black beans, picked over
1 onion, chopped
2 garlic cloves, chopped
2 fresh green chili peppers, seeded and chopped (cautionary note, page 9)
½ tsp. salt
4 egg whites
1 lb. carrots, sliced into rounds, plus 1 carrot cut lengthwise into strips with a vegetable peeler, soaked in ice water for 45 minutes and drained, for garnish
1 tsp. paprika
¾ cup low-fat cottage cheese
1½ tbsp. freshly grated Parmesan cheese
2 tbsp. capers, rinsed and drained
salad greens for garnish

Rinse the black beans under cold running water, then put them into a large saucepan with enough cold water to cover them by about 3 inches. Discard any beans that float to the surface. Cover the saucepan, leaving the lid ajar, and slowly bring the liquid to a boil. Boil the beans for two minutes, then turn off the heat and let the beans soak, covered, for at least an hour. (Alternatively, soak the beans overnight in cold water.)

Rinse the beans and place them in a clean saucepan with enough cold water to cover them by about 3 inches. Add the onion, garlic, and chili peppers to the pan, and bring the water to a boil. Cover the pan, lower the heat, and simmer the beans until they are tender—45 minutes to one hour. Check the water level from time to time and add more hot water if necessary.

Drain the cooked beans thoroughly and place them in a food processor. Add ¼ teaspoon of the salt and two of the egg whites, and process the bean mixture to a smooth purée. Set the mixture aside.

Meanwhile, simmer the carrots in water until they are tender—about eight minutes. Drain the carrots and allow them to cool a little. Process them to a smooth purée in a food processor with the paprika and the remaining salt and egg whites.

Preheat the oven to 425° F. Lightly oil a loaf pan 9 by 5 by 3 inches.

Spoon the bean mixture into the prepared pan and press it down with the back of the spoon to make an even layer. Top the bean layer with the cottage cheese, spreading it out evenly. Scatter on the Parmesan cheese and the capers, and press them down lightly. Lastly, spoon the carrot mixture into the pan and spread it evenly. Cover the terrine with foil and bake it until a skewer inserted into the center meets with little resistance—50 minutes to one hour. Allow the terrine to cool in the pan.

Turn out the terrine onto a flat serving platter and cut it into slices. Serve each portion with a garnish of salad greens and carrot curls.

Indian Spiced Pâté

Serves 10 as a first course
Working time: about 20 minutes
Total time: about 4 hours (includes soaking)

Calories **125**
Protein **6g.**
Cholesterol **0mg.**
Total fat **4g.**
Saturated fat **trace**
Sodium **165mg.**

1¼ cups dried black-eyed peas, picked over
2 tbsp. safflower oil
1 large onion, finely chopped
1 garlic clove, crushed
1½ tbsp. black mustard seeds
1 tbsp. fennel seeds
½ tsp. chili powder
½ tsp. ground coriander
½ tsp. garam masala
2 tbsp. tomato paste
1 tbsp. red wine vinegar
1 tsp. salt
freshly ground black pepper
fresh oregano sprigs for garnish (optional)

Rinse the black-eyed peas under cold running water, then put them into a large saucepan with enough cold water to cover them by about 3 inches. Discard any peas that float to the surface. Cover the saucepan, leaving the lid ajar, and slowly bring the liquid to a boil. Boil the peas for two minutes, then turn off the heat and let the peas soak, covered, for at least an hour.

(Alternatively, soak the peas overnight in cold water.)

Drain and rinse the peas, and place them in a clean saucepan with enough cold water to cover them by about 3 inches. Bring the water to a boil, lower the heat, and simmer the peas, covered, until they are tender—about 40 minutes. Check the water level from time to time and add more hot water if necessary. Drain the peas when they are cooked, reserving 6 tablespoons of the cooking water.

Heat the oil in a large, heavy-bottomed saucepan. Add the onion and garlic, and sauté them over medium heat until they are soft but not browned.

Add the mustard seeds, fennel seeds, chili powder, ground coriander, garam masala, and tomato paste to the mixture in the pan. Stir the spices in well and continue sautéing these ingredients for five minutes more. Mix in the red wine vinegar and sauté for one minute more.

Place the cooked peas in a food processor with the reserved cooking liquid, and process them until they are smooth. Stir them into the onion and spice mixture with the salt and some freshly ground black pepper.

Transfer the pâté to a large bowl and allow it to cool before serving. Garnish the pâté, if desired, with sprigs of oregano.

SUGGESTED ACCOMPANIMENT: *hot pita bread or toast.*

EDITOR'S NOTE: *Black mustard seeds are available in Indian and Middle Eastern groceries.*

4 *A terrine of thinly sliced peaches suspended in layers of jellied apple purée and blackberry purée (recipe, page 126) provides a perfect harmony of sweet and tart flavors.*

Terrines for Dessert

Light, refreshing, and pleasing to the eye, the terrines in this chapter reflect a new and highly imaginative approach to the making of desserts. In this innovative style of cooking, spectacular sweets are created without undue reliance on the cream pitcher, the butter dish, or the sugar bowl. The glorious desserts on the following pages are as healthful as they are glamorous, with little or no saturated fat, a modest calorie count, and all the life-sustaining nutrients that fresh fruit, nuts, and low-fat dairy products supply.

The foundation for a number of these preparations is a mousse of beaten egg whites combined with yogurt. The use of low-fat cheeses or yogurt as a base, instead of heavy cream or egg-yolk-laden custards, makes it possible to incorporate ingredients that would otherwise send fat and calorie counts soaring: The caramel and chocolate Bavarian cream with its caramel sauce on page 117, for instance, becomes a permissible indulgence. Another foundation much used in this chapter is fruit, whether in the form of a purée or a clear jelly.

Fruit, indeed, is the chief source of inspiration for these terrines. Here are delicacies to celebrate the best of the market's offerings, whatever the time of year. The soft fruits of summer are put to good use in the strawberry cheese loaf *(page 120)*, with its liqueur-spiked sauce, and in the marbled blueberry dessert, with its garnish of lightly caramelized berries *(page 126)*. Yet there is no shortage of alternatives for winter, when dried fruits and tropical imports come into their own: The prune and almond terrine, with its mousse of yogurt, honey, and brandy-soaked prunes *(page 114)*, and the assemblage of exotic fruits in champagne jelly *(page 125)* are only two of many options available.

A number of the molds used for recipes in this chapter are first lined with either plastic wrap or parchment paper. This step will protect delicately flavored ingredients from taking on any metallic taste if metal molds are used, and—whatever the container—will make it easy to turn out the finished dish.

To fully appreciate the vibrant colors and lively flavors of fresh fruit, it is best to make these terrines on the day you intend to serve them. They should be assembled several hours in advance, cooled, chilled or set in the refrigerator or the freezer as the recipe specifies, and served cold.

gelatin has dissolved completely. Strain the juice into a mixing bowl and let it cool. Chill the mixture until it has partially set—about two hours.

Using an electric beater, whisk the orange jelly until it is slightly foamy—30 to 60 seconds—then whisk in the yogurt. Chill this mixture until it has almost set —about 30 minutes more. Stir the jelly lightly at this stage to eliminate any lumps.

Mix together the walnuts, breadcrumbs, and cinnamon. Line a terrine or loaf pan 7½ by 3¾ by 2 inches with plastic wrap, pulling the wrap as tight as possible and pressing it carefully into the corners of the terrine. Spoon a quarter of the orange jelly mixture into the bottom of the terrine and sprinkle a quarter of the walnut mixture on top in a thin, even layer. Repeat this process to create another three layers of each mixture, finishing with the walnut mixture. Chill the assembly until it has set completely—about three hours.

To unmold the terrine, invert it onto a flat serving plate and carefully remove the plastic wrap. Decorate the terrine with a dusting of ground cinnamon along the center and the reserved curls of orange zest. Cut it into slices to serve.

SUGGESTED ACCOMPANIMENT: *sour cream or yogurt.*

Orange and Walnut Layered Terrine

Serves 6
Working time: about 40 minutes
Total time: about 6 hours (includes chilling)

Calories **170**
Protein **6g.**
Cholesterol **0mg.**
Total fat **6g.**
Saturated fat **1g.**
Sodium **75mg.**

2 to 3 slices whole-wheat bread, crusts removed
4 oranges
1 tbsp. powdered gelatin
¼ cup sugar
⅔ cup plain low-fat yogurt
2 oz. walnuts (about ½ cup), finely chopped
½ tsp. ground cinnamon, plus a little ground cinnamon for dusting

Preheat the oven to 325° F. Place the bread on a baking sheet and toast it in the oven until it is crisp and dry—about 25 minutes. Allow the bread to cool, then place it in a plastic bag and use a rolling pin to crush it into fine crumbs.

Finely grate the zest of two of the oranges and set it aside. Using a vegetable peeler, pare short, wide strips of zest from the remaining two oranges. Place the strips in a small, nonreactive saucepan, cover them with cold water, and bring the water to a boil. Lower the heat and simmer the strips for five minutes. Drain the strips, and set them aside on paper towels until they are required.

Squeeze the juice from all four oranges. Put the juice and the finely grated zest in a small, nonreactive saucepan. Sprinkle the gelatin over 2 tablespoons of water in a small bowl and let it soften for five minutes.

Add the sugar to the orange juice and stir the juice over medium heat until the sugar has dissolved— about three minutes. Remove the pan from the heat and add the softened gelatin; stir the liquid until the

Tropical Fruit Terrine with Passionfruit Sauce

Serves 8
Working time: about 1 hour
Total time: about 6 hours

Calories **180**
Protein **6g.**
Cholesterol **0mg.**
Total fat **trace**
Saturated fat **trace**
Sodium **50mg.**

1 mango, peeled, flesh cut into ½-inch-wide strips
1 small papaya, peeled and seeded, flesh cut into ½-inch-wide strips
1 kiwi fruit, peeled and cut lengthwise into thin slivers
⅔ cup skim milk
1 vanilla bean, or ½ tsp. pure vanilla extract
4 tsp. powdered gelatin
1¾ lb. bananas
⅓ cup fresh lime juice
2 tbsp. plain low-fat yogurt
1 tsp. sugar (optional)
Passionfruit sauce
4 tsp. sugar
1 lime, grated zest only
4 passionfruits

Place the mango, papaya, and kiwi fruit strips in a fine sieve over a bowl, and let them drain. Heat the milk in a small, heavy-bottomed saucepan until it is just sim-

mering, then remove it from the heat. Split the vanilla bean lengthwise and add it to the milk. Cover the pan and set it aside for 30 minutes, to allow the milk to become infused with the vanilla flavor. (If you are using vanilla extract, infusion is not necessary.)

Remove the vanilla bean from the milk and scrape out all of the seeds. Stir the seeds into the milk. Soften the gelatin in 2 tablespoons of water *(technique, page 13, Step 1)*. Heat the vanilla-flavored milk to the simmering point again and remove it from the heat. Add the softened gelatin and stir until it has dissolved completely. Set this mixture aside; if it starts to set, place the pan in hot water.

Peel the bananas and cut them into chunks. Toss the chunks in the lime juice to prevent them from discoloring, then purée them with the lime juice in a food processor or blender. Add the vanilla-flavored milk and the yogurt, and process the mixture again until it is smooth. Add the sugar at this stage if a sweeter mixture is desired.

Dampen the insides of a terrine or loaf pan 7½ by 3¾ by 2 inches with water. Spread a layer of the banana mousse about ¼ inch thick in the bottom of the terrine. Place the terrine in the refrigerator to set the mousse—about 15 minutes. Spread another layer of mousse in the terrine—this time about ½ inch thick. Arrange a selection of the fruit strips, lengthwise, on top of the mousse, in two or three rows; leave at least ½ inch between each row of fruit strips and make sure none is touching the sides of the terrine. (Write down

the position of fruit varieties on a piece of paper to make sure the arrangement differs between layers.) Gently press the strips down through the soft mousse to the set layer beneath and spread another ½ inch of mousse over the top. Tap the base of the terrine gently on the work surface, to eliminate any air bubbles, then return it to the refrigerator for 30 minutes, to set the new layers of mousse. Repeat this process twice. Once the final layer of mousse has been added, chill the dessert for three hours, to set it firmly.

Meanwhile, prepare the passionfruit sauce. Bring ⅓ cup of water to a boil in a small, nonreactive pan. Add the sugar and lime zest and simmer, stirring occasionally, until the liquid has thickened slightly. Cut three of the passionfruits in half crosswise, and spoon the pulp and seeds into the syrup. Simmer for two minutes more. Remove the pan from the heat, cover it, and let the sauce cool for 30 minutes. Chill it until required.

Just before serving the terrine, press the passionfruit sauce through a fine sieve. Halve the remaining passionfruit, spoon the pulp and seeds into the sauce, and stir them in well.

To unmold the terrine, dip the base and sides of the pan in hot water for two or three seconds and turn the dessert out onto a flat serving plate. Serve it cut into slices, accompanied by the sauce.

SUGGESTED ACCOMPANIMENTS: *Cape gooseberries, sliced star fruit, or extra slices of any of the fruits featured in the dessert.*

Terrine of Prunes and Almonds

Serves 12
Working time: about 1 hour and 30 minutes
Total time: about 1 day (includes
marinating and chilling)

Calories **205**
Protein **8g.**
Cholesterol **10mg.**
Total fat **9g.**
Saturated fat **3g.**
Sodium **40mg.**

1 lb. large pitted prunes
2 tsp. Earl Grey tea leaves
7 tbsp. brandy
1 oz. slivered almonds (about ⅓ cup)
5 tbsp. sugar
3½ oz. whole almonds (about ⅔ cup), ½ cup blanched, the remainder unskinned
1¼ cups skim milk
2 drops pure almond extract
2½ tbsp. powdered gelatin
7 tbsp. heavy cream
3 egg whites
2 tbsp. honey
¼ cup sour cream
⅓ cup plain low-fat yogurt

First prepare the prunes. Steep the tea leaves in 1 cup of boiling water for five minutes. Place the prunes in a saucepan and strain the tea over them. Bring the tea just to a boil, lower the heat, and simmer the prunes until they are tender—about 10 minutes. Allow the prunes to cool in the tea, then drain and pit them, discarding the tea. Place the prunes in a bowl and pour 5 tablespoons of the brandy over them. Cover the bowl and let the prunes marinate for at least 12 hours. When you are ready to make the terrine, drain the prunes and reserve the liquid. Select six firm prunes, slice them, and set them aside until required. Purée the remaining prunes in a food processor or blender, and set them aside.

Place the slivered almonds in a dry, heavy-bottomed skillet and cook them over medium heat, stirring them from time to time, until they are golden brown—about five minutes. Add 1 tablespoon of the sugar, and continue cooking until the sugar caramelizes and coats the almonds—one to two minutes. As soon as the nuts have caramelized, remove them from the pan and spread them out on a sheet of lightly oiled wax paper. Let them cool and harden, then place them in a plastic bag and crush them coarsely with a rolling pin.

Grind the blanched and unskinned almonds in a food processor. With the food processor running, gradually pour in ½ cup of water. Add the milk, process again to mix the ingredients, then pour the mixture into a small, heavy-bottomed saucepan. Bring the liquid to a boil and simmer it gently over very low heat for about 10 minutes. Allow the mixture to cool a little, then strain it through a fine sieve, pressing down hard on the almonds to extract all the flavored liquid. Discard the solids. Stir the almond extract and the remaining sugar into the liquid, and let it cool slightly.

Dissolve 1 tablespoon of the gelatin in 2 tablespoons of water (technique, page 13). Stir the gelatin solution into the warm almond-flavored milk and set the mixture aside until it begins to thicken—about 45 minutes. Whip the cream until it just holds its shape, and fold it into the almond cream. Chill the mixture until it has almost set—about 20 minutes. Beat two of the egg whites until they form soft peaks. Stir 1 tablespoon of the whites into the almond cream, then fold in the remainder. Fold in the sliced prunes and the crushed caramelized almonds.

Rinse a terrine 11 by 3½ by 3½ inches with cold water; leave some water clinging to the insides of the terrine. Pour in the almond mixture and chill it until it is firm—about 30 minutes.

Blend the honey, sour cream, and yogurt into the puréed prunes. In a small bowl, add the remaining brandy to the reserved prune-soaking juices and dissolve the rest of the gelatin in this liquid, using the same method as before. Mix the gelatin solution thoroughly into the prune purée.

Beat the remaining egg white until it forms soft peaks. Stir 1 tablespoon of the egg white into the prune purée, then gently fold in the rest. Spoon the mixture into the terrine and chill it until it is firmly set—at least four hours.

Unmold the terrine onto a flat serving dish and serve it cut into slices.

Hazelnut Praline Block with Fresh Figs

Serves 16
Working time: about 30 minutes
Total time: about 4 hours (includes chilling)

Calories **135**	¼ lb. hazelnuts (about 1 cup)
Protein **13g.**	⅔ cup sugar
Cholesterol **trace**	7 tsp. powdered gelatin
Total fat **3g.**	2 lb. low-fat cottage cheese
Saturated fat **1g.**	1½ tbsp. brandy or Armagnac
Sodium **25mg.**	5 fresh figs, tops sliced off

Preheat the oven to 350° F. Line a terrine or loaf pan 11 by 3½ by 3½ inches with parchment paper *(technique, page 34)*. Lightly oil a marble slab, or lightly grease a baking sheet.

Spread the hazelnuts out on a dry baking sheet and roast them in the oven until they are evenly browned —about 10 minutes. Wrap them in a dishtowel, and roll them back and forth, then peel off the loosened skins. Put the roasted nuts and ½ cup of the sugar in a small, heavy-bottomed saucepan, and stir them over low heat until the sugar has dissolved and turned a golden caramel color. Pour the mixture onto the oiled slab or baking sheet, and spread it out with a wooden spoon. Let it cool and harden for about 30 minutes.

Dissolve the gelatin in 3 tablespoons of water *(technique, page 13)*. Break the hazelnut praline into pieces and chop them coarsely in a food processor. Scatter enough praline over the base of the prepared terrine to form a layer ½ inch deep. Process the remaining praline in the food processor until it is a fine powder. Add the remaining sugar, the cottage cheese, brandy, and dissolved gelatin. Process the mixture again until all the ingredients are smoothly combined.

Pour the praline cream into the terrine until it is 1½ inches deep. Arrange the figs in a row down the center of the terrine and pour in the remaining praline cream to cover the figs. Refrigerate the terrine until it has set firmly—two to three hours.

Dip the bottom and sides of the terrine in hot water for two to three seconds. Invert it onto a flat serving plate and peel off the lining paper. Cut the terrine into slices using a sharp, long-bladed knife that has been dipped in hot water.

Chestnut and Fig Terrine

Serves 12
Working time: about 1 hour and 10 minutes
Total time: about 5 hours and 40 minutes (includes cooling and freezing)

Calories **280**
Protein **2g.**
Cholesterol **0mg.**
Total fat **12g.**
Saturated fat **3g.**
Sodium **110mg.**

1½ lb. fresh chestnuts, or ¾ lb. dried chestnuts, soaked overnight in cold water and drained thoroughly
6 tbsp. Marsala
1 stick (¼ lb.) polyunsaturated margarine
½ cup sugar
6 oz. dried figs (about 1 cup), chopped
Chocolate coating
2 oz. semisweet chocolate, chopped
2 tbsp. Marsala
1 tbsp. polyunsaturated margarine

Cut a deep cross in the hull of each fresh chestnut. Drop the nuts into a saucepan of boiling water and parboil them to loosen their hulls—about 10 minutes. Remove the pan from the heat. Using a slotted spoon, lift the nuts out of the water a few at a time, and peel off the hulls and inner skins while the chestnuts are hot. About 1 pound of peeled nuts will result.

Put the fresh or dried chestnuts into a saucepan, and cover them with fresh cold water. Bring the water to a boil over medium heat, then reduce the heat to low, and cook the chestnuts gently until they are tender—15 to 20 minutes. Drain the chestnuts and return them to the pan. Pour the Marsala over the nuts, and cook them gently until the Marsala has been completely absorbed and the nuts are very soft—5 to 10 minutes. Remove the pan from the heat and allow the nuts to cool for about one hour. Meanwhile, line a terrine or loaf pan 7½ by 3¾ by 2 inches with parchment paper *(technique, page 34).*

Put the cooled chestnuts into a food processor and process them until they form a smooth paste. Alternatively, pass them through a ricer or sieve.

Cream the margarine and sugar together in a mixing bowl until they are soft and fluffy. Beat in the chestnut purée, then fold in the chopped figs. Spoon the mixture into the lined terrine and smooth the surface. Put the terrine in the freezer until the mixture has frozen solid—about three hours.

To make the coating, put the semisweet chocolate and Marsala into a small saucepan. Stir over low heat until the chocolate melts and blends smoothly with the Marsala. Remove the pan from the heat and stir in the margarine. Allow the coating to cool—about five minutes—but do not let it set.

Cover a flat board with foil. Remove the terrine from the freezer and turn it out onto the board; carefully peel off the lining paper. Using a small metal spatula, quickly spread the chocolate coating evenly all over the terrine. Mark the surface to create a pattern. Return the terrine to the freezer until the chocolate has set hard—about 15 minutes. Cover the dessert with plastic wrap and keep it in the freezer until required.

Thirty minutes before serving the terrine, remove it from the freezer. Unwrap it, place it on a flat serving plate, and put it in the refrigerator. To serve, cut the terrine into thin slices using a sharp, long-bladed knife.

EDITOR'S NOTE: *The terrine may be stored in the freezer for as long as six months.*

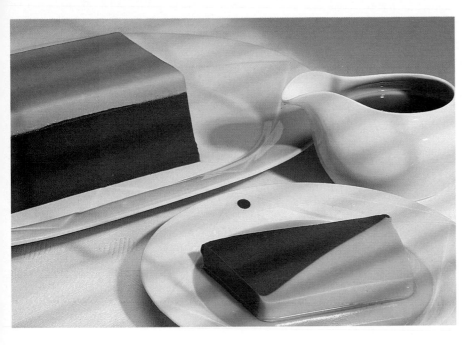

Caramel and Chocolate Bavarian Cream

Serves 12
Working time: about 1 hour and 40 minutes
Total time: about 8 hours (includes chilling)

Calories **190**	1 cup less 2 tbsp. sugar
Protein **8g.**	1 quart skim milk
Cholesterol **95mg.**	4 eggs
Total fat **8g.**	3 tbsp. powdered gelatin
Saturated fat **4g.**	2 tbsp. cocoa powder
Sodium **90mg.**	⅔ cup heavy cream
	1 egg white

First make the caramel Bavarian cream. Put 6 tablespoons of sugar into a large, heavy-bottomed saucepan with 3 tablespoons of cold water. Stir them together over low heat until every granule of sugar has dissolved, brushing down the sides of the pan from time to time with a pastry brush dipped in hot water. Bring the syrup to a boil over high heat and boil it rapidly until it has turned a rich golden color. Remove the pan from the heat and pour in 2 cups of the milk. Set the pan over low heat until the caramel has dissolved completely in the milk—about five minutes. Stir the liquid occasionally. Do not let it boil.

Meanwhile, lightly beat two of the eggs together in a large bowl. Soften half the gelatin in 3 tablespoons of cold water (technique, page 13, Step 1), and set it aside until needed.

Whisk the hot, caramel-flavored milk into the beaten eggs. Set the bowl over a pan of gently simmering water and stir the mixture until it forms a smooth, thin custard—about 20 minutes. Alternatively, microwave the custard on high for three minutes, stirring it every minute. As soon as the custard is ready, pour it through a fine sieve into a clean bowl. Add the softened gelatin and stir the mixture until the gelatin has completely dissolved. Set the caramel custard aside to cool, stirring it frequently to prevent a skin from forming.

To make the chocolate Bavarian cream, blend the cocoa powder and 1 cup of the remaining milk together in a saucepan. Bring the mixture to a boil over medium heat, stirring continuously. Lower the heat, cook the mixture gently for one to two minutes, then stir in the remaining milk. Continue heating the mixture until it is very hot but not boiling.

Meanwhile, in a large bowl, lightly beat the remaining two eggs and 2 tablespoons of sugar together. Soften the remaining gelatin in 3 tablespoons of cold water as before.

Whisk the hot milk into the egg and sugar mixture. Set the bowl over a pan of gently simmering water, and cook the chocolate custard in the same way as the caramel custard. When the chocolate custard is ready, pour it through a fine sieve into a clean bowl. Add the softened gelatin and stir the mixture until the gelatin has completely dissolved. Allow the custard to cool, stirring it frequently to prevent a skin from forming. Refrigerate both custards until they begin to thicken —about 30 minutes.

Beat the cream and egg white together until the mixture will hold soft peaks. Divide the cream mixture equally between the two custards and lightly whisk it in until evenly blended.

Wedge a nonreactive terrine or loaf pan 7½ by 3¾ by 3½ inches on its side at a 45-degree angle in a large bowl of ice. Pour the caramel custard into the terrine until it is level with one edge of the terrine, forming a triangular cross section lengthwise. Leave the terrine in position until the custard has set firmly—about 30 minutes; alternatively, carefully transfer the bowl to the freezer for 10 to 15 minutes. Meanwhile, keep the chocolate custard at room temperature to prevent it from setting. If necessary, place the bowl in warm water to soften the mixture, but do not let the custard become hot.

When the caramel custard has set, remove the terrine from the ice and stand it flat on the work surface. Pour in the chocolate custard to fill the terrine, then place the terrine in the refrigerator until the custard has set firmly—three to four hours.

Meanwhile, make a caramel sauce. Put the remaining sugar into a small saucepan with 3 tablespoons of cold water and make a rich golden caramel in the same way as before. Pour in ⅔ cup of hot water, reduce the heat to low, and leave the pan on the heat until the caramel has completely dissolved in the water to make a syrupy sauce. Allow the sauce to cool, then refrigerate it until required.

Unmold the Bavarian cream onto a flat serving dish. Serve it sliced, with the caramel sauce.

Orange and Almond Terrine

Serves 12
Working time: about 30 minutes
Total time: about 2 hours and 30 minutes
(includes chilling)

Calories **185**
Protein **18g.**
Cholesterol **trace**
Total fat **6g.**
Saturated fat **1g.**
Sodium **30mg.**

6 oranges
2 tbsp. powdered gelatin
2 cups low-fat cottage cheese
1½ cups plain low-fat yogurt
4 oz. ground almonds (about 1 cup)
¼ cup sugar
2 tbsp. orange-flavored liqueur
mint sprigs for decoration

Line the bottom of a nonreactive loaf pan 9 by 5 by 3 inches with parchment paper.

Using a sharp knife, slice off the peel at both ends of the oranges. Stand each orange on one of its flat ends and cut off the remaining peel by slicing downward in vertical strips; be sure to cut off all of the pith. Working over a bowl to catch the juice, cut four of the oranges into segments by slicing between the flesh and membrane. Cut the orange segments in half crosswise and set them aside, with the juice, until required. Slice the remaining two oranges crosswise into thin rounds, then cut each round in half to make semicircles. Set the semicircles aside.

Dissolve the gelatin in 3 tablespoons of water *(technique, page 13)*. Pour the juice from the oranges into a food processor or blender, and add the cottage cheese and yogurt, ground almonds, sugar, orange-flavored liqueur, and dissolved gelatin. Process the mixture until it is smooth.

Place a row of orange semicircles, slightly overlapping them, down the center of the prepared pan. Reserve the rest for decoration. Stir the orange segments into the cottage cheese and yogurt mixture, and spoon the mixture into the pan without disturbing the orange semicircles on the bottom. Refrigerate the terrine until it is firmly set—two to three hours.

To unmold the terrine, dip the bottom and sides of the pan in hot water for two to three seconds, then turn it out onto a flat serving plate. Cut the terrine into slices with a sharp knife, and decorate each portion with sprigs of mint and a few of the reserved orange semicircles.

Champagne and Melon Terrine

THIS TERRINE CAN BE SERVED EITHER AS A DESSERT OR AS A FRESH AND UNUSUAL FIRST COURSE.

Serves 8
Working time: about 45 minutes
Total time: about 10 hours and 30 minutes
(includes chilling)

Calories **180**
Protein **16g.**
Cholesterol **trace**
Total fat **trace**
Saturated fat **trace**
Sodium **35mg.**

3 tbsp. powdered gelatin
3 cups dry champagne or sparkling white wine
1 cantaloupe (about 1¾ lb.)
1½ cups plain low-fat yogurt
2 tbsp. sugar
1-inch piece fresh ginger, peeled and finely chopped
mint sprigs for garnish

Dissolve 2 tablespoons of the gelatin in 4 tablespoons of cold water *(technique, page 13)*. Pour the champagne or wine into a mixing bowl, and gradually stir in the gelatin solution.

Line a loaf pan 9 by 5 by 3 inches with champagne jelly as follows. Pour ⅔ cup of the champagne and gelatin mixture into the pan and place the pan, on a tray, in the freezer. When the jelly has set—after 5 to 10 minutes—tilt the pan over onto one of its long sides and place a small wedge under the rim of the pan to raise it a little. Pour another ⅓ cup of the jelly mixture into the pan, and adjust the position of the wedge if necessary to ensure that the mixture just reaches the rim of the pan, but does not flow out. Let the jelly set in the freezer for 5 to 10 minutes, then repeat the process to cover the other long side. Cover the two short sides of the pan in the same way, using about ¼ cup of jelly mixture for each side. When the jelly has set firmly, transfer the pan to the refrigerator while you prepare the melon.

Halve the melon, scoop out and discard the seeds, and cut the melon into wedges; cut away and discard the skin. Using a sharp knife, cut enough flesh into very thin slices to line the bottom and sides of the loaf pan. Remove the pan from the refrigerator, and working quickly, arrange overlapping melon slices over the jelly-lined bottom and sides. (Do not worry about any slices that may stand above the rim; these can be trimmed off later.) Return the pan to the refrigerator while you make the filling.

Cut the remaining melon into small chunks. Dissolve the remaining gelatin in 1 tablespoon of water, using the same method as before. In a large bowl, mix together the yogurt, melon chunks, sugar, ginger, and the remaining champagne jelly mixture. Stir in the dissolved gelatin and chill the filling until it has almost set—about 30 minutes. Spoon the filling into the lined pan and chill it overnight.

Before unmolding the terrine, trim any protruding melon slices that rise above the top of the pan. Dip the pan into boiling water for two to three seconds, then invert it onto a flat serving plate. Serve the terrine, either cut into slices or spooned into portions, garnished with sprigs of mint.

Strawberry Cheese Loaf

Serves 10
Working time: about 30 minutes
Total time: about 8 hours and 30 minutes
(includes chilling)

Calories **130**
Protein **12g.**
Cholesterol **10mg.**
Total fat **2g.**
Saturated fat **1g.**
Sodium **240mg.**

1 lb. low-fat cottage cheese
¾ cup plain low-fat yogurt
1 tsp. pure vanilla extract
3 tbsp. sugar
2 tsp. powdered gelatin
1 egg white
1¾ lb. strawberries, hulled
2 tsp. red-currant jelly
Strawberry-orange sauce
½ lb. strawberries, hulled
2 tbsp. sugar
3 tbsp. fresh orange juice
2 tbsp. orange-flavored liqueur

Press the cottage cheese through a sieve into a mixing bowl. Beat in the yogurt, vanilla extract, and sugar. Dissolve the gelatin in 2 tablespoons of water (technique, page 13), then slowly pour it into the cheese mixture, beating well all the time. Beat the egg white until it forms soft peaks. Stir 1 tablespoon of the egg white into the cheese mixture, then fold in the remaining egg white.

Line a loaf pan or terrine 7½ by 3¾ by 2 inches with a piece of dampened cheesecloth. Spread one-third of the cheese mixture in the bottom of the pan. Reserve 4 ounces of the strawberries for decoration. Halve 13

of the remaining strawberries and arrange six halves, stem ends down and cut sides against the cheesecloth, along each long edge of the pan. Between these rows of strawberry halves, make a single layer of whole strawberries. Spoon half of the remaining cheese mixture over the strawberries, then lay another seven strawberry halves against the cheesecloth on each long side of the pan—as before, but this time with stem ends up. Pack the remaining whole strawberries over the cheese mixture in an even layer and spread the last of the cheese mixture evenly on the top, pressing it down with the back of a spoon. Put the terrine into the refrigerator and chill it overnight, or until the cheese mixture is well set.

To make the sauce, purée the strawberries in a food processor or blender, and press the purée through a sieve into a small saucepan. Stir in the sugar, orange juice, and orange-flavored liqueur, and cook the sauce over low heat, stirring it gently, until the sugar has dissolved—about two minutes. Let the sauce cool.

Just before serving the dessert, slice all but a few of the reserved strawberries. Mix the red-currant jelly with 1 tablespoon of water in a small saucepan over low heat. Unmold the dessert onto a flat serving dish and arrange the sliced strawberries on top. Brush them with the red-currant glaze and decorate the dish with the remaining whole strawberries. Serve the terrine cut into slices, accompanied by the sauce.

EDITOR'S NOTE: *Once it has reached room temperature, this terrine becomes soft and difficult to slice. If you wish, return it to the refrigerator to firm it up once more, or alternatively, spoon it into portions.*

Red-Currant and Passionfruit Terrine with Vanilla Sauce

Serves 12
Working time: about 20 minutes
Total time: about 1 hour

Calories **70**	2 passionfruits
Protein **3g.**	4 egg whites
Cholesterol **35mg.**	6 tbsp. sugar
Total fat **1g.**	¼ lb. red currants, picked over and stemmed
Saturated fat **trace**	**Vanilla sauce**
Sodium **35mg.**	1 tbsp. cornstarch
	2 egg yolks
	½ vanilla bean, split lengthwise, seeds only scraped out and reserved, or ½ tsp. pure vanilla extract
	1 tbsp. sugar
	1¼ cups skim milk

Preheat the oven to 325° F. Line a collapsible-sided mold 12 by 4 by 2¾ inches with parchment paper.

Cut the passionfruits in half, and spoon out the pulp and seeds into a small bowl. Beat the egg whites in a mixing bowl until they form soft peaks. Beat in the sugar in three batches, ensuring that the mixture is stiff and glossy each time before adding more sugar. Lightly fold in the passionfruit pulp and seeds and the red currants. Spoon the mixture into the prepared mold and level the surface with a spatula.

Place the mold in a roasting pan and pour in suffi-

cient boiling water to come halfway up the sides of the mold. Bake the terrine until a fine skewer inserted in the center comes out clean—about 40 minutes. Watch the surface of the terrine while it is cooking, and cover it with a sheet of parchment paper if it appears to be browning too quickly. When the terrine is cooked, remove the mold from the water bath and gently invert it onto a flat serving plate. Carefully release the collapsible sides of the mold and lift them off. Peel off the lining paper and set the terrine aside to cool.

To prepare the sauce, whip the cornstarch and egg yolks together in a mixing bowl. Combine the vanilla seeds, or vanilla extract, and the sugar, pressing down on the seeds with the back of a spoon to separate them and disperse them evenly in the sugar. Stir the sugar and vanilla mixture into the egg yolks.

Heat the milk in a heavy-bottomed saucepan until it just reaches the boiling point. Pour the milk into the egg yolks and beat the mixture well with a whisk. Pour it back into the pan through a sieve. Stir the vanilla sauce over gentle heat until it just thickens—do not allow it to boil. Pour the sauce into a bowl to cool; stir the sauce from time to time to prevent a skin from forming on the surface.

Transfer the vanilla sauce to a pitcher. Serve the terrine cut into slices, accompanied by the sauce.

SUGGESTED ACCOMPANIMENT: *small bunches of fresh red currants, dipped in lightly beaten egg white and sugar.*

EDITOR'S NOTE: *This terrine can be kept in the refrigerator for up to 24 hours before it is served, but it should not be frozen. Raspberries, blueberries, or sliced strawberries may all be used in place of red currants.*

Rice and Apricot Ring

Serves 8
Working time: about 1 hour and 10 minutes
Total time: about 3 hours and 30 minutes
(includes chilling)

Calories **125**	2½ cups skim milk
Protein **6g.**	⅓ cup short-grain rice, washed
Cholesterol **trace**	½ tsp. pure almond extract
Total fat **1g.**	5 large ripe apricots, peeled, halved, and pitted,
Saturated fat **trace**	or 14 oz. canned apricot halves
Sodium **60mg.**	in their own juice, drained
	¼ cup plain low-fat yogurt
	1 tbsp. powdered gelatin
	2 egg whites
	⅓ cup sugar
	6 oz. fresh raspberries (about ¾ cup)

Bring the milk to a boil in a heavy-bottomed saucepan. Reduce the heat to low, and add the rice and the almond extract. Simmer the mixture uncovered, stirring from time to time, until the rice has absorbed all of the milk—about 50 minutes.

If you are using fresh apricots, place them cut sides down in a nonreactive saucepan and pour in ¾ cup of boiling water. Simmer the fruit gently until it is just tender—two to three minutes—then drain it.

Arrange eight apricot halves in the bottom of an 8-inch ring mold. Reserve the remaining apricot halves.

When the rice has absorbed the milk, remove it from the heat and allow it to cool slightly, then stir in the yogurt. Dissolve the gelatin in 2 tablespoons of water (technique, page 13) and stir it into the rice mixture. Beat the egg whites until they stand in soft peaks. Beat in all but 1 tablespoon of the sugar in three batches, ensuring that the mixture is stiff and glossy each time before adding more sugar.

Stir a spoonful of the egg whites into the rice to lighten the mixture, then fold in the remainder of the egg whites. Spoon the mixture into the prepared ring mold, being careful not to disturb the apricot halves. Level the surface of the mixture and refrigerate the ring until it is set—at least two hours.

Meanwhile, put the raspberries in a nonreactive saucepan and add the remaining sugar. Heat the berries and sugar gently until the juice runs, then simmer the berries until they fall apart—two to three minutes. Allow them to cool.

Purée the cooked raspberries with the reserved apricot halves in a food processor or blender. Press the purée through a fine sieve to remove the seeds.

To unmold the dessert, dip the bottom of the ring mold in hot water for two to three seconds, then turn the contents out onto a flat serving plate. Serve the dessert cut into slices and garnished with the raspberry-apricot purée.

SUGGESTED ACCOMPANIMENT: *fresh raspberries, placed in the center of the ring.*

EDITOR'S NOTE: *The ring may be stored in the refrigerator for up to four days, but it should not be frozen.*

Molded Chocolate Mousse with Orange-Caramel Sauce

Serves 8
Working time: about 25 minutes
Total time: about 3 hours and 25 minutes

Calories **210**
Protein **5g.**
Cholesterol **5mg.**
Total fat **7g.**
Saturated fat **4g.**
Sodium **50mg.**

1 tbsp. powdered gelatin
5 oz. semisweet chocolate
1 tbsp. dark rum (optional)
½ cup sour cream
1 cup plain low-fat yogurt
1 orange, grated zest only
2 egg whites
1 tbsp. sugar
2 tangerines, peeled and segmented, all pith removed
Orange-caramel sauce
1 cup fresh orange juice
½ cup sugar
1 tsp. ground cinnamon

Line a 2-cup decorative mold with plastic wrap, pulling the wrap as tight as possible and pressing it into the contours of the mold.

Dissolve the gelatin in 2 tablespoons of water *(technique, page 13).* Melt the chocolate, with the rum if you are using it, in a flameproof bowl set over a pan of simmering water; stir the chocolate until it is smooth. In a mixing bowl, whisk together the sour cream and yogurt, then whisk in the melted chocolate, the orange zest, and finally the dissolved gelatin.

In a separate bowl, beat the egg whites until they form soft peaks. Add the sugar, and beat again until the whites are stiff and glossy.

Gently fold the beaten egg whites into the chocolate mixture, then turn the mixture into the prepared mold. Level the surface of the mousse and put it in the refrigerator to set—three to four hours.

To make the sauce, put 3 tablespoons of the orange juice in a heavy-bottomed pan with the sugar. Heat these ingredients gently until the sugar has dissolved, then increase the heat and bring the liquid to a boil. Add the remaining orange juice to the pan (cover your hand with a towel when doing this, in case the mixture splatters), and stir in the cinnamon. Boil the sauce for five minutes, to reduce it a little. Strain the sauce into a bowl through a paper coffee filter or a layer of cheesecloth, to remove the sediment. Allow the sauce to cool thoroughly.

To serve the mousse, invert the mold onto a flat serving dish and carefully peel off the plastic wrap. Pour the sauce around the mousse, and arrange the tangerine segments decoratively along the top of the mousse and in the sauce.

Cassis, Peach, and Raspberry Layered Pudding

Serves 8
Working time: about 35 minutes
Total time: about 5 hours

Calories **160**
Protein **3g.**
Cholesterol **0mg.**
Total fat **0g.**
Saturated fat **0g.**
Sodium **5mg.**

1¼ lb. peaches, peeled, halved, and pitted
¾ cup sugar
4 tbsp. powdered gelatin
1½ cups fresh raspberries
1 tbsp. cassis
3 egg whites
Raspberry sauce
1 cup fresh raspberries
2 tbsp. gin
1 tbsp. confectioners' sugar

Place the peaches in a small, nonreactive saucepan with ⅔ cup of water and half of the sugar. Poach them gently for a few minutes, to soften them. Drain the peaches, reserving the syrup, and set them aside to cool. Purée the peaches in a food processor or blender.

Put 3 tablespoons of the reserved poaching syrup in a small bowl and dissolve 2 tablespoons of the gelatin in this liquid *(technique, page 13)*. Stir the dissolved gelatin into the remaining poaching syrup, then stir in the peach purée. Set the mixture aside until it has partially set—about 40 minutes.

Meanwhile, purée 1 cup of the raspberries in a food processor or blender, and press the purée through a fine sieve into a bowl. Stir the remaining sugar into 4 tablespoons of water in a small pan and heat the mixture gently to dissolve the sugar.

Soften 1 tablespoon of the gelatin in 2 tablespoons of water *(technique, page 13, Step 1)*. Add the softened gelatin to the hot sugar syrup and stir until the gelatin has dissolved completely, then mix it into the raspberry purée. Set this mixture aside until it has partially set—about 25 minutes.

While the raspberry mixture is setting, stir the cassis into 1¼ cups of water. Place 3 tablespoons of this liquid in a small bowl and dissolve the remaining tablespoon of gelatin in it, as with the poaching syrup. Stir the dissolved gelatin thoroughly into the remaining cassis and water mixture.

Pour a thin layer of the cassis jelly mixture into the bottom of a nonreactive terrine or loaf pan 8½ by 4½ by 2 inches and let it set in the refrigerator for 10 minutes. When it has set, place the remaining ½ cup

of raspberries on top of the jelly in an even layer. Pour the remaining cassis jelly mixture over the berries. Return the pan to the refrigerator, and let it chill until the jelly is set—about 15 minutes.

Beat the egg whites until they form soft peaks. Fold one-third of the egg whites into the partially set raspberry mixture and fold the remainder into the partially set peach mixture. Spoon half of the peach mixture into the pan and return it to the refrigerator to set—about 30 minutes.

When the peach layer has set, spoon in the raspberry mixture and refrigerate it until it has set—about 30 minutes. Finally, add the remaining peach mixture and thoroughly chill the terrine again to set the top layer—about two hours.

To make the raspberry sauce, purée the berries in a food processor or blender until they are smooth. Press the purée through a fine sieve into a bowl to remove the seeds, then beat the gin and confectioners' sugar into the sieved purée.

To unmold the terrine, dip the bottom and sides of the pan in hot water for two or three seconds, then turn it out onto a serving plate. Serve it cut into slices, accompanied by the raspberry sauce.

Exotic Fruits in Champagne Jelly

Serves 8
Working time: about 1 hour and 30 minutes
Total time: about 5 hours and 30 minutes

Calories **165**
Protein **6g.**
Cholesterol **0mg.**
Total fat **0g.**
Saturated fat **0g.**
Sodium **10mg.**

3 tbsp. powdered gelatin
2 cups dry champagne or good-quality sparkling white wine
¼ cup sugar
1 small ripe mango, peeled, pitted, and cut into strips
1 small star fruit, thinly sliced crosswise
10 oz. fresh lychees, peeled, pitted, and quartered, or 8 oz. canned lychees, pitted and quartered
6 oz. kumquats, thinly sliced crosswise, slices seeded
1 small papaya, peeled, seeded, and thinly sliced
1 cup watermelon, peeled, seeded, and thinly sliced

Soften the gelatin in 6 tablespoons of water (technique, page 13, Step 1). Pour 1¼ cups of the champagne or wine into a saucepan, add the sugar, and stir well. Heat this mixture gently until the sugar has dissolved. Remove the pan from the heat and add the softened gelatin; stir until the gelatin has completely dissolved. Set this jelly mixture aside and let it cool to room temperature.

When the jelly has cooled, stir in the remaining champagne and spoon a little of the mixture into a loaf pan 9 by 5 by 3 inches, covering the bottom with a thin layer. Chill the jelly until it has set—about 10 minutes. Arrange a few pieces of mango, star fruit, lychee, kumquat, papaya, and watermelon in an attractive pattern on the jelly. Spoon a little more jelly over this first layer of fruit and chill until it has set—about 10 minutes. Continue layering the fruit in the pan—either using a variety of fruits in each layer or creating layers of each individual fruit—and coat each layer with a little of the champagne jelly. Chill the mold for 10 minutes between each layer, to set the jelly. When the pan is filled with fruit and jelly, chill the terrine thoroughly to ensure that it is completely set—at least three hours.

To unmold the terrine, dip the bottom and sides of the pan in hot water for two to three seconds, then invert it onto a flat serving plate. Use a sharp knife to cut the terrine into slices for serving.

SUGGESTED ACCOMPANIMENT: *thin cookies.*

EDITOR'S NOTE. *For the most attractive result, select small fruits and arrange the best pieces in the first layer at the bottom of the pan. The selection of fruits may be varied to take advantage of what is in season, but avoid using pineapple and kiwi because they contain enzymes that inhibit the setting power of gelatin.*

Put ⅔ cup of cold water into a nonreactive saucepan with the remaining sugar. Stir the ingredients together over medium heat until the sugar dissolves. Bring the solution to a boil and boil it rapidly for one minute. Reduce the heat to low and stir in the kirsch, then add the sliced peaches and poach them gently until they have softened—two to three minutes. Using a slotted spoon, transfer the peaches from the syrup to a wire rack lined with paper towels. Let them drain and cool. (The syrup may be saved for poaching fruits for use in another recipe; it will keep in the refrigerator for about three weeks.)

Dissolve 1½ tablespoons of the gelatin in 3 tablespoons of water (technique, page 13). Stir the hot gelatin solution into the apple purée.

Pour one-third of the apple purée into the bottom of a nonreactive loaf pan 8½ by 4½ by 2½ inches. Place the pan in the refrigerator until the purée has set—30 to 40 minutes. Keep the remaining apple purée at room temperature, to prevent it from setting.

Meanwhile, dissolve the remaining gelatin in 3 tablespoons of water as before, and stir it into the blackberry purée.

Arrange half of the peach slices evenly over the set apple purée, then carefully pour in the blackberry purée. Return the pan to the refrigerator until the blackberry purée has set—30 to 40 minutes.

Place the remaining peach slices evenly over the set blackberry purée, and carefully spoon in the remaining apple purée. Refrigerate the terrine to set it firmly— three to four hours, or overnight.

Unmold the terrine onto a flat serving plate. Serve it cut into slices.

Peach, Apple, and Blackberry Terrine

Serves 12
Working time: about 1 hour and 20 minutes
Total time: about 6 hours (includes chilling)

Calories **120**
Protein **3g.**
Cholesterol **0mg.**
Total fat **0g.**
Saturated fat **0g.**
Sodium **5mg.**

2 lb. cooking apples, peeled, quartered, cored, and sliced
½ lemon, juice only
⅔ cup sugar
1 lb. fresh or frozen blackberries
2 tbsp. kirsch
3 large peaches, peeled, pitted, and sliced
2½ tbsp. powdered gelatin

Put the apples, lemon juice, and ¼ cup of the sugar into a nonreactive, heavy-bottomed saucepan. Cover the pan and cook over low heat, stirring frequently, until the apples are soft and fluffy—15 to 20 minutes.

Meanwhile, put the blackberries into another nonreactive, heavy-bottomed saucepan with ¼ cup of the remaining sugar. Cover the pan and cook the berries over low heat until they are soft—8 to 10 minutes.

Purée the apples and their juice in a food processor, or press them through a fine sieve into a flameproof measuring cup. There should be about 2½ cups of purée; if necessary, make up the quantity with apple juice. Press the blackberries and their juice through a fine sieve into another flameproof measuring cup. There should be about 2 cups of purée; add water if necessary.

Marbled Blueberry Dessert

Serves 12
Working time: about 35 minutes
Total time: about 3 hours

Calories **105**
Protein **7g.**
Cholesterol **5mg.**
Total fat **2g.**
Saturated fat **1g.**
Sodium **40mg.**

3 oz. fresh blueberries, stemmed and picked over
⅔ cup sugar
1 cup sour cream
1 cup plain low-fat yogurt
8 tsp. powdered gelatin
4 egg whites

Line a loaf pan or terrine 7½ by 3¾ by 2 inches with plastic wrap, pulling the wrap as tight as possible and pressing it well into the corners of the pan.

Place the blueberries in a small, nonreactive saucepan with 1 tablespoon of water and 2 tablespoons of the sugar. Cover the pan and cook the fruit gently over low heat to soften the berries—four to five minutes. Remove the pan from the heat and allow the berries to cool in the syrup.

Put the sour cream and yogurt in a mixing bowl. Dissolve the gelatin in 6 tablespoons of water *(technique, page 13),* and whisk all but 1 tablespoon of the gelatin solution into the sour-cream and yogurt mixture. Stir the remaining tablespoon of gelatin into the cooled blueberries.

Beat the egg whites until they form soft peaks, then beat in the remaining sugar a little at a time, ensuring that the mixture is stiff and glossy after each addition of sugar. Gently fold the beaten egg whites into the sour-cream and yogurt mixture.

Spoon alternate layers of the sour-cream and yogurt mixture and the blueberries into the prepared loaf pan or terrine. To marble the filling, plunge a skewer into the mixture and draw it back and forth along the length of the pan a few times. Level the surface of the filling with a spatula and refrigerate the dessert until it has set firmly—two to three hours.

Invert the dessert onto a flat serving plate and carefully remove the plastic wrap. Cut the dessert into slices for serving.

SUGGESTED ACCOMPANIMENT: *a bowl of berries, with a light caramel poured over the top.*

EDITOR'S NOTE: *Prepare a light caramel for the berry accompaniment with 6 tablespoons of sugar and 3 tablespoons of water, following the method described in the recipe for the caramel and chocolate Bavarian cream on page 117.*

5 *Thinly pounded chicken breasts wrapped in spinach leaves (recipe, opposite) reveal a green-flecked, basil-scented mousseline when sliced.*

Microwaved Terrines and Pâtés

All the particular virtues and benefits of microwave cooking come to the fore in the making of terrines and pâtés. The microwave oven reduces much of the time, effort, and cleanup required for the most labor-intensive preparations, making it possible to produce delicacies worthy of a banquet table in a matter of minutes. Its ability to preserve and, indeed, intensify the full flavor and color of fresh vegetables and fish, all within the briefest possible cooking time, makes the microwave oven an ideal medium for the repertoire of light, healthful dishes on the following pages.

Only nine minutes are required to cook the eggplant for the Middle Eastern-style pâté on page 137, and it is unnecessary to salt the vegetable in advance to rid it of its acrid juices: The microwave process eradicates any bitterness while the vegetable cooks. Garlic lovers will appreciate the ease with which the aromatic cloves are softened and mellowed to provide the foundation for a creamy pâté *(page 136)*. Where visual appeal is important, colors remain bright and true: The trout and asparagus terrine on page 138, for instance, displays a delicate interplay of pink and green.

Sauces thicken smoothly, without the need for constant stirring. Gelatinous stocks, prepared in advance and kept in the refrigerator, can be melted rapidly in the microwave oven for use in jellied dishes. Delicate meats such as chicken livers can be cooked gently and thoroughly, in a few minutes, to provide the starting point for a warm, port-spiked pâté *(page 131)*.

Microwave cooking takes place at such high speeds that mixtures in small, individual serving dishes seem to finish cooking almost before they have started. To avoid the risk of the contents boiling over, do not leave small dishes unattended even for a few moments; microwave oven timers often may not be reliable for cooking times under 60 seconds.

When recipes call for a food to be covered with plastic wrap, be sure to use only microwave-safe wrap. When covering a dish that contains liquid, prevent any potentially dangerous accumulation of steam by pulling back a corner of the wrap.

The recipes in this chapter have been tested in 650-watt and 700-watt microwave ovens. The term "high" indicates 100 percent power, "medium high" 70 percent power, and "defrost" 30 percent power. In calculating cooking times, remember that food continues to cook after its removal from the microwave oven.

Chicken Ballotines

Serves 8 as a first course
Working time: about 45 minutes
Total time: about 3 hours (includes chilling)

Calories **155**
Protein **23g.**
Cholesterol **55mg.**
Total fat **7g.**
Saturated fat **3g.**
Sodium **180mg.**

4 boneless chicken breast halves, skinned (about 5 oz. each)
1 tbsp. crème fraîche or sour cream
1 tbsp. plain low-fat yogurt
½ tsp. salt
⅛ tsp. ground white pepper
12 large spinach leaves, washed and stemmed, blanched in boiling water for 10 seconds, drained, and spread out on paper towels to dry
mixed salad greens for garnish
Mixed-herb pesto
½ oz. pine nuts (about 2 tbsp.)
1 cup loosely packed fresh basil leaves
1 cup loosely packed parsley leaves
1 tbsp. freshly grated Parmesan cheese
1 tbsp. virgin olive oil

Lay the chicken breast halves skinned side down on a board. With a small knife, open out the two flaps of flesh on the inner side of the breasts, taking care not to sever the flaps. Place the opened-out breasts between two sheets of plastic wrap or wax paper. Using a wooden rolling pin or a meat mallet, pound them out as thin as possible, without tearing the meat. Trim off the edges of the chicken from each breast to form a rectangle measuring about 4½ by 5 inches. Set the flattened breasts aside and reserve the trimmings for use in the filling.

To make the mixed-herb pesto, grind the pine nuts to a coarse powder in a food processor or blender, then add the basil, parsley, Parmesan cheese, and the olive oil. Process the mixture briefly until it is just smooth. Transfer the pesto to a bowl and wash out the food processor.

Put the reserved chicken trimmings in the food processor together with the crème fraîche or sour cream, yogurt, half of the salt, and the white pepper, and blend the mixture to a smooth paste. Add the pesto and process until the filling is completely mixed.

Place three large spinach leaves vein side up on a square of plastic wrap. Overlap the leaves to form a square slightly larger than a flattened chicken breast. Place one of the chicken breasts on top of the spinach, sprinkle it with a little of the remaining salt, and spoon on a quarter of the pesto filling, shaping it into a cylinder along the length of the piece of chicken. ▶

With the aid of the plastic wrap, roll up the chicken breast around the filling, ensuring that the spinach leaf encloses the chicken completely. Seal the plastic wrap tightly around the roll, twisting the ends firmly and tucking them under. Repeat with the remaining chicken breasts, then place the four rolls in the refrigerator to chill for at least one hour.

Arrange the chilled rolls in a single layer in a shallow dish, and puncture the plastic wrap in several places.

Microwave the rolls on high for four minutes, giving the dish a quarter turn after every minute. Turn and rearrange the chicken rolls, and microwave them on high for one minute more.

Let the chicken cool, still wrapped in plastic, then chill thoroughly in the refrigerator, keeping the rolls wrapped until required. Unwrap the chicken rolls, cut them into slices, and serve garnished with the mixed salad greens.

Cucumber Timbales

Serves 6 as a first course
Working time: about 25 minutes
Total time: about 1 hour and 25 minutes
(includes chilling)

Calories **70**
Protein **11g.**
Cholesterol **trace**
Total fat **trace**
Saturated fat **trace**
Sodium **185mg.**

3 tsp. powdered gelatin
1½ tbsp. cornstarch, mixed with 3 tbsp. cold water
⅔ cup skim milk
1 cucumber (about 1 lb.), 12 thin slices reserved for garnish, the rest finely chopped
3 tbsp. chopped mint, plus 6 mint sprigs for garnish
2 garlic cloves, crushed
¾ cup plain low-fat yogurt
2 tbsp. fresh lemon juice
¼ tsp. salt
ground white pepper

Sprinkle the gelatin over 3 tablespoons of water in a small bowl, let it soften for two minutes, then microwave the mixture on high for 30 seconds; stir to dissolve the granules.

In a large bowl, whisk the cornstarch and water mixture into the milk. Microwave the milk on high, whisking several times, until the sauce has thickened—one and a half to two minutes. Beat the gelatin mixture and chopped cucumber into the sauce. Add the chopped mint, garlic, yogurt, lemon juice, salt, and some white pepper, and mix well.

Rinse six small, round ramekins in cold water. Spoon the cucumber mixture into the ramekins and refrigerate them for at least one hour. Unmold the timbales onto individual plates, and serve garnished with the reserved cucumber slices and the mint sprigs.

SUGGESTED ACCOMPANIMENT: *warm pita bread.*

Chopped Chicken Livers

LIVER IS A RICH SOURCE OF VITAMINS BUT HAS A
RELATIVELY HIGH CHOLESTEROL CONTENT, WHICH SHOULD BE
TAKEN INTO ACCOUNT WHEN PLANNING THE REST
OF THE DAY'S MENU.

Serves 8 as a first course
Working time: about 10 minutes
Total time: about 1 hour and 30 minutes

Calories **85**
Protein **7g.**
Cholesterol **110mg.**
Total fat **4g.**
Saturated fat **1g.**
Sodium **120mg.**

¼ lb. shallots, chopped
1 garlic clove, crushed
1 tbsp. virgin olive oil
½ lb. chicken livers, soaked in skim milk to cover for 30 minutes, drained and patted dry with paper towels
3 tbsp. port or red wine
6½ tbsp. fresh whole-wheat breadcrumbs
¼ tsp. salt
freshly ground black pepper
flat-leaf parsley for garnish

Place the shallots and garlic in a bowl, and stir in the olive oil. Cover the bowl with plastic wrap, pull back one corner of the wrap, and microwave on high for three minutes.

Add the livers and the port or red wine to the bowl, re-cover it with plastic wrap, again pulling back one corner, and microwave the mixture on high for five minutes more. Allow the chicken livers to cool slightly, then place all the cooked ingredients, together with the breadcrumbs, salt, and some freshly ground black pepper, in a food processor or blender, and process them to form a coarse pâté. Pile the pâté onto a serving plate and garnish with the parsley.

SUGGESTED ACCOMPANIMENTS: *toast; gherkins.*

Smoked Cod Brandade

BRANDADE IS A FRENCH DISH OF SALT COD MIXED WITH OLIVE
OIL, POTATOES, AND CREAM, THEN FLAVORED WITH GARLIC
TO PRODUCE A FRAGRANT PASTE. THIS MODERN VERSION
GREATLY REDUCES THE FAT AND SALT CONTENT.

Serves 6 as a first course
Working (and total) time: about 25 minutes

Calories **150**
Protein **8g.**
Cholesterol **20mg.**
Total fat **8g.**
Saturated fat **1g.**
Sodium **465mg.**

½ lb. smoked cod fillet, skinned
½ cup skim milk
1 bay leaf
¾ lb. potatoes, scrubbed
1 large garlic clove
ground white pepper
3 tbsp. virgin olive oil

Place the cod, milk, and bay leaf in a dish. Cover the dish with plastic wrap, leaving one corner open, and microwave on high for four minutes. Remove the cod and let it stand while you cook the potatoes.

Prick the potatoes all over. Place them on a double layer of paper towels in the microwave oven, and microwave them on high for 10 minutes, rearranging them once. The potatoes should feel soft in the center when pierced with a skewer; if they still feel firm, cook them for two minutes more. Set the potatoes aside.

Drain the cod, discarding the bay leaf, and reserve the cooking liquid. Break the fish into chunks, removing any bones, and place it in the bowl of a food processor. Process the fish in bursts, scraping down the sides of the bowl, until it is very finely shredded.

Peel and quarter the potatoes, then add them to the fish in the food processor. Using short bursts of power, process the potatoes and fish until they form a coarse purée. Add one-half to two-thirds of the fish-cooking liquid to the purée and process briefly until well mixed. Use the flat of a knife or a mortar and pestle to crush the garlic, then add it to the brandade with some white pepper. With the food processor running, slowly pour in the olive oil through the feeder funnel. Stop the motor and check the consistency of the brandade: The mixture should be light and soft. If it is too stiff, add more of the fish-cooking liquid. Transfer the brandade to a microwave-proof serving bowl.

Cover the bowl with plastic wrap, leaving one corner open, and microwave the brandade on medium low for two minutes. Serve immediately.

SUGGESTED ACCOMPANIMENT: *crackers or fresh vegetables.*

EDITOR'S NOTE: *The brandade may be prepared in advance and warmed just before serving. If cold, microwave the brandade on high for three minutes, stirring and fluffing it up with a fork once or twice during this time.*

Spiced Tomato Rice Mold

Serves 6 as a first course
Working time: about 20 minutes
Total time: about 2 hours (includes cooling)

Calories **235**
Protein **5g.**
Cholesterol **0mg.**
Total fat **6g.**
Saturated fat **1g.**
Sodium **10mg.**

1 large onion, coarsely chopped
4 medium tomatoes, quartered
1 large sweet red pepper, coarsely chopped
½ cup dry white wine
2 tbsp. virgin olive oil
¼ tsp. cayenne pepper
1 tbsp. paprika
1 bouquet garni
1¼ cups short-grain rice
3 tbsp. finely chopped parsley
cherry tomatoes for garnish (optional)
sweet yellow or red pepper slices for garnish (optional)
lettuce leaves for garnish (optional)

Put the onion, tomatoes, and chopped sweet pepper in a large bowl with the wine, oil, cayenne pepper, paprika, and bouquet garni. Cover the bowl with plastic wrap, pulling back one corner, and microwave on high until the vegetables are soft—12 to 14 minutes.

Remove the bouquet garni and press the vegetables through a sieve into a large bowl. Stir the rice into the resulting purée, cover the mixture with plastic wrap, again pulling back one corner, and cook on high for 10 minutes, stirring twice. Microwave on defrost for about 10 minutes more, stirring twice; the rice should have absorbed all the liquid.

Lightly oil six 3½-inch brioche molds. Mix the parsley into the rice, then spoon the spiced rice into the molds, packing it down and smoothing the surface. Let the rice cool and set for about one hour.

To serve, turn out the rice molds onto individual plates. Garnish, if you like, with cherry tomatoes, sweet pepper slices, and lettuce.

Paupiettes of Sole in Aspic

Serves 4 as a first course
Working time: about 30 minutes
Total time: about 2 hours (includes chilling)

Calories **110**
Protein **19g.**
Cholesterol **40mg.**
Total fat **3g.**
Saturated fat **1g.**
Sodium **190mg.**

4 small lemon or Dover sole fillets (about 10 oz.), skinned
1 tbsp. fresh lemon juice
⅛ tsp. salt
freshly ground black pepper
3 oz. white crabmeat, picked over and flaked
2 tbsp. sour cream
1½ tsp. chopped fresh tarragon
3 tbsp. dry white wine or dry vermouth
2 cups vegetable aspic (recipe, page 13), melted
dill or tarragon sprigs for garnish
Tarragon yogurt sauce
⅔ cup plain low-fat yogurt
½ tsp. grated lemon zest
1 tbsp. fresh lemon juice
1½ tsp. chopped fresh tarragon

Lay the fillets of sole on a flat surface skinned side up and trim them to form neat, even-size rectangles; reserve the trimmings. Sprinkle the fillets with the lemon juice, and season them with the salt and some black pepper. Chop the sole trimmings, and mix them with the crabmeat, sour cream, and chopped tarragon. Place one-quarter of the crab mixture in a mound at the thick end of each fillet, then carefully roll up the fish from head to tail, keeping the filling in the middle.

Place the paupiettes in the center of a shallow dish so that they almost touch each other. Pour the wine or vermouth over them, and cover the dish loosely with plastic wrap, leaving a corner open. Microwave the paupiettes on high for two minutes, rearranging them after one minute to ensure that they cook evenly. Set the fish aside to cool completely, still covered. Drain the cooled paupiettes thoroughly and chill them in the refrigerator for at least one hour.

Spoon a very thin layer of the vegetable aspic into the bottom of four small, round molds or ramekins and refrigerate until the aspic is set—about 10 minutes. Place one paupiette, standing on end, in each mold, then pour in the remaining aspic to cover the paupiettes completely. Chill the molds until the aspic is set—about 30 minutes.

To make the sauce, mix the yogurt, lemon zest, lemon juice, and chopped tarragon in a small bowl. Carefully unmold the jellied paupiettes onto four small serving plates. Spoon a little of the sauce onto each plate, and serve at once, garnished with sprigs of either dill or tarragon.

Monkfish and Shrimp Terrine

Serves 8 as a first course
Working time: about 20 minutes
Total time: about 1 hour and 30 minutes
(includes chilling)

Calories **95**
Protein **20g.**
Cholesterol **75mg.**
Total fat **2g.**
Saturated fat **trace**
Sodium **450mg.**

3 tsp. powdered gelatin
1 lb. monkfish or other firm white fish fillets, skinned, cut into ½-inch cubes
¼ bunch watercress, washed, thick stems discarded, chopped
5 oz. low-fat cream cheese
⅛ tsp. salt
freshly ground black pepper
2 tbsp. fresh lemon juice
2 tbsp. chopped parsley, plus parsley sprigs for garnish
2 egg whites
¼ lb. peeled cooked shrimp
6 tbsp. vegetable aspic (recipe, page 13), melted
4 lemon slices, halved, for garnish
8 whole cooked shrimp with their heads on, for garnish (optional)

Sprinkle the gelatin over 3 tablespoons of water in a small bowl and let it soften for two minutes. Microwave on high for 30 seconds, then stir to dissolve the granules; set the gelatin aside to cool.

Place the fish in a shallow dish and sprinkle it with 1 tablepoon of water. Cover the dish with plastic wrap, leaving one corner open, and microwave on medium high until the fish is just firm—about four minutes. Let the fish cool, still covered, then drain off any cooking liquid and pat the fish dry on paper towels.

Place the watercress, cream cheese, salt, some black pepper, the lemon juice, and half of the chopped parsley in a bowl, and stir well. Stir the cooled gelatin solution into the watercress mixture.

In a mixing bowl, beat the egg whites until they form soft peaks. Gently stir 1 tablespoon of the whites into the watercress mixture, then fold in the remaining whites. Let the mixture rest until it has almost set—about 20 minutes—then gently stir in the fish and half of the peeled shrimp.

Lightly grease a loaf pan 7½ by 3¾ by 2 inches. Place the remaining peeled shrimp in the bottom of the pan, pour on the aspic, and refrigerate until the aspic is partially set—about 10 minutes. Sprinkle the remaining chopped parsley evenly over the aspic, then carefully pour the watercress, fish, and shrimp mixture into the pan, and chill until the terrine is set—about one hour. Unmold and slice the terrine, and serve garnished with parsley sprigs and lemon slices and, if you like, with whole cooked shrimp.

Garlic Pâté

Serves 4 as a first course
Working time: about 15 minutes
Total time: about 20 minutes

Calories **140**
Protein **8g.**
Cholesterol **trace**
Total fat **6g.**
Saturated fat **2g.**
Sodium **350mg.**

18 large garlic cloves
½ cup fresh whole-wheat breadcrumbs
6 oz. low-fat cream cheese
⅛ tsp. salt
freshly ground black pepper
1 tbsp. virgin olive oil

Peel and quarter the garlic cloves. Place the pieces in a bowl and add just enough cold water to cover them.

Microwave on medium high for three and a half minutes; drain the garlic and discard the water.

Place the garlic in a food processor or blender with half of the breadcrumbs, and blend for a few seconds. Add the remaining breadcrumbs, the cream cheese, the salt, and a generous amount of black pepper; continue to process the mixture until it is smooth. With the machine running, slowly dribble in the olive oil.

To serve the pâté, transfer it to a small bowl and smooth the surface.

SUGGESTED ACCOMPANIMENTS: *an assortment of crisp, colorful raw vegetables; chunks of French bread.*

Eggplant Pâté

Serves 6 as a first course
Working time: about 10 minutes
Total time: about 50 minutes

Calories **60**
Protein **2g.**
Cholesterol **trace**
Total fat **4g.**
Saturated fat **1g.**
Sodium **75mg.**

3 large eggplants (about 3 lb. total)
4 tbsp. fresh lemon juice
6 tbsp. plain low-fat yogurt
3 tbsp. sesame paste (tahini)
1/8 tsp. salt
2 garlic cloves, finely chopped
paprika for garnish

Prick the eggplants in several places with a skewer or the tip of a sharp knife, and place them in the micro-wave oven on a double thickness of paper towels. Microwave the eggplants on high for about nine min-utes, turning them over halfway through the cooking time. When cooked, the eggplants should be soft throughout. Set them aside until they are cool enough to handle. Cut each eggplant in half and scoop out the soft flesh, then set it aside in a bowl to finish cool-ing—about 30 minutes.

Purée the eggplant flesh in a food processor or blender with the lemon juice, yogurt, sesame paste, salt, and garlic. Transfer the purée to a bowl and sprinkle it with paprika before serving.

SUGGESTED ACCOMPANIMENT: *whole-wheat bread.*

Trout and Asparagus Terrine

Serves 6 as a main course
Working time: about 30 minutes
Total time: about 3 hours and 40 minutes
(includes chilling)

Calories **120**
Protein **18g.**
Cholesterol **trace**
Total fat **4g.**
Saturated fat **1g.**
Sodium **300mg.**

½ lb. asparagus spears, trimmed and peeled
2 trout (about ½ lb. each), cleaned, filleted, and skinned
½ lemon, juice only
1 tbsp. powdered gelatin
½ cup dry white wine
¾ lb. low-fat cream cheese
4 scallions, finely chopped
1 tbsp. chopped parsley
2 egg whites
fresh chervil or parsley leaves for garnish
lemon wedges for garnish

Place the asparagus in a large, shallow bowl, tips toward the center. Pour in ⅔ cup of water and cover with plastic wrap, pulling one corner back a little. Microwave on high for two minutes. Remove the asparagus from the oven and let it cool, still covered.

Cut each trout fillet into three long strips. Lay the strips flat on a plate and sprinkle them with the lemon juice. Cover the plate loosely with plastic wrap and microwave on high for three and a half minutes. Uncover the plate and let the fish cool.

Line the bottom of a loaf pan 7½ by 3¾ by 2 inches with wax paper or plastic wrap. In a small bowl, sprinkle the gelatin over the wine and let it soften for two minutes. Microwave the mixture on high for 30 seconds, then stir to dissolve the granules; let the mixture cool. Beat the cheese until it is soft and creamy. Add the scallions and parsley, and whisk in the wine and gelatin mixture. Beat the egg whites until they are just stiff, then fold them into the cheese mixture.

Pour a little of the cheese mixture into the bottom of the loaf pan, and top it with a third of the asparagus, laid lengthwise. Pour in a little more cheese and top with trout strips. Continue building up the terrine, alternating the cheese mixture with asparagus and trout strips, and finishing with a thin layer of cheese mixture. Refrigerate the terrine for at least three hours.

To serve the terrine, turn it out and cut it into slices. Garnish the slices with the chervil or parsley leaves and wedges of lemon.

SUGGESTED ACCOMPANIMENT: *boiled potatoes with chives.*

Parslied Duck

Serves 6 as a main course
Working time: about 30 minutes
Total time: about 9 hours (includes marinating and chilling)

Calories **235**
Protein **27g.**
Cholesterol **110mg.**
Total fat **10g.**
Saturated fat **2g.**
Sodium **160mg.**

4 lb. duck, cut into four pieces, skinned
1¼ cups loosely packed flat-leaf parsley, stems reserved, leaves finely chopped, plus 2 large leaves for garnish
1 lemon, thinly pared zest only
10 black peppercorns
2½ cups dry white wine
1 tbsp. powdered gelatin

Place the duck pieces in a large bowl, and add the parsley stems, lemon zest, peppercorns, and wine. Cover the bowl with a lid or plastic wrap, and let the duck marinate in a cool place for two to three hours, turning it once.

Place the duck, still in its marinade, in the microwave oven; if it is covered with plastic wrap, pull back one corner. Microwave the duck on high for 10 minutes; microwave on defrost for 30 minutes more, turning the pieces once after 15 minutes, until the juices run clear when a thigh is pricked with a skewer. Transfer the duck pieces to a plate. Strain the cooking juices through a sieve lined with a paper towel and allow them to cool. Chill the stock for at least three hours, then discard the fat that rises to the top.

Remove the duck meat from the bones, cut it into small cubes, and place it in a large bowl together with the chopped parsley leaves. Cover the bowl and set it aside in a cool place.

Put 4 tablespoons of the defatted stock into a small bowl, sprinkle the gelatin over the liquid, and let it soften for two minutes. Microwave the stock and gelatin on high for 30 seconds, then stir to dissolve the granules. Pour the gelatin into the remaining stock and leave it until it just begins to thicken—about 30 minutes. Reserve 4 tablespoons of the stock and gelatin mixture, and add the remainder to the duck and parsley, mixing well. Pour the duck and stock mixture into a 2½-cup serving dish, and refrigerate it until it just begins to set—about 10 minutes. Pour the reserved stock over the duck, garnish with the large parsley leaves, and return the dish to the refrigerator until it is completely set—at least two hours.

SUGGESTED ACCOMPANIMENTS: *green beans; crusty bread.*

Glossary

Acidulated water: a dilute solution of lemon juice in water, used to keep certain vegetables and fruits from discoloring after they are peeled.

Bain-marie: see Water bath.

Balsamic vinegar: a mild, intensely fragrant wine-based vinegar made in northern Italy; traditionally it is aged in wooden casks.

Belgian endive: a small, oval vegetable, composed of tightly wrapped white-to-pale-yellow leaves.

Blanch: to partially cook food by briefly immersing it in boiling water. Blanching makes such thin-skinned vegetables as tomatoes easier to peel; it can also mellow strong flavors.

Bok choy (also called Chinese chard): a sweet-tasting cruciferous vegetable that grows in a celery-like bunch, with smooth, white stalks and wide, dark green leaves.

Bouquet garni: several herbs—the classic three are parsley, thyme, and bay leaf—tied together or wrapped in cheesecloth and used to flavor a stock, sauce, or stew. The bouquet garni is removed and discarded at the end of the cooking time.

Calorie (or kilocalorie): a precise measure of the energy a food supplies when it is broken down for use in the body.

Capers: the pickled flower buds of the caper plant, a shrub native to the Mediterranean. Preserved in vinegar, capers should be rinsed before use.

Caramelize: to heat sugar, or a food naturally rich in sugar such as fruit, until the sugar turns brown and syrupy.

Cassis: a liqueur made from black currants.

Caul fat: a weblike fatty membrane that surrounds a pig's stomach. When wrapped around a filling, it melts during cooking and moistens the mixture.

Cayenne pepper: a fiery powder ground from the seeds and pods of red peppers; used in small amounts to heighten other flavors.

Ceps (also called porcini): wild mushrooms with a pungent, earthy flavor that survives drying or long cooking. Dried ceps should be soaked in warm water before they are used.

Chanterelle (also called girolle): a variety of wild mushroom that is trumpet shaped and yellow-orange in color. Chanterelles are available fresh or dried; dried chanterelles should be soaked in warm water before use.

Chervil: a lacy, slightly anise-flavored herb often used with other herbs, such as tarragon and chives. Because long cooking may kill its flavor, chervil should be added at the last minute.

Chicory (also called curly endive): a curly-leafed green with a bitter taste similar to Belgian endive. The lighter leaves are sweeter and tenderer than the dark green ones.

Chiffonade: a leafy vegetable sliced into thin shreds.

Chili peppers: hot or mild red, yellow, or green members of the pepper family. Fresh or dried, most chili peppers contain volatile oils that can irritate the skin and eyes; they must be handled carefully. *(See cautionary note, page 9.)*

Chili powder: a peppery red powder made from ground dried chili peppers. It is available in various strengths from mild to hot.

Chinese five-spice powder: see Five-spice powder.

Cholesterol: a waxlike substance manufactured in the human body and also found in foods of animal origin. Although a certain amount of cholesterol is necessary for proper body functioning, an excess can accumulate in the arteries, contributing to heart disease. See also Monounsaturated fat; Polyunsaturated fat; Saturated fat.

Cloud-ear mushrooms (also called tree-ear mushrooms, tree fungus, mu ehr, and wood ears): silver-edged, flavorless lichen used primarily for their crunchy texture and dark color. Sold dried, the mushrooms should be soaked in hot water for 20 minutes before they are used.

Cod: a saltwater fish, normally weighing between 6 and 15 pounds, which is caught all year round in the Atlantic and Pacific. Its lean, white flesh flakes easily when cooked.

Cornstarch: a starchy white powder made from corn kernels and used as a thickening agent. Like arrowroot, it is transparent when cooked and makes a more efficient thickener than flour.

Court-bouillon: a flavored liquid used for poaching fish or shellfish. It may contain aromatic vegetables, herbs, wine, or milk.

Crab: a crustacean with five pairs of jointed legs, the first of which have pincers. It is often sold cooked because of the short shelf life of raw crab.

Cumin: the aromatic seeds of an umbelliferous plant similar to fennel, used whole or powdered as a spice, especially in Indian and Latin American dishes. Toasting gives it a nutty flavor.

Debeard: to remove the fibrous threads from a mussel. The mussel uses these threads, called the beard, to attach itself to stationary objects.

Deglaze: to dissolve the browned bits left in a pan after roasting or sautéing by stirring in wine, stock, water, or cream.

Devein: to remove the intestinal vein that runs along the outer curve of a shrimp. To devein a shrimp, peel it first, then make a shallow cut along the line of the vein and scrape out the vein with the tip of the knife.

Dijon mustard: a smooth or grainy hot mustard once manufactured only in Dijon, France; it may be flavored with herbs, green peppercorns, or wine.

Dover sole: a lean, highly prized fish native to the waters around Great Britain, with firm, white flesh and a delicate flavor. It is available in limited quantities in the United States.

Eel: an Atlantic fish that resembles a snake, with firm, rich flesh and a mild flavor. Eels migrate downriver to the sea to spawn. They are generally skinned before they are cooked.

Fennel (also called Florence fennel or finocchio): a vegetable with feathery green tops and a thick, white, bulbous stalk. It has a milky, licorice flavor and can be eaten raw or cooked. The tops are used both as a garnish and as a flavoring.

Five-spice powder: a pungent blend of ground Sichuan pepper, star anise, cassia, cloves, and fennel seeds; available in Asian food shops.

Garam masala: a mixture of ground spices used in Indian cooking. It usually contains coriander, cumin, cloves, ginger, and cinnamon. It is available in Asian markets and some supermarkets.

Gelatin: a virtually tasteless protein, available in powdered or leaf form. Dissolved gelatin is used to firm liquid mixtures so that they can be molded.

Ginger: the spicy, buff-colored rhizome, or rootlike stem, of the ginger plant, used as a seasoning either fresh, or dried and powdered. Dried ginger makes a poor substitute for fresh ginger.

Grape leaves (also called vine leaves): the tender, lightly flavored leaves of the grapevine, used in many ethnic cuisines as wrappers for savory mixtures. Preserved grape leaves, usually packed in brine, should be rinsed before use.

Grouper: a fish caught in temperate and tropical waters around the world. Its flesh is lean, moist, and sweet. Depending on the species, groupers range in size from 1 to 700 pounds. The most important fisheries in the United States are from North Carolina to Florida.

Haddock: a silver-gray member of the cod family, with lean, delicately flavored flesh. The average weight of a haddock is 2 to 5 pounds; it is caught in the Atlantic.

Halibut: the largest of the flatfish, with lean, moist, firm, white flesh. The Pacific variety weighs from 10 to 800 pounds, the rare Atlantic variety up to 700. Because of its large size, halibut is generally sold in steak or fillet form.

Hazelnut (also called filbert): the fruit of a tree found primarily in Turkey, Italy, Spain, and the United States. Filberts, which are cultivated, have a stonger flavor than hazelnuts, which grow wild.

Hot red-pepper sauce: a hot, unsweetened chili sauce.

Julienne: the French term for vegetables or other food cut into strips.

Juniper berries: the berries of the juniper tree, used as the key flavoring in gin as well as in pork dishes and sauerkraut. Whole berries should be removed from a dish before it is served.

Kirsch (also called Kirschwasser): a clear cherry brandy distilled from black cherries grown in Switzerland, Germany, and the Alsace region of France.

Lemon sole: not a true sole, this flatfish is an important food fish in Britain and France and is available in limited quantities in the United States.

Mace: the pulverized aril, or covering, that encases the nutmeg seed.

Macerate: to soften a food by soaking instead of cooking, usually in an aromatic or spiced liquid.

Madeira: a fortified wine, often used in cooking, that is produced on the island of Madeira. There are four classes of Madeira, ranging from sweet to dry in flavor and brown to gold in color.

Marinade: a mixture of aromatic ingredients in which meat or vegetables are allowed to stand before cooking to enrich their flavor.

Marsala: a dark Sicilian dessert wine with a caramelized flavor.

Monkfish (also called anglerfish): an Atlantic fish with a scaleless, thick-skinned body and a large, ugly head; only the tail portion is edible. Although most monkfish weigh from 8 to 15 pounds, some specimens reach 50 pounds. The lean, firm, somewhat dry flesh is thought by some to resemble lobster in flavor and texture.

Monounsaturated fat: one of the three types of fat found in foods. Monounsaturated fat is believed not to raise blood-cholesterol levels.

Morel: a delicious fungus with a pitted, conical cap. It is usually sold dried and should be soaked in warm water to remove all grit before use.

Mullet, red: a delicious fish, the red mullet is small, weighing between 6 ounces and 1 pound.

Mussel: a bivalve mollusk with bluish black shells found along the Atlantic and Pacific coasts as well as in the Mediterranean. The mussel's flesh varies from beige to orange-yellow in color when cooked.

Nan: a flat, leavened, Afghan bread. Available in Middle Eastern groceries and some supermarkets.

Nonreactive pan: a cooking vessel whose surface does not react chemically with food. Materials used include stainless steel, enamel, glass, and some alloys. Untreated cast iron and aluminum may react with acids, producing off colors and tastes.

Nori: paperlike dark green or black sheets of dried seaweed, often used in Japanese cuisine as a flavoring or as wrappers for rice and vegetables.

Olive oil: any of various grades of oil extracted from olives. Extra virgin olive oil has a full, fruity flavor and very low acidity. Pure olive oil, a processed blend of olive oils, has the lightest taste and the highest acidity. For salad dressings, virgin and extra virgin olive oils are preferred.

Oyster mushroom: a variety of wild mushroom, now cultivated. Stronger tasting than button mushrooms, they are pale brown, gold, or gray.

Papaya (also called pawpaw): a fruit native to Central America. The skin color ranges from green to orange, and the flesh from pale yellow to salmon. Ripe papayas are sweet and edible raw; unripe papayas may be cooked as a vegetable.

Paprika: a slightly sweet, spicy, brick-red powder produced by grinding dried red peppers. The best type of paprika is Hungarian.

Parchment paper: a reusable paper treated with silicone to produce a nonstick surface. It is used to line loaf pans and baking sheets.

Passionfruit: a juicy, fragrant, egg-shaped tropical fruit with wrinkled skin, yellow flesh, and small black seeds. The seeds are edible; the skin is not.

Peppercorns: the berries of the pepper vine picked at various stages of ripeness and then dried. Black, white, pink, and green peppercorns are available.

Pesto: a paste made by pounding basil, garlic, pine nuts, and salt with olive oil. It can be bought ready-made from delicatessens and supermarkets. In Italian, *pesto* simply means "pounded."

Pine nuts: seeds from the cone of the stone pine, a tree native to the Mediterranean. Pine nuts are used in pesto and other sauces; their buttery flavor can be heightened by light toasting.

Pistachio nuts: prized for their flavor and green color, pistachios must be shelled and boiled for a few minutes before their skins can be removed.

Poach: to cook in simmering liquid. The temperature of the liquid should be about 200° F., and its surface should merely tremble.

Polyunsaturated fat: one of the three types of fat found in foods. It is abundant in such vegetable oils as safflower, sunflower, corn, and soybean. Polyunsaturated fat lowers blood-cholesterol levels.

Poppadom: a thin, crisp pancake made of lentil flour. Poppadoms are often served with curry and are available in Asian markets.

Quatre épices: a blend of ground spices often used in French cuisine, consisting of white pepper—which gives it its predominantly peppery taste—cloves, nutmeg, and ginger.

Radicchio: a purplish red Italian chicory with a chewy texture and a slightly bitter taste.

Ramekin: a small, round, straight-sided glass or porcelain mold, used to bake a single serving.

Recommended Dietary Allowance (RDA): the average daily amounts of essential nutrients that healthy people should consume. RDAs are established by the National Research Council.

Red-leaf lettuce: a red-tinged, frilly lettuce.

Reduce: to boil down a liquid to concentrate its flavor and thicken its consistency.

Rice vinegar: a fragrant vinegar that is milder than cider or white vinegar. It is available in dark, light, seasoned, and sweetened varieties; Japanese rice vinegar is usually milder than Chinese.

Ricotta: soft, mild, white Italian cheese, made from cow's or sheep's milk. Full-fat ricotta has a fat content of 20 to 30 percent, but low-fat ricotta has a fat content of only about 8 percent.

Roe: refers primarily to fish eggs, but edible roe is also found in scallops, crabs, and lobsters.

Safflower oil: a vegetable oil that contains a high proportion of polyunsaturated fats.

Saffron: the dried, yellowish red stigmas (or threads) of the saffron crocus, which yield a powerful yellow color as well as a pungent flavor. Powdered saffron may be substituted for threads but has less flavor.

Salmon, Atlantic: a fish that is supplied chiefly by Canada and Norway. Atlantic salmon weigh between 5 and 10 pounds; the flesh is light pink and denser than that of its Pacific cousins.

Salmon, Pacific: a popular fish from the Pacific Northwest. King salmon (or chinook), the fattiest and largest of the salmon, weighs up to 30 pounds; the color of its flesh is red. Red (or sockeye) salmon ranges from 3 to 7 pounds, with flesh that is a deep red-orange. Silver (or coho) salmon, weighing from 6 to 15 pounds, has silvery skin and bright orange flesh. (Farm-raised baby coho is available at 12 ounces.) At 3 to 6 pounds, pink (or humpback) salmon is the smallest of the Pacific varieties.

Saturated fat: one of the three types of fat found in foods. It exists in abundance in animal products and coconut and palm oils; saturated fat raises the level of cholesterol in the blood. Because high blood-cholesterol levels may contribute to heart disease, saturated fat consumption should be restricted to less than 10 percent of the calories provided by the daily diet.

Savoy cabbage: a variety of round cabbage with a mild flavor and crisp, crinkly leaves.

Scallop: a bivalve mollusk found along the east and west coasts of North America. The round adductor muscle of the animal is the part usually eaten by Americans, although all of the mollusk's meat is edible. Bay, sea, and calico scallops are the commercially important species. The bay scallop, found in bays and estuaries along the Atlantic and Gulf coasts, is small—only ½ inch across—and cream or pink in color. Deep-sea scallops are collected in the waters of the Atlantic and Pacific and measure up to 2½ inches. Any white connective tissue still attached to sea scallops should be removed before cooking. The calico scallop, measuring ½ to ¾ inch, is found from North Carolina to Florida and in the Gulf.

Sea bass: a handsome fish with firm, lean flesh, the sea bass is found in the Atlantic.

Sesame seeds: small, nutty-tasting seeds used frequently, either raw or toasted, in Middle Eastern and Indian cooking. They are also used to make an oil with a nutty, smoky aroma.

Shallot: a mild species of onion, with a subtle flavor and papery, red-brown skin.

Shiitake mushroom: a variety of mushroom, originally grown only in Japan, sold fresh or dried. The dried form should be soaked and stemmed before use.

Shrimp: a crustacean that lives in Atlantic and Pacific waters. Although there are hundreds of species, the most popular are white, brown, and pink shrimp. Also available are northern shrimp, caught in the North Atlantic and North Pacific, and rock shrimp, so named because of their tough shells. Rock shrimp are found primarily around Florida. Virtually all commercially caught shrimp is immediately beheaded and frozen. It is sold according to count per pound; the range is from fewer than 10 per pound to more than 70. Shrimp can be cooked in or out of the shells. Shrimp is moderately high in cholesterol but very low in fat. See also Devein.

Sichuan pepper (also called Chinese pepper, Japanese pepper, or anise pepper): a dried shrub berry with a tart, aromatic flavor that is less piquant than black pepper.

Skim milk: milk from which almost all the fat has been removed.

Snow peas: flat green pea pods eaten whole, with only the stems and strings removed.

Sodium: a nutrient essential to maintaining the proper balance of fluids in the body. In most diets, a major source of the element is table salt, which is 40 percent sodium. Excess sodium may contribute to high blood pressure, which increases the risk of heart disease. One teaspoon of salt, with 2,132 milligrams of sodium, contains almost two-thirds of the maximum "safe and adequate" daily intake recommended by the National Research Council.

Soy sauce: a savory, salty brown liquid made from fermented soybeans and available in both light and dark versions. One teaspoon of ordinary soy sauce contains 1,030 milligrams of sodium; lower-sodium variations may contain half that amount.

Squab: a young pigeon, weighing from 8 ounces to 1 pound when sold. Domestic pigeons have paler flesh and a mellower taste than wild pigeons.

Squid: a shell-less mollusk of the cephalopod family found in North American coastal waters. The two main varieties are short-finned and long-finned squid. Eighty percent of the squid—including the tentacles, body pouch, fins, and ink—is edible. If it is bought whole, the pen, beak, ink sac, and gonads should be removed before the squid is consumed. Squid is high in cholesterol.

Star anise: a woody, star-shaped spice, similar in flavor to anise. See also Five-spice powder.

Stock: a savory liquid made by simmering aromatic vegetables, herbs, and spices, and usually meat bones and trimmings, in water. Stock forms a flavor-rich base for sauces.

Sun-dried tomatoes: tomatoes that have been dried in the open air to concentrate their flavor; some are then packed in oil.

Timbale: a creamy mixture of vegetables or meat baked in a mold. The term, French for "kettle-drum," also denotes a drum-shaped baking dish.

Tomato paste: a concentrated tomato purée, available in cans, used in sauces and soups.

Total fat: an individual's daily intake of polyunsaturated, monounsaturated, and saturated fats. Nutritionists recommend that fats constitute no more than 30 percent of a person's total calorie intake. The term as used in the nutrient analyses in this book refers to all the sources of fat in a recipe.

Tree-ear mushrooms: See cloud-ear mushrooms.

Trout, rainbow: a freshwater fish, with an average weight of 8 ounces to 1 pound. Most of

the commercial supply is farm raised. The flesh is soft and rich in flavor.
Trout, salmon (also called sea trout): the same species as the brown river trout, the sea trout has a migratory life and habits similar to salmon, which is why it is called salmon trout. The flesh is pale pink and moist with an excellent flavor and texture.
Tuna: refers to several varieties of fish, found in both the Atlantic and the Pacific; some tuna can weigh as much as 1,500 pounds. The flesh is dense, full flavored, and oily; it can be white, as in albacore tuna, or light brown, as in bigeye and skipjack tuna. Bluefin has a dark, nearly red flesh.
Turmeric: a yellow spice from a plant related to ginger, used as a coloring agent and occasionally as a substitute for saffron. Turmeric has a musty odor and a slightly bitter flavor.
Virgin olive oil: see Olive oil.
Water bath (also called bain-marie): a large pan partially filled with hot water and placed in a preheated oven as a cooking vessel for foods in smaller containers. The combination of ambient hot water and air cooks the food slowly and evenly.
Whole-wheat flour: wheat flour that contains the entire wheat grain with nothing added or taken away. It is valuable as a source of dietary fiber and is higher in B vitamins than white flour.
Yogurt: a smooth-textured, semisolid cultured milk product made with varying percentages of fat. Yogurt can be substituted for sour cream in cooking, or it can be combined with sour cream to produce a sauce or topping that is lower in fat and calories than sour cream alone.
Zest: the flavorful outermost layer of citrus-fruit peel, cut or grated free of the white pith, which lies beneath it.

Acknowledgments

The editors wish to thank: Rachel Andrew, London; Steve Ashton, London; Paul van Biene, London; René Bloom, London; Maureen Burrows, London; Sean Davis, London; Jonathan Driver, London; Ellen Galford, Edinburgh; Jamie Griffiths, London; Bridget Jones, Guildford, Surrey; Jim Murray, London; Sharp Electronics (U.K.) Ltd., London; Jane Stevenson, London; Toshiba (U.K.) Ltd., London; Ian Watson, London.

Picture Credits

Credits from top to bottom are separated by dashes.
Cover: Andrew Whittuck. 4: John Elliott, except bottom left, Chris Knaggs. 5: David Johnson. 6: Chris Knaggs. 12-16: John Elliott. 17: David Johnson. 18: Chris Knaggs. 19, 20: John Elliott. 21: David Johnson. 22: Chris Knaggs. 23: David Johnson. 24: Andrew Whittuck. 26: John Elliott. 27: Chris Knaggs. 29: John Elliott. 30: Andrew Whittuck. 31: Chris Knaggs. 33: Andrew Whittuck. 34: Chris Knaggs. 35: Andrew Williams. 36: John Elliott. 37: Andrew Whittuck. 39: John Elliott. 40: David Johnson. 41: Andrew Whittuck. 43: Chris Knaggs. 44: David Johnson. 45, 46: John Elliott. 47: David Johnson. 48: Andrew Whittuck. 49: John Elliott. 50: Andrew Whittuck. 51: Chris Knaggs. 52: David Johnson. 53: Andrew Whittuck. 54, 55: James Murphy. 56: John Elliott. 57: David Johnson. 58: James Murphy. 59: Andrew Whittuck. 60, 61: John Elliott. 63: Andrew Williams. 64: David Johnson. 65, 66: John Elliott. 67, 68: David Johnson. 69: John Elliott. 70: Chris Knaggs. 71: John Elliott. 72: David Johnson. 73: Chris Knaggs. 74, 75: John Elliott. 76: David Johnson. 77: Andrew Williams. 79: John Elliott. 80: David Johnson. 81: Andrew Whittuck. 82: Chris Knaggs. 83: David Johnson. 84, 85: James Murphy. 86: Chris Knaggs. 87-89: John Elliott. 90: David Johnson—Taran Z Photography. 91: John Elliott. 92: Andrew Whittuck. 93: Andrew Williams. 94: John Elliott. 95: David Johnson. 96, 97: John Elliott. 98: Chris Knaggs. 99: Andrew Williams. 101: David Johnson. 102: Chris Knaggs. 103: John Elliott. 104, 105: David Johnson. 106: John Elliott. 107: David Johnson. 108: Andrew Williams. 109-112: Chris Knaggs. 113: Andrew Whittuck. 114, 115: David Johnson. 116-119: John Elliott. 120: David Johnson. 121: Andrew Whittuck. 122: Chris Knaggs. 123: John Elliott. 124: Andrew Whittuck. 125: David Johnson. 126: John Elliott. 127: Andrew Whittuck. 128, 130: Chris Knaggs. 131: David Johnson. 132: John Elliott. 133-135: David Johnson. 136: Chris Knaggs. 137: Andrew Whittuck. 138: Chris Knaggs. 139: David Johnson.

Props: The editors wish to thank the following outlets and manufacturers; all are based in London unless otherwise stated. 14, 15: marble, W. E. Grant & Co. (Marble) Ltd.; plate, Mappin & Webb Silversmiths. 16: china, Royal Worcester, Worcester; cutlery, Mappin & Webb Silversmiths. 18: plate and dish, David Winkley, The Craftsmen Potters Shop. 19: china, Hutschenreuther (U.K.) Ltd. 39: cloth, Ewart Liddell; plate, Royal Worces-ter, Worcester. 44: cloth, Ewart Liddell; silver, Mappin & Webb Silversmiths. 50: cloth, Ewart Liddell; china, Royal Worcester, Worcester. 53: plate, Villeroy & Boch. 60: china, Hutschenreuther (U.K.) Ltd. 61: silver, Mappin & Webb Silversmiths. 64: plates, Villeroy & Boch. 65: platter, Hutschenreuther (U.K.) Ltd. 66: marble, W. E. Grant & Co. (Marble) Ltd. 67: china, Royal Worcester, Worcester. 68: work surface, Formica, Newcastle, Tyne and Wear. 69: plate, Royal Worcester, Worcester. 70: platter, Villeroy & Boch. 74, 75: silver, Mappin & Webb Silversmiths. 82: plate, Hutschenreuther (U.K.) Ltd. 84, 85: marble, W. E. Grant & Co. (Marble) Ltd.; plate, Chinacraft. 98: platter, Villeroy & Boch. 99: plate, Royal Worcester, Worcester. 101: dark marble, W. E. Grant & Co. (Marble) Ltd. 102: work surface, Formica, Newcastle, Tyne and Wear. 114: marble, W. E. Grant & Co. (Marble) Ltd. 116: cake server, Mappin & Webb Silversmiths. 117: cloth, Ewart Liddell. 120: cloth, Ewart Liddell; platter, Hutschenreuther (U.K.) Ltd. 121: china, Royal Worcester, Worcester. 123: plate, Royal Worcester, Worcester. 124: linen, Ewart Liddell; china, Hutschenreuther (U.K.) Ltd. 128: cloth, Ewart Liddell; plate, Augarten Gesellschaft MBH, Augarten, Austria. 135: plate, Royal Worcester, Worcester. 138: plate, Rosenthal (London) Ltd.

Index